# DATE DUE

| | |
|---|---|
| DEC 0 2 2013 | |
| JUL 1 6 2014 | |
| JUN 2 1 2018 | |
| | |
| | |
| | |
| | |
| | |
| | |
| | |
| | |
| | |
| | |

BRODART, CO.  Cat. No. 23-221

# Cyber Bullying

# Cyber Bullying

Protecting Kids and
Adults from Online Bullies

Samuel C. McQuade, III
James P. Colt
Nancy B. B. Meyer

Westport, Connecticut
London

**Library of Congress Cataloging-in-Publication Data**

McQuade, Samuel C.
 Cyber bullying : protecting kids and adults from online bullies /
Samuel C. McQuade III, James P. Colt, Nancy B. B. Meyer.
   p. cm.
 Includes index.
 ISBN 978–0–313–35193–8 (alk. paper)
 1. Cyberbullying.   2. Bullying.   3. Bullying in schools—Automation.
4. Computer crimes.   I. Colt, James P.   II. Meyer, Nancy B. B.   III. Title.
 HV6773.M395   2009
 364.15—dc22       2008045523

British Library Cataloguing in Publication Data is available.

Library of Congress Catalog Card Number: 2008045523
ISBN: 978–0–313–35193–8

First published in 2009

Praeger Publishers, 88 Post Road West, Westport, CT 06881
An imprint of Greenwood Publishing Group, Inc.
www.praeger.com

Printed in the United States of America

The paper used in this book complies with the
Permanent Paper Standard issued by the National
Information Standards Organization (Z39.48–1984).

10  9  8  7  6  5  4  3  2

# Contents

# Preface

Cyber bullying, or what some people call "Internet aggression," "Internet bullying," or "digital harassment," involves using computers or other information technology (IT) devices, such as personal digital assistants or cell phones, to embarrass, harass, intimidate, threaten, or otherwise cause harm to individuals targeted for such abuse. This definition takes into account our view that bullying typically evolves over time to include more extensive use of the Internet and IT devices, along with escalating forms of aggression when these are not prevented. Most bullying does not result in property damage, or physical injury, nor does it cause prolonged or extensive psychological or emotional trauma. In addition, most children probably face some type and level of bullying as they grow up, which is not to say that bullying is normal or acceptable behavior.

Our fear and concern in writing this book is that online bullying, especially by and among youth and including adults of any age, appears to be becoming so prominent, technologically insidious, and severe in its consequences that classical forms of bullying may also be spreading as a consequence of youth interacting online. In other words, online and classical forms of bullying are increasingly intertwined behaviors. This condition exists throughout modernized societies in which the Internet is relied on to support various types and combinations of written or audible interpersonal communications such as e-mail, instant messaging, texting via cell phones, and myriad other social computing activities including electronic gaming, blogging, chatting or posting messages, images and videos onto web pages and so on.

Online activities that support communications for interpersonal, recreation, commercial, education, and government purposes have enabled variations of so-called Internet culture to emerge throughout the amorphous realm of cyberspace. In cyberspace, youth and adults interact in ways that extend their activities, experiences, and associations. They do so in largely unmonitored, unregulated, and unsanctioned ways. What a person would rarely—if ever—contemplate doing in person, they may do online because they can, or believe they can, get away with it. When it comes to bullying online, this is especially true of youth and young adults. Hence, online bullying by and among youth and young adults is today an integral aspect of what we will explain as the digital culture of contemporary youth.

Cyber bullying is now ubiquitous and involves to varying extents tens-of-millions of children, adolescents, and young adults throughout the world, as well as older adults and especially vulnerable populations of people such as the elderly and individuals with special needs. Essentially anyone and everyone who stands out for some reason in comparison to a dominant individual or group is vulnerable to being picked on in person and/or online. Children attending primary school, adolescents of secondary school age, and young adults in colleges and universities are now constantly at risk of standing out and being portrayed online in ways that incite others to intentionally embarrass, harass, intimidate, or threaten them. When this happens they will become victims, offenders, and/or witnesses of incivility online or in person, one form of abuse leading to another as aggressive behaviors spin out of control through a ganging up process commonly known as "piling on."

As bullying occurs within and transcends cyberspace and physical places that people must occupy, children, youth, and adults in the Digital Age experience immeasurable and various kinds of emotional, psychological, sociological, economic, and even physical harm, as do many of their parents, siblings, and friends. Millions of people throughout the world are now impacted by bullying that has changed and intensified as the result of uncivil social computing activities. The specter of cyber bullying in traditional and online media—and increasingly voiced as a major concern in school and community meetings—is bringing about greater concern among parents, educators, law enforcement officials, and legislators. The 2006 suicide of Megan Meier allegedly stemming from a cruel hoax was particularly sad, bringing cyber bullying under closer scrutiny by social networking firms, legislative bodies, and society in general.

Unlike other useful resources on the subject, this book addresses bullying from the perspective of technological and cultural evolution that bring about changes in the way people think and behave. Specifically we will address ways in which computers and other types of electronic devices along with the Internet and social computing activities enable changing youth attitudes, behavioral patterns, and their contemporary culture. Although youth culture in various societies has always existed and changed in various ways over time, and has probably always included bullying in some forms, this book explains the ways in which bullying is increasingly carried out online using IT devices to erode if not destroy *joy, trust,* and *hope* in the lives of youth already struggling to survive adolescence within the Digital Age. In the process we also address bullying by and among adults, especially young adults who have grown up accustomed to interacting with each other online.

Our book is also distinct because it is based on extensive original interview and survey research, including: (1) semistructured interviews about cyber bullying with hundreds of youth and adults encountered by Nancy B.B. Meyers since 2004 in the course of her travels throughout the world; (2) original survey and structured doctoral dissertation interviews by Dr. Jim Colt in 2007–2008 of school officials in Monroe County, New York that explored student behaviors, school discipline, school district security policies, and educational program challenges associated with cyber bullying; and (3) survey research conducted by Dr. Sam McQuade and several colleagues from 2004–2006 in New York universities, and in primary and secondary schools from 2007–2008 that included responses to cyber bullying and other Internet-related abuse and crime questions by more than 40,000 K through 12th grade students, along with hundreds of parents and teachers.

Space constraints prohibit our including statements made by scores of people interviewed or otherwise involved in our research, however each chapter in the book includes several case experiences of real people. Bullying stories represent those of victims living in North America, Central America, South America, Australia, Europe, and Asia. Stories include detailed and sometimes graphic experiences of victims of all ages, race, gender, and many ethnicities: bullying by young persons of each other; by older people of younger people and vise-versa; among people of the same or different genders; and hate crimes, especially of gay people or victims portrayed as being gay, which is quite common. Statements and testimonials scattered throughout each chapter reveal key things about traditional and high-tech versions of bullying, and of course lessons for protecting kids and adults from online bullying. Occasionally we quote foul language reported during interviews because this reflects the reality of online communications and how people feel about online bullying experiences. We apologize if some readers may be offended by this.

A few stories are well-known examples of cyber bullying. Most experiences reported in our book have never been previously reported. Several are shocking or heartbreaking. Others will have you rooting for the victims some of whom resort to bullying as a means of retaliation or self-defense. All give evidence of ways in which cyber bullying is creeping into our lives to erode online and off-line civility. Except when referring to well-documented cases published prior to the writing of this book, the names and locations of everyone interviewed or otherwise indicated in this book have been changed to protect their identities. However, all instances of bullying described in the book are known, or believed by one or more authors, to have actually occurred, and descriptions of events are based on facts as reported by people who voluntarily agreed to be interviewed.

Despite the scholarly effort that has gone into this book, it is not intended to be an academic treatise on cyber bullying. Rather we have concentrated on writing a thorough book about a serious problem, and done so in a way that is readily understandable by adults of any age regardless of their being in a position to intervene to prevent or respond to cyber bullying in some official capacity. When discussing what parents, educators, criminal justice, and others in society can do to stop bullying we provide suggestions that go beyond practical tips. We also take on common myths about how to deal with bullying in recognizing that social computing is now effectively mobile computing, and bullying is no longer what it used to be. In doing so we thoughtfully consider the perspectives of stakeholders and what they are up against as society attempts to grapple with bullying in all its forms. For example, as we focus on ways in which youth and adults in modernized societies like the United States now use IT devices to routinely interconnect with each other, we explore what they are experiencing along with the views of parents, educators, and public officials who are caught up in the problem or otherwise have special responsibility for supervising youth in society, but whose online activities may from a practical, technical, or legal standpoint be unknowable.

As you may already realize, we take the position that cyber bullying is a complex social problem that must be addressed through careful development of policy, program, and legal interventions. There are no quick fixes, and even individual cases can be very complicated. This is so because bullying in modernized societies is a systemic problem being tolerated if not inadvertently perpetuated and worsened in its effects via various ways in which people (especially youth) communicate online, and because each person who is victimized or otherwise involved in cyber bullying causes or experiences special circumstances through their online interactions. Although we focus on bullying by and among youth and young adults, we recognize that older adults are also involved in bullying sometimes because, as parents, their children may be bullies and/or victims of bullying, or because they themselves are bullies or victims of bullying. We also recognize that in the broadest sense, bullying is integral to many forms of abuse and crime (e.g., exploitation of youth and women for sexual purposes), and as an institutionalized condition within certain portions of the world such as when women are legally or socially discriminated against and/or sanctioned for certain types of behaviors that their societies deem inappropriate. For these reasons, we also include a limited number of case examples that describe cultural conditions or perceptions that exist around the world and pertain in some way to bullying.

Finally, by way of introduction, we wish to mention that our purpose in writing this book is not to rid the world of verbal and written abuse, though we wish that were possible. Bullying has been going on for centuries, as learned behaviors that unfortunately exist in all cultural settings. Instead we merely wish to help people realize that: (1) cyber bullying has evolved from traditional forms of bullying, and it is becoming more insidious as technologies enable new forms of online abuse to occur; (2) it occurs frequently because it is integral to the ways in which youth and young adults now interact increasingly online; (3) consequences of cyber bullying range from the innocuous to devastating over short and longer time periods for affected individuals, families, and organizations like schools; and (4) entire communities must work together to intervene and prevent bullying in its classical and new forms, especially now that worldwide Internet connections have created real possibilities for harm extending far beyond school yard and neighborhood spats. Only in this way can we ensure that youth everywhere preserve their inherent right to being *joyful*, free to develop and *trust* friends, and also safe in their daily routines while they maintain *hope* for bright futures.

# Acknowledgments

The authors wish to acknowledge and thank numerous individuals and organizations that made this work possible. First, Nathan Fisk and Neel Sampat are recognized for their outstanding support as graduate research assistants to Dr. McQuade while studying under his supervision at the Rochester Institute of Technology. Each provided research design help, online survey technical assistance, community presentations, and analytical support to make sense of massive amounts of data with an understanding of technology-enabled youth culture. The authors also acknowledge and thank dozens of colleagues who shared multidisciplinary perspectives and expertise from several pertinent fields, including but not limited to human and child development, education administration, sociology, psychology, criminal and juvenile justice administration, criminology, public policy, cultural anthropology, and fields otherwise related to science, technology, and society.

Many professionals consulted in the course of our work are affiliated with educational institutions, nonprofit organizations, or professional membership associations that care to prevent bullying. Several are executive board members of The Cyber Safety and Ethics Initiative, founded in Rochester, New York, to understand and prevent all forms of cyber abuse and cyber crime through research and community-level education. Lastly we wish to extend sincere thanks, empathy and sympathy to the victims of cyber bullying who agreed to be interviewed, and to officials and parents who daily do the best they can to confront the problem. Their contributions to societal understanding of cyber bullying and ways to protect people from becoming involved or experiencing its consequences are invaluable.

# The New Reality of Bullying and Cyber Bullying

*There is no such thing as cyber bullying. Adults make up these things to suppress kids and not let them have fun with their own friends on the Internet.*

— *13-year-old female*

Enter the terms "cyber bully" or "cyberbully" into Google or another Web browser and you will receive over 1,000,000 Web page hits. These Web sites will list scores of real life bullying stories, resource agencies, professional conferences, and training workshops along with cyber bullying prevention and intervention tips for kids, parents, and educators. A few Web sites even serve as cyber memorials for youth who died as the result of some form of online bullying up to and including hate crimes. Other Web sites will describe impending or existing laws that criminalize hostile behaviors including the use of computers or other electronic devices, such as cell phones, to intentionally embarrass, harass, intimidate, or threaten people. No matter how it is phrased, "cyber bullying" (spelled as one word or two), always results in real harm to real people. For this reason Web sites springing up throughout cyberspace, the mainstream media, and a small but important set of research studies, are providing increasing evidence about the new reality of bullying and cyber bullying made possible as the result of people abusing computers, other types of information technology (IT) devices and the Internet.

In this first chapter we explain what cyber bullying is and that it may generally be regarded as a technological extension of traditional in-person bullying. We provide examples of recent prominent cases of bullying and we analyze those cases to identify seven common aspects of modern bullying that distinguish high-tech elements of contemporary bullying that occur completely, or to some extent, online. Next we provide a realistic, though hypothetical, example of what it has been like for young adults to grow up with computers, the Internet, and more recently portable IT devices that has enabled social and mobile computing. This provides a foundation for understanding ways in which cyber bullying is linked to the aggressive, abusive, and uncivil aspects of the digital culture of contemporary youth. This concept establishes the foundation for why youth and young adults use technology in the ways that they do, which unfortunately now integrates bullying into their largely inadequately supervised cyber lifestyles.

## What Is Cyber Bullying?

Cyber bullying occurs when a person uses IT to embarrass, harass, intimidate, threaten, or otherwise cause harm to individuals targeted for such abuse. Cyber bullying amounts to a technological extension of physical bullying that has traditionally been carried out face-to-face or indirectly over the telephone or through typed or handwritten messages. Regardless of technologies employed, bullying has traditionally involved one person or multiple aggressive people who seek out victims they perceive to be weak or vulnerable, and then pick on them over time. Name-calling, shoving, tripping, kicking, spitting, knocking books out of a classmate's hands, making threats, fistfights, hang-up phone calls, threatening messages, bad-mouthing, spreading malicious gossip, and excluding people from peer groups as social outcasts are among the most prominent forms of traditional bullying.

It is interesting to note that mean-spirited or prank messages originated with the telegraph system in the early nineteenth century. Later telephones made possible hang-up calls and threatening messages more immediate. Telegraph and phone system operators could easily listen in on conversations and spread gossip throughout their local community and in time over long-distance networks of telephone wires. Early forms of cyber bullying undoubtedly involved people using electronic communication systems to do what is still done today: gossip, embarrass, harass, intimidate, coerce, or threaten. There are other enduring aspects of bullying that rely on even simpler technology to communicate mean-spirited messages. Remember the "Kick Me" signs taped to somebody's backside? Remember how although intended as a joke, these kinds of messages and pranks were actually mean-spirited attempts to hurt and embarrass someone?

Pranks and bullying often involve actions that involve communicating messages designed to make known and light of someone else's perceived or actual shortcomings. The idea is sparked by one person or perhaps a small group of individuals who need to show off or dominate someone else or a situation. Typically bullies bolster support for themselves by getting others to join in, and often technology is used in some way to facilitate communications. This sort of thing has been going on for as long as people have used technology to enable the ways they communicate and interact.

Many adults may remember the angst they felt as children when excluded from a group of their friends. They may remember the fear they experienced as youngsters when groups of students who disliked them would lay in wait for them after school hours, or make fun of them for some reason: the way they dressed, had their hair cut, performed in class (positively or negatively), or simply because they wore glasses! Anything could and still can spark being picked on. Remember, "Hey four eyes . . . "? Looking back adults may smirk at or dismiss these memories in recognition that "kids can be mean" or feel that unfortunately "being bullied is a natural part of growing up." In truth, as students and then young adults, they and millions of people like them have historically feared and endured bullying in some form—some more successfully than others—and people everywhere cringe at the prospect of being bullied regardless of their age.

Kids and young adults today face the same bullying challenges as their parents did and much more. This is because people increasingly use computers, gaming consoles, and cell phones to access the Internet, communicate, and interact with one another. Modern technology has empowered human abilities to communicate in ways that obviously did not exist when people relied only on the telegraph and conventional phone systems. The Internet, computers, and technological devices now make creating and conveying mean messages to individuals or groups potentially and tremendously more efficient and effective. These technologies have enabled messages consisting of text, images, photos, videos, and/or audio recordings to be easily created and used for any purpose including bullying.

Today online bullying messages consisting of images or graphics can be used in numerous ways along with text to imply or convey all sorts of threats in weird or sinister ways. Receiving such messages can be like discovering a dead chicken on a porch, finding your dog hanging from a tree in your front yard, or some other creepy and disturbing action that are sometimes used to *really* intimidate someone in an off-line or traditional sense. In the Digital Age, sexual coercion is also made easy and is commonplace. So are insidious conspiracies among youth that play out online as well as in physical environments. Some youth today, as in prior times, endure bullying in silence for fear of reprisals. Others strike back in ways they believe necessary or think they can get away with in person or online. In any case, computerization has enabled modern bullying through online communications to be more efficient and effective than ever. Cyberspace has changed everything for all ages.

## PROMINENT EXAMPLES OF MODERN BULLYING AND CYBER BULLYING

People throughout the connected world are taking notice and beginning to realize that for all the wonderful things associated with the Internet—computers and mobile devices such as cellular phones, personal digital assistants (PDAs), and portable gaming consoles—using these and other technological devices also enable unintended negative spin-offs. One of these spin-offs is cyber bullying by youth and some adults who, having been empowered with computerized technology, use electronic devices without adequate positive role models and supervision or instruction in how to be safe and responsible when online. Indeed, a major consequence of computerization and largely unfettered youth access to digital technology, especially in the absence of needed guidance and oversight, is cyber bullying. Sometimes the results of this are nothing short of tragic, as the following cases well reported by the news media reveal.

### BILLY WOLFE

In the spring of 2008, Billy Wolfe was a high school sophomore living in Fayetteville, Arkansas, population 60,000. As reported by the New York Times and substantiated through school and online records of events, Billy was bullied for years and at the time of this writing reportedly remains concerned about making it through a school day without getting beat up. Beginning at the age of 12 he began suffering bruises and black eyes at the hands of classmates. One example follows: while one boy records with a cell phone, another boy walks up to an unsuspecting Billy and lands a punch to Billy's forehead, leaving a welt the size of a baseball. The cell phone video records Billy staggering from the blow, dropping his book bag to defend himself, and then stopping after hearing the screams of his sister calling for someone to come to his aid. The aggressor goes to school and shows the video to friends, while Billy goes home. School has not yet even started, but in short order the video clip will be posted online for the entire world to view.

Another example shows Billy in ninth grade: some other boys who knew Billy created a Web page on a social networking site called "Every One That Hates Billy Wolfe." The page contained an image of Billy's face placed on a likeness of Peter Pan. The image contained a message stating, "There is no reason anyone should like Billy he's a little bitch. And a homosexual that NO ONE LIKES."[1] Although the page was taken down, it didn't take long before a student in Billy's Spanish class punched Billy so hard that his braces were caught on the inside of his cheek. In a previous incident in junior high school, some boys in a wood shop class convinced a bigger student that Billy was saying bad things about his mother. Again, an unsuspecting Billy working on constructing a miniature house was hit so forcefully in the cheek that he briefly lost consciousness. Billy's mother later recalled that a school official declined to report the incident to police because Billy had been cast as the original aggressor and got what he deserved.

Since the last bullying incident, lawsuits were filed by the Wolfe family against some of the bullies, and another lawsuit is impending against the school district for allegedly not doing enough to protect Billy.

## MEGAN MEIER

On October 17, 2006, a 13-year-old girl named Megan Meier, who lived in Dardenne Prairie, Missouri committed suicide allegedly due to cyber bullying. While on the popular social networking site MySpace, Megan had been called a liar and a whore. However, a 16-year-old boy named Josh Evans befriended her and told her she was hot. For over a month, Josh was very kind and flattering. But the flattery ended quickly and turned to insults with Josh telling Megan that he hated her. Other girls on the social networking site also insulted Megan in a series of episodes. A short time after one of these episodes, Megan, who also suffered from depression, hanged herself in her bedroom with a belt. A few weeks later the investigation into Megan's death revealed that Josh was actually a fake profile allegedly created by a 48-year-old mother of another girl who Megan knew and lived just four residences away from on the same street! The mother, a woman named Lori Drew, reportedly admitted to police that she collaborated with a 19-year-old male to create the profile of Josh Evans in order to secretly monitor what Megan was saying on MySpace about her own daughter. However, the episode ended tragically with a message posted by confused and despondent Megan to Josh on the day she committed suicide, which read: "I just don't understand why u acttin like this."[2]

Unfortunately, there were no state laws in Missouri at the time that could be interpreted to the facts of this case as being a crime. Therefore, there were no charges filed against the suspects. However, this changed following efforts of the Meier family to make cyber bullying explicitly illegal along with media portrayal of extreme injustice in Megan's case. Almost two years later, on May 15, 2008, a federal grand jury indicted Lori Drew on three counts of illegally accessing an interstate computer system to inflict emotional distress, and one count of conspiracy for plotting the incident with assistance from at least one other individual. In November 2008, a federal court jury convicted Drew of three counts of the lesser crimes of accessing a computer without authorization. Megan's case has now inspired the Megan Meier Cyberbullying Prevention Act, the first proposed national cyber bullying crime legislation in the United States.

## RYAN HALLIGAN

The story of Ryan Patrick Halligan is another tragic example of bullying in the Digital Age again involving suicide by a 13-year-old boy. In 2003 Ryan lived with his family in Essex Junction, Vermont. He had a learning disability, was described as not being very athletic, and was reportedly bullied by other students beginning in 5th grade when he was about a 10-year-old. Given his personality and sensitive nature, the verbal bullying made Ryan feel very insecure about himself. With some counseling and the passage of time, the situation seemed to improve, however in the 7th grade an online rumor that Ryan was gay resulted in a new, wider and more intensive round of bullying from other students.

The rumor that Ryan was gay spread like wildfire with other students using technological devices and instant messaging to fan the flames of self-esteem destruction. Having made a deal with his parents to keep a computer in his room provided that his school progress reports were positive, Ryan began using the Internet as a means of solitude and escape from the in-person bullying he experienced in the real world. Ryan was subsequently befriended by a girl who engaged him in online conversations, allegedly to find out more about him and later betray him in school as a loser. When Ryan's grades revealed declining classroom performance, his father, John Halligan, disabled the computer. Shortly afterward, Ryan hanged himself in a family bathroom.

In the aftermath of the suicide Mr. Halligan diligently read every record of the online conversations held between Ryan and other students, all of which had been saved on the computer hard drive as the result of a particular software application that Ryan had installed. Review of the online conversations revealed Ryan's story, the details of which he had kept from his father and others. Mr. Halligan later described the reading as heartbreaking and the most difficult thing he had ever done. For example, one part of an instant message conversation held between Ryan and another boy prior to the suicide went like this:

> Other Boy: the last time I hear u complain?
> Other Boy: ur finally gonna kill urself?!
> Ryan: yep
> Other Boy: phew
> Other Boy: its about fXXXin time
> Ryan: you'll hear about it in the papers tomorrow.[3]

## GHYSLIAN RAZA

Also in 2003, Ghyslian Raza, then a 15-year-old boy living in Quebec, Canada, made a two minute video clip of himself pretending to be in a *Star Wars* fight scene.[4] The video, which was made in a school lab, showed an overweight boy as not being very athletic or graceful and becoming more energetic while making his own sound effects to engage an imaginary foe. Some of his classmates came into possession of the clip and doctored the video by adding the dramatic musical sound score used in the *Star Wars* movie. They also used computer technology to create special effects that made the golf-ball retriever that Ghyslian was holding appear to be a double-blade light saber such as that used by the fictional character and aspiring Jedi Knight Luke Skywalker, or his evil counterpart Darth Maul from *Star Wars Episode I, The Phantom Menace.*

Having doctored the video to make Ghyslian look and sound ridiculous, the boys then posted the clip online. Within three days the video was reportedly downloaded over 1 million times, and within weeks it was downloaded more than 15 million times! This understandably caused Ghyslian incredible public embarrassment, because although humorous to many people, Ghyslian never intended for his own video to be seen by other people much less doctored and then viewed publicly. The added sound and technical lighting effects intensified his humiliation, as did being known as "The Star Wars Kid" throughout the online world. With the support of his parents, Ghyslian subsequently sought professional counseling and continued his education in a different school environment. His parents sued the parents of the four male students involved in creating and distributing the video online.

## COMMON ASPECTS OF MODERN BULLYING CASES

The four cases described above were given broad media or Internet attention because they involved a range of severe results that were caused, hastened, or worsened by youth using IT devices. Cases that involved widespread public embarrassment, a need to discontinue normal school routines while receiving mental health treatment, enduring physical beatings with substantial injury, or despair leading to suicide. While not all instances of bullying have such severe results, a closer analysis of the four cases above reveal several common and important aspects of bullying in computerized societies, including:

1. *Victims were perceived as being relatively weak or vulnerable:* Megan suffered from depression, Ghyslian was overweight, Ryan had a learning disability, and Billy was comparatively frail in physical appearance.
2. *Abuse involved social computing activities:* Megan and Ryan chatted online, Ghyslian had his video posted to one social networking location only to have it spread virally throughout the online world, and a special Web forum for posting hate speech directed at Billy was created.
3. *Computer technology was used creatively to deceive and heighten bullying effects:* A profile created in MySpace was used to manipulate Megan into believing Josh existed, Ghyslian had his video doctored with special lighting and sound effects, rumors about Ryan were spread rapidly online, and beatings suffered by Billy were video recorded with a cell phone and posted online.
4. *Physical place and cyberspace behaviors were intertwined:* The primary indicted offender in Megan's case was a mother of a peer who lived four residences away, the boys who bullied Ghyslian were classmates, the same was true for Billy who feared for his physical safety even when attending school, and Ryan also experienced physical bullying that resurfaced as online bullying within three years.
5. *Sexuality and perceived relationships were exploited:* Megan was deceived into imaginary love, Ryan was rumored to be gay and later befriended and then

betrayed by a girl who struck up a relationship only to find out more about him, and Billy was also accused of being gay in order to harass him and incite additional bullying.

6. *Parents or other adults may not have been positioned to intervene effectively:* At 13 Megan was actively involved for several weeks in an online courtship with someone purportedly aged 16, but whose identity or existence was never confirmed. Ryan was allowed to keep a computer in his bedroom until his grades declined and only after his suicide did his father read the heartbreaking logs of his online conversations. School and criminal justice officials positioned to prevent the bullying of Billy allegedly failed to accurately perceive a growing problem and intervene sufficiently despite numerous records documenting bullying incidents. Moreover, all the parents of the bullies in these cases may have been negligent in not adequately supervising the online and off-line activities of their children.

7. *Youth involved were not sufficiently provided with adequate instruction in Internet safety, information security and cyber ethics:* For example, offenders were generally not afforded instruction about how to responsibly use IT devices in ways that would not offend or harm other people, or they disregarded these lessons. Similarly, victims were generally not taught how to block digital messages or the importance of discontinuing online dialog after it becomes hostile.

Our purpose here is not to blame parents, public officials, and certainly not young people, especially those who are victims of bullying. Rather our goal is to advance public awareness and understanding about the increasingly complex societal problem of bullying, and particularly with respect to how it is being exacerbated by online practices of kids and young adults. As indicated in the common aspects of cases listed above, cyber bullying is not so much different than traditional bullying (that some youth engaged in prior to availability of the Internet). Indeed, the modern cases discussed here have elements of both traditional bullying (i.e., involving verbal, written, and physical abuse that occurs among individuals or groups) and cyber bullying involving the use of IT devices and the Internet to intentionally embarrass, harass, intimidate, or threaten).

The implication is that bullying should not be conceived as traditional bullying versus cyber or online bullying. To think of bullying in this way reflects a very simplistic view of the problem that does not adequately consider the role and evolution of technology in enabling human behaviors. Rather, bullying is today a problem that remains in and yet transcends the physical realm in which people actually live into cyberspace where youth are increasingly spending time; through which millions now derive their self-esteem, develop creativity and attitudes, make and maintain relationships, and establish interactive behavioral patterns that rely on using various types of technological devices for all sorts of purposes. As will be explained in the following sections, cyber bullying is about growing up with information technology or IT (meaning with both IT devices and bullying that ranges from being relatively low- to high-tech in nature).

## Growing Up with Information Technology (IT)

To better understand the technological and behavioral factors that have lead to modern cyber bullying let's consider the life of a typical American teenager who was born in 1990, about the time in which the Internet began to expand exponentially. When the child was just 1-year-old the first Web site was created. When this child was a 2-year-old, the number of computers connected via the Internet exceeded 1 million, and digital audio and video capabilities were just beginning to be installed in home computers. During this time period, the Internet began to explode in popularity, and started to become part of the popular culture, especially with the emergence of the World Wide Web.

When our typical American child was a 3-year-old, less than one-tenth of one percent of people throughout the world connected to the Web using companies like America Online or other Web browsers most of which no longer exist (or at least not by the same name). Google, for example, had not yet come of age. By the time the child was a 4-year-old, the child's parents (if they were connected) could order dinner from Pizza Hut online without ever picking up a telephone. When the child was a 5-year-old, the first Wiki had been created at about the same time as Ebay and Hotmail. In just 5 years, in approximately 1995, the number of Internet users worldwide had exceeded 16 million people (or .4% of the world's population). As the child became a 6-year-old, Google came into being along with the Palm Pilot. Cellular phones not equipped with today's small and long-lasting batteries tended to be large handheld "bricks" or affixed to vehicle dashboards. Society was still using pay telephones, even those that accepted coins rather than "swipe cards" for payment.

When the child was a 7-year-old and in the 1st or 2nd grade, Microsoft Corporation had expanded from small beginnings on the south side of Redmond, Washington into a worldwide transnational organization. Its founder, Bill Gates, was the richest man on the planet. When the child was an 8-year-old, the first Web blogs began to appear and a year later, when our youngster was only a 9-year-old, Sean Fanning created the popular and controversial music file sharing program called Napster. In the year 2000, when the child became a 10-year-old, about 361 million people had an Internet connection, less than 6 percent of the world population. When the child became an 11-year-old, Wikipedia.com was created giving rise to "wiki-wisdom" experts including young people who were coming to expect and believe Internet content was truth to be accessed and discerned almost instantly. (Perhaps it is, if you're adept at cross-checking contributors to Internet knowledge and their sources of information—the need for some things never change!)

By the young person's 12th birthday, the popular social networking site, Friendster, had been created and by their 13th birthday, and MySpace was activated. At this time, in about 2002, nearly half of the youth between the ages of 12 and 17 owned, controlled, or were the primary user of a cellular phone small enough to fit into a pocket with ease. As the teen became a 14-year-old, podcasts that included downloadable video or audio presentations were becoming more popular, and kids seemingly everywhere had learned to create their own Web sites in addition to creating profiles on social networking sites like MySpace. YouTube was all the rage when the teen became a 15-year-old, but by the time our teenager is a 16-year-old MySpace had grown to 100 million users! (Bear in mind that this was about the number of worldwide Internet users when the child was only a 3-year-old.)

Finally, as the teen becomes a 17-year-old, computing and telecommunications technology inventions and innovations had culminated with Apple's iPhone—the first "do-it-all device" replacing the need to carry separate PDAs, MP3 players and cell phones. In 2008, now an 18-year-old, our teenager is considered throughout the United States (at least for most purposes) to be legally an adult with all rights and responsibilities that go along with that. They probably graduated from high school and may be on their way to college. Chances are they own at least two electronic devices (e.g., a computer and a cell phone) that enable them to go online at anytime from home or while on the move. They may spend as many or more hours online each day as they do watching television (to the extent there is even a difference in the versions of these technologies that they own or use), and they probably still and always will enjoy electronic gaming and chatting with friends online even as they establish careers and families of their own.

What does age 18 and beyond hold for our teenager? Besides the right to vote and drink (in most states), move about, associate, marry, and work (or not), who can say? What is clear is that our hypothetical teenager grew up in a period of history that is still unfolding and remains arguably unprecedented technologically. Not since the combination of telegraphy, telephones, and automobiles, combined with other inventions of the early twentieth century, has the world witnessed so many technological changes. What is alarming is how quickly this all happened, all since about 1990 when our hypothetical teenager was born, along with the extent that youth and adults throughout the world are now using IT devices and the Internet to interact with each other as friends or associates as well as with strangers, in so many different ways, and for so many different reasons.

As of the publishing of this book, our hypothetical youth is about a 19-year-old. This person is among approximately 21 percent of the world population of 6.6 billion people who have Internet connectivity. About 37 percent of this connectivity is in Asia with 550 million (or 14%) of its people connected, and Europe has 382 million (or 48%) of its people connected. Overall Internet usage increased 290 percent from 2000–2008 with the fastest growing regions during this time frame being the Middle East (1176%), Africa (1030%) and Latin America/Caribbean (660%). North America however, consisting of the United States and Canada, was the earliest and fastest growing region in the world during the 1990s when our typical American child was growing up with information technology. Today North America with approximately 337 million people consisting of only 5 percent of the world population has 73 percent of its residents connected to the Internet.[5]

## TECHNOLOGY-ENABLED GENERATION SHIFT AND THE ONSET OF SOCIAL COMPUTING

Since the advent of the telegraph and telephone, people have used electronic technology to socialize and socially network. The sensation of social networking with computers originated as college and university students and other adults began using the Internet routinely to interact with each other using text messages for personal as well as professional purposes. That was over 50 years ago, in the late 1950s. Since that time, as we have already indicated through the growing up experiences of our hypothetical teenager, the Internet was invented, eventually commercialized (in 1993) and effectively transformed into what most people now generally know as the World Wide Web. Today we simply refer to this as either "the Web" or "the Net." Along the way in this history we had Generation X and Generation Y, and what recent observers now call the Web or Net Generation. Somehow these terms do not quite capture the new reality that social computing and mobile computing are fast becoming one in the same thing and that the couch potatoes of yesterday have been replaced by *mouse-potatoes* of one kind or another!

Welcome Generation WiFi. Teenagers and young adults today are surrounded by and are active participants in a wired and wireless IT-enabled world. According to recent research findings of the Pew Internet and American Life Project, 93 percent of American teens (approximately 20 million) now use the Internet,[6] and more than half of all teenagers access the Net on a daily basis.[7] When teenagers go online, research indicates that 90 percent send or receive e-mail, and 84 percent visit Web sites for popular entertainment information such as movies, television shows, music groups, or sports/sports stars.[8] Other online activities in order of popularity include playing electronic games, getting information about current events, sending or receiving instant messages, retrieving information about colleges, researching politics, buying things, researching health information, looking for employment information, and looking for religious information.

Increasingly, youth are using cell phones and other portable devices to access the Net and to interact with one another. For example, one in three American teens reportedly use a cell phone to text message.[9] Online social networks can rapidly form, expand, and now span the world with any number of individuals involved. Mobile computing made possible by cell phones and other portable devices accentuates possibilities for simultaneous in person and online interactions, resulting in a world where friends are everywhere!

Unfortunately, teens who are quickly becoming social computing experts and who have created online digital content are also more likely to report being cyber bullied.[10] Indeed, as will be explained later in the book, opportunities to connect and share information online go right along with opportunities to be harmed or to harm others online.

The lion's share of youth Internet activity involves what is commonly called "social computing." This occurs via social networking sites, electronic games, blogs and similar online forums where a majority of today's youth hangout in their free time. Recent research shows that 55 percent of teenagers who are between the ages of 12 to 17 who are online have a profile on a social networking site, with 42 percent of social networkers also indicating that they blog.[11] Perhaps escalating gasoline and food prices are forcing more youth into cyberspace in lieu of physical places such that social computing forums are steadily replacing or at least augmenting traditional youth hangouts like parking lots, food joints and shopping malls. After all, in the online world, youth can band together to share ideas and their creativity in all sorts of ways without spending money or being hassled by parents or law enforcement officers. Generally speaking, very few people in positions of authority or responsibility over kids actually know what those kids do when they are online or why.

## DIGITAL YOUTH CULTURE

As personal computers and worldwide computerization provide steadily more access to the Web, more and younger people connect to the online world, and in the process, to each other. Today millions upon millions of kids and young adults, having grown up with the Net and incorporated IT devices into their lifestyles, instinctively jump online whenever they have a question or wish to socially interact in some way. Essentially they are youth in an emerging worldwide Internet or digital culture. More accurately, and if you prefer, *they are creating and representing the digital culture of contemporary youth*. Put differently, more and more youth are routinely participating in myriad Internet activities that involve socially engaging each other online. Surely this is no surprise since we all know that societies continually evolve and are moved along in part if not substantially by the desires and needs of youth.

The challenges of describing the digital culture of contemporary youth are twofold. First, creating new labels for old problems is not trivial when it comes to addressing complex societal problems seriously. People in institutions like the media, legislative bodies, and advocacy organizations sometimes create appealing labels without much consideration of problematic effects new labels can introduce, such as increasing taxes to pay for expensive programs that may not work! Unfortunately most people do not give new or sensational labels much thought. Take *cyber bullying* for example. This relatively new label for an old problem has triggered a good deal of interest, concern, arguments, and even the need for this book. The central issue is whether cyber bullying is actually something different or merely the ongoing technological evolution of ways in which kids beat each other up along with, of course, who should be held responsible.

Academics understand the labeling challenge in terms of what they call construct validity (i.e., how do you know that you know something seemingly new or different actually exists?). The worse thing we could do as a society is not carefully consider the issue and what can and should be done about it (which by the way are not the same thing). Regardless of labeling challenges and controversy and the need to get it right, society, in fact, needs to understand and manage new problems, as well as new variations of old problems that periodically develop. Just as we cannot afford to pay for ineffective prevention programs, we cannot always afford to sit back on our thumbs and wait for problems to resolve themselves. Therefore, along the way, we necessarily create labels for phenomena that seem different or important in some way. So what? Practically speaking, catchy labels for problems can help to inspire needed attention and command resources to help solve societal problems, like cyber bullying, provided we genuinely understand the foundations, elements, causes, and correlations of the phenomenon.

Society continually struggles with new terms to describe changing circumstances in the world. As we will explain throughout this book, cyber bullying represents the changing nature of traditional face-to-face verbal, written, and physical bullying. We contend that cyber bullying represents transforming traditional bullying methods that are continuing to change right along with digital technologies that are radically changing our world in many ways. So just as we have embraced the term cyber bullying to help readers understand these changes and what all the fuss is about, we will also throughout the book use the term *digital youth culture* as an abbreviation for youth in digital culture or (as indicated above) the digital culture of contemporary youth.

The second challenge defining these or other such concepts is explaining what we mean by a label, and why a new term like *digital youth culture* makes sense. This term began appearing incidentally in online forums and academic articles in approximately 2001. Although a few scholars have referred to digital youth culture with respect to electronic or video gaming, no one has previously attempted to articulate the concept in more general ways to the best of our knowledge. Sam McQuade's theory is that digital youth culture pertains to why and ways in which young people use computers, cellular phones, and other types of portable technology devices to interact with each other. The label does not imply something inherently good or bad, though it does brand today's youth and young adults with regard to their online activities. Contemporary digital youth culture needs to be understood in several ways, ranging from its social and psychological properties to aspects of enabling forces such as technology for commerce in our increasingly high-tech society.

Like all cultures, digital youth culture evolves over time with changes in technology, language, social mores, laws, and the collective experiences of people who participate. As youngsters become more adept technologically they learn to navigate cyberspace and survive within the digital youth culture that places high value on actively participating in social computing via electronic gaming, blogs, chat rooms, Web sites (like MySpace, Facebook, and YouTube), instant messaging (IM) with computers, or text messaging with cell phones. As technological devices continue to become more interoperable and multifunctional, the machines—as well as users of them—are more able to talk to each other and carry out far ranging activities that involve the exchange of data.

Digital youth culture inspires, enables, and reflects new realities about youth coming of age in the Digital Age who more or less share attitudes about issues and activities as they interact through social computing activities like online gaming; creating profiles, and posting information onto networking forums (i.e., MySpace, Facebook, and YouTube); and blogging, instant messaging (i.e., IM-ing) with computers and text messaging (i.e., texting) with cell phones. To be sure, not all youth are able—or choose not to—engage in social computing, or do so in different ways and to different extents. Nonetheless, in order to understand why technology is so important in the changing nature of traditional bullying, consider that a vast majority of today's youth actively use the Internet and that the age of onset for their using computers and other types of electronic devices gets younger every year.

Remember our hypothetical teenager born in 1990? Now consider additional survey research conducted by Samuel McQuade and his colleagues from April 2004 through January 2005 at the Rochester Institute of Technology (RIT) and at the State University of New York (SUNY) at Brockport. When our teenager was a 14- or 15-year-old, hundreds of college students at these universities were randomly surveyed.[12,13] As a group they reported beginning to use computers on average as 10-year-olds (in about 1995). However, in a major follow-up study involving over 40,000 K–12th grade students surveyed in 2007–2008 reported they began using computers on average as 7-year-olds.[14] This would have been in about 1997, when our hypothetical student was also a 7-year-old! This larger and most recent study also revealed that more than half of children now attending kindergarten or 1st grade (who are between 5- to 7-year-olds) are using home computers to connect to the Internet.

Can you see how the age for the onset of computing and accessing of the Internet is steadily earlier? Can you also understand that as computing begins at younger and younger ages active engagement in social networking and thus creation of digital youth culture by kids themselves is being extended downward into tween ages (9–12-year-olds) and childhood years? Consider the following additional findings from RIT's 2007–2008 "Internet and At Risk Behaviors Survey" of K–12th grade students:

- Of the 63 percent of 4,459 kindergarten and 1st grade students surveyed in 2007–2008 who use a home computer to access the Internet, 92 percent use their home computer to play electronic games, 66 percent watch videos or listen to music, 48 percent read or write e-mail, 41 percent talk with people on a Web site and 49 percent look at Web sites for schoolwork. As children age they use more types of devices to access the Internet and they spend more time online doing more kinds of things.
- Many students first report cyber bullying experiences in 2nd grade, with 18 percent of 2nd–3rd graders surveyed reporting that someone was mean to them online, and 9 percent admitting they have been mean to someone online, within the year preceding the survey.
- In addition, 68 percent of 2nd–3rd graders surveyed reported their parents do not watch them when they are using a computer at home, 50 percent reported parents do not limit their home computer use, 63 percent reported that when they use a computer they do so for a long time and 30 percent reported they did not tell a grown-up after experiencing content that made them feel uncomfortable.

By the beginning of the 4th grade most kids in urban, suburban, and rural school settings have been well equipped to access the Internet and participate in all forms of online learning, entertainment, and social computing. In contrast to their younger counterparts, RIT's research reveals that among 9,350 4th–6th graders surveyed in 2007–2008 about their Internet activities, 92 percent reported they play electronic games, 87 percent visit Web sites designed for kids, 80 percent listen to music, 72 percent watch videos or do schoolwork online, 54 percent read or write e-mail, 38 percent instant message (IM), 26 percent participate in chat rooms, and 24 percent text message. Having grown up using computerized devices and never having known a world without the Internet, they eagerly learn new information technology skills and assume their place as members in the worldwide digital youth culture. Technology savvy kids today are what Marc Prensky in 2001 referred to as "digital natives" as opposed to "digital immigrants who are adults now over thirty years of age."[15]

Digital youth culture must be considered in the context of prevailing youth attitudes about computing throughout its technological history. The elements of today's attitudes toward using the Internet and IT devices have been significantly shaped by philosophies espoused by the Hacker Ethic, the Open Source Community, online gamers, and innumerable commercial, technical, and recreational special interest groups that have blossomed within the Digital Age. In general, these philosophies hold in common and value notions that access to information should be universal, unregulated, and relatively inexpensive if not free. In addition, people are naturally curious and enjoy exploring and discovering knowledge through computing, which can be rewarding in its own right not unlike any other hobby, athletic interest, or intellectual pursuit. Computing (and now mobile computing) are choices of lifestyle if not a necessity in modernized societies. Computing is here to stay.

Like it, live it or not, it's a choice everyone must make for themselves limited only by their time, money, and technological aptitude.

These general principles combine to form the first in a collection of elements that foster attitudes, choices, and behaviors of youth engaged in or otherwise subsumed by digital youth culture and in the quest to create original content that distinguishes who they are. Digitized data or "content" as it is commonly referred to, can take the form of text, still photos of images, video clips, sound, animation, and so forth. As you probably know, figuring out how to make IT devices do what they are capable of can be initially challenging, so youth who continually track the latest gadgets to hit the market are known to help each other out online. The result is infinite exploration of the Net and explosive creativity among youth who work together to solve problems, and to create and share content that reflects who they are. In the process, dozens of "friends" begin to associate online in a process known as "friending" and everyone engaged shares a love of social computing and technology devices that make life as they know it possible.

Members of digital youth culture promote and reward things that have to do with demonstrating technological prowess in interactive forums, including: (1) demonstrating competitive, teaming, and creative capabilities when electronic gaming or developing Web sites or social networking profiles; (2) providing rapid-fire mutual aid responses to technical questions (e.g., Person A asks Person B something he does not know, but who then poses the question to Group 1 resulting in Person A getting her answer from any member of the group and/or from Person B, and so on); and (3) using abbreviations and cryptic syntax called "netspeak" or more specifically "leetspeak" (i.e., elite speak, like "lol"= laughing out loud) to creatively abbreviate and thereby quicken responses while disguising the meaning of messages to the prying eyes of parents or other supervising grown-ups. (More will be said about leetspeak in Chapter 3.)

Creatively expressing oneself online is central to the concept of digital youth culture. Nearly 40 percent of online teens now share their own creations such as art, music, photos, and stories online while also showcasing their creativity in other ways as indicated above.[16] Digital youth culture continues to evolve and is already different from that which existed when 20-somethings or older individuals grew up, and it continues to change rapidly with technology that makes it possible if not inevitable. Always the emphasis is on being online and interacting quickly in ways that are deemed cool by other youth. (Note: Some academics refer to the inevitability of technology as "technology determinism," which is something we do not necessarily ascribe to because people decide what technologies are worthwhile; technologies decide nothing, though once established its existence bears heavily in all kinds of decision making along with individual and collective behaviors of people.)

Unlike youth of previous generations who grew up without using the Internet and myriad portable IT devices as learning resources and for communication along with stimulation, today's youth have literally integrated computers, cell phones, and entertainment devices into nearly all of their free time activities. Unable to use their devices or connect to the Net for extended periods of time (e.g., more than a day), many young people will literally feel disoriented, socially isolated, and out of control. A popular television sitcom recently portrayed this when the leading youth actor, sent to his room without his cell phone asked his parents, "So what I am suppose to do now?" Response: "read a book." Youth actor: "No *SERIOUSLY*—what am I suppose to do?" What the sitcom did not reveal is the reality that many youth today have more than one means of accessing the Net, engaging friends online or otherwise using IT devices to occupy themselves. Many youth are now known to text each other using cell phones from their bedrooms or other private places well after midnight.

This sitcom example represents an underlying theme of this book, which is how the new reality of social computing and digital youth culture skews and challenges acceptable behaviors in civil society. As indicated in the opening quote of this chapter, many youth interviewed for this book had never heard about cyber bullying prior to being asked about it. For them, online insults, embarrassment, harassment, or threats is simply a condition of being online and active in cyberspace. Their attitude toward this reality is similar to the expectation of getting at least a little wet if you walk in the rain even with an umbrella and while wearing a raincoat. With respect to online bullying, some days are cloudier than others, on some days it rains a little, and on other days the Net is filled with cyber bullying thunder and lighting! And as with places in the real world, some spaces in the online world (e.g., particular social networking forums) are more prone to storms than are others, and youth who spend time in these environments vary in their temperaments and ability to handle or engage in various kinds of foul weather. Digital youth culture in part if not in the main, clearly tolerates and may actually perpetuate stormy conditions online that involve abusive, harmful, and criminal behaviors.

## HARMFUL ASPECTS OF DIGITAL YOUTH CULTURE

Studies about what we call digital youth culture are now just beginning to emerge albeit not by this name (e.g., works by the Pew Foundation, MacArthur Foundation, and independent scholars throughout the world). Nonetheless from this research we are able to formulate impressions about digital content that youth now create and post online, which obviously to some extent is a reflection of their online groups and collective mindset. While millions of youth engage in harmless and positive online exchanges, millions of other *and the same* youth and young adults also engage in various types of cyber abuse and offending behaviors, such as: academic dishonesty, cyber bullying, online crimes like pirating of music, movies, and software, and password cracking, "data snooping," and computer hacking among other types of cyber crimes. Many youth and adults also participate in sexually suggestive and explicit conversations and posting nude photographs of themselves or someone else online (i.e., pseudo child pornography). It is now also understood that youth as well as adults are increasingly committing several forms of traditional crime in higher tech ways, which is a subject that we also explore in more detail later in Chapter 3.

Increasingly, cyber abuse and online offending behaviors are engaged in or at least affecting youth at astonishingly young ages. Data from the Rochester Institute of Technology "Survey of Internet and At-Risk Behaviors" involving over 40,000 K–12th grade students in 14 New York State school districts is also now revealing important correlations between cyber abuse and offending behaviors among young people who routinely interact with each other online. As the old saying goes, "kids can be cruel" but we are discovering that this reality applies to online as well as off-line behaviors.

As youth mature and struggle through adolescence, their creative capacity to harm other people, whether intentionally or unintentionally, multiplies with their natural drives to become more independent combined with the number of people, circumstances, ideas, and *technologies they are exposed to and use.* This has always been the case, but today widespread and rapidly growing Internet connectivity and powerful personal computers, along with interoperable and mobile technology devices, may be accelerating generational differences between relatively young and old people. We think this is the case, and that it represents an unprecedented period in history with enormous implications for parenting and for adult-youth relations. In time, differing attitudes toward and aptitudes for actively engaging in social computing among generations of people will undoubtedly be reduced—eventually nearly everyone gets on board with new technologies, though new technologies invariably create new differences and variations of old problems—and so it goes. Cyber bullying is a point in case.

Perpetuation of cyber bullying and other illicit behaviors is evident in millions of Web pages, chat rooms, and blogs containing content created by youth. We wish to stress, however, that it is only the abusive, aggressive, and uncivil aspects of digital youth culture that is of concern. Rochester Institute of Technology's 2007–2008 "Survey of Internet and At-Risk Behaviors" of approximately 10,000 middle school students found that within the previous year: 6 percent were asked online for a nude photo of themselves, 8 percent were shown a nude photo of someone else, 10 percent were requested to engage in sexual chat, and 13 percent actually engaged in sexual chat. Survey findings substantiate that in most instances this content was sent by other youth such as a boy, girl, classmate, friend, or online friend. Data also reveal that pirating via peer-to-peer (p2p) file sharing of music, movies, and software begins in 4th grade, and that cyber bullying is commonly experienced through primary and secondary grades. Additionally, RIT survey findings also show that online sexual promiscuity, social computing, and cyber bullying positively, significantly, and highly correlate. This means that kids involved in any one of these three things are likely to be involved in the other two.

Given these data we conclude that contemporary digital youth culture is much more accepting of abusive, illicit, and illegal behaviors than society in general, and that this along with the timeless creed not to "snitch on friends" amounts to a fourth element deserving of special attention. Abuses and violations of laws are common and collectively fuel enjoyable-to-menacing conditions for youth Internet users who have come to expect, tolerate, and/or even endorse such behaviors. This occurs in the absence of adequate supervision and positive role modeling by parents or other adults who are respected by youth. But whenever cyber abuse or cyber crime occurs, and no matter what form it takes, if online or in-person friends are involved, reporting violators to adults or authorities is absolutely forbidden! Paradoxically, it is OK within the digital youth culture for youth to tell friends about their problems, and seek their support. Sadly, given the fickleness of youth relationships (especially prior to high school years) friends often betray friends by exposing their secrets online for large numbers of other kids to read and make fun of. This by the way may help to explain why cyber bullying may peak during middle school, especially among female students, a subject that will be discussed in more detail later.

Despite its harmful aspects, we embrace digital youth culture for what it is: a logical and naturally occurring outcome of genuinely cool technology that unfortunately is frequently abused in various ways by great numbers adolescents and young adults (as well as older adults). Like all cultures, digital youth culture has its pros and cons, including those things that relate to all matters of the human condition: knowledge, faith, social bonds, love, sex, conflict, violence, and so forth. In the final analysis, the Net provides youth with exciting opportunities to communicate, share, learn, and have fun. It also provides them with requisite knowledge and skills they will need to be successful as adults in an increasingly high-tech and interconnected world. The Net also exposes kids to many things they are not prepared to handle very well, including, but not limited to, sexually explicit content often generated and exchanged among youth themselves.

Researchers who carried out the 1999 National Youth Internet Safety Survey found that 48 percent of all unwanted online solicitations for sex received by youth younger than an 18-year-old were sent by other youth also younger than an 18-year-old.[17] Parents need to understand that adolescents who are naturally exploring their sexuality actively use their IT devices and the Internet to do so. In the process they socially engage one another to chat and romance, they discover and view pornography, and they hit on each other. When things don't go well, some youth write, create, send, or post mean content online. No one can do this better than youth who have grown up using the technology and fused it with who they are becoming as individuals and collectively as the WiFi Generation.

### GOOD AND HARMFUL ELEMENTS OF DIGITAL YOUTH CULTURE

Youth love IT devices and the Internet. Social computing via Web site forums, chat rooms, blogs, electronic gaming, IM-ing, and texting are integral aspects of their living in the modern world.

Competition, teaming to solve problems and creativity pervade and combine to provide for rich and intellectually stimulating online interactions. Youth and young adults get hooked on these things.

Being online (a lot), always available to chat or help out and rapid-fire sending and receiving of electronic messages are highly valued. To be cool, youth must possess and use their cell phone or other technology devices often (though being overly geeky can also become the basis for someone to be cyber bullied).

Communicating with abbreviations and cryptic syntax earns praise, respect, and status. It also enables messages to be sent quicker and in ways not readily understood by parents or other adults.

Online incivility, promiscuity, abuse, and crime are common, to be expected, and tolerated. Sending and receiving mean or nasty messages is done routinely by many, though not all, youth online, as is lying about age, appearance, and other personal matters.

In the abbreviated rapid-fire environment in which youth thrive online, some individuals never fully learn how to interface with the larger society using established—or what are conventionally considered—proper communication skills whether in writing or verbally.

Through time, as youth explore themselves and their places in the world and through spaces in cyberspace, networks of actual friends and invisible believed-in friends are created.

Online time spent with other people reduces traditional ways (and arguably more natural and effective ways) through which people come to bond and learn to genuinely trust each other.

In the end, many youth come to develop a false sense of real friendships, associations, and what it means to trust. The concept of trust itself may become distorted or even questioned with regard to its true value and necessity for maintaining friendships, associations, and elements of a functioning society. Online activities that erode rather than promote civility within and across societies become less deviant and more widespread. Cyber bullying is now an obvious example of what is occurring in this regard.

## CONTEMPLATING THE FUTURE

While not completely endorsing of social networking forums, as educators, researchers, authors, adults, and parents who care deeply about youth, we recognize the reality and positive aspects of social computing and digital youth culture *when* youth are solidly educated about risks involved and adequately supervised while engaging other people online. We also recognize and understand that the Net provides youth with boundless realms through which they can discover things, share ideas, express their creativity, or otherwise interact in seemingly private places about private things that becomes increasingly necessary and their right as they age. Further, the Net provides many and various opportunities for youth and young adults to learn about and befriend people throughout the world, which on the whole may promote appreciation, tolerance, and even acceptance of differences and thereby build potentially lasting and trusting relationships.

However, cell phones and other portable devices now typically carried around by kids in modern societies converge with lifestyle choices and necessities. These forces and processes increasingly equate social computing with mobile computing. The result is that MySpace, Facebook, and dozens of similar social networking forums and mediums through which people can connect with each other online effectively enable youth to maintain a social life with family and friends without ever having to leave or go home. At anytime, and from anywhere that offers a cellular phone or Internet connection, they can write to, speak with, or literally see their online friends simply depending on the technological capabilities of the devices they use. And of course online friends may include people they have never actually met in person and/or who live in another part of the world.

In yesteryear, prior to the onset of the World Wide Web and the more recent phenomenon of social computing, kids expressed themselves and formed a sense of identity in face-to-face manners such as through personal contacts, participating in school activities, musical preferences, or wearing a certain fashionable style of clothing. Today, kids still do these things, but also can instantly share their digital identities with the world on a social networking site. Rochester Institute of Technology's research substantiates that beginning in the 4th grade students are not shy about posting their real or perhaps false identities, residential addresses, school location, or personal phone numbers online. As previously indicated, they also readily share interests, opinions, music, pictures, and lists of friends. Today it is difficult if not impossible to purchase a cell phone without a built-in digital/video camera, and computer Webcams are inexpensive and commonly used by youth to literally perform (sometimes sexually) while social computing.

Since youth believe that their cyber world is private or should be, meaning outside the awareness of parents and older adults, the harmful and/or alarming aspects of digital youth culture become even murkier to understand or prevent. Teenagers often do not want their parents to know what they are doing online because they know it is wrong and/or believe it is personal stuff that parents have no right to know about much less butt into! Whether they are engaging in positive Internet use or participating in unacceptable behaviors like cyber bullying, social networking forums like MySpace, Facebook, and YouTube are *their* spaces, at least in their minds. Of course this begs the question of what happens when youth and young adults grow up to begin families of their own, and whether parents or other adults masquerading as youth should access, view, or even go so far as to participate in online forums considered by young people as being their digital turf. Unresolved control of social networking forums and ethical considerations about what constitutes social deviancy and responsible parenting in the Digital Age confounds, rather than bridges, gaps between parents, young adults, and youth. These issues are given more and careful consideration in Chapter 2 in which we further explore reasons why individuals become involved in and/or experience bullying and cyber bullying.

Given amazing and continually expanding levels of technological connectivity and associated vulnerabilities to becoming abused or slipping into harmful behavioral patterns online, some important questions must be considered: Are tweens (kids between the ages of 9 and 12), teens, and young adults being adequately prepared to safely and responsibly interact with an online world? For that matter, are older adults any more or less prepared to use technological devices responsibly? Do people have the judgment to navigate rocky social networking streams and dangerous information content rapids on the Web? Have we as a society been systematically provided with Internet safety, information security, and cyber ethics education, along with technical training needed to prevent cyber bullying, among other forms of online abuse and offending? Do parents have the technological awareness and skills to provide positive role modeling and sound advice to their children and teenagers? Are schools implementing bullying prevention and ethics instruction initiatives, and to what extent have these intervention strategies been shown to be effective?

Unfortunately, at this point, the answer to these questions is most likely, "no" or "not much" or "who knows?" There simply has not been enough time and not enough serious attention paid to such questions, nor to the reality of bullying among youth, young adults, and other people who are actively engaged in online activities, to satisfactorily know all the answers to online bullying. For the sake of the safety of our children and their children however, the time to start figuring out real answers to the questions above is now! This book is a start.

# Characteristics and Causes of Bullying Among Individuals and Groups

*I get the greatest feeling of power when I destroy someone, especially when it's behind their back and not face to face. So what? Everybody does it. It's fun! Adults are never going to step up. We're way ahead of them. Stop us one way and we'll invent another way.*

*—13-year-old female*

So far we have discussed the reality that social computing now effectively equates to mobile computing that is integral to digital youth culture. We also explained in Chapter 1 that kids today rely on social and electronic gaming networks to interact with their online and in-person friends. Also that cyber bullying is an extension of classical in-person bullying methods and is a key type of incivility that increasingly occurs online by and among youth. In this chapter we next explore what is known about bullies and their victims. In the first section of the chapter we will review what is known about their ages, gender, and issues pertaining to juvenile crime. We also discuss the psychological traits of bullies and their victims, what is generally known about their ethnicity and family structure, as well as their school settings and other characteristics.

In the second section of this chapter we will consider 10 commonly believed myths about bullying. Each myth is explained with a real life example of bullying often reported in the words of a bully or their victim.

In the third section we discuss online deceit and incivility. Here we'll take a look at how feelings of invincibility and anonymity combine in what is known as "disinhibition" that contributes to youth misbehaving online. We also examine how these issues can affect judgment about what is harmful when clouded by excessive playing of online games that feature aggression, violence, and sex. This section ends with some comments about the role that societal culture reinforced by mass media now has in also creating, condoning, and disseminating content that does little to advance online civility and may help to explain why many youth are so uncivil to each other when online.

We conclude the chapter in a fourth section by addressing several things that may also contribute to bullying in society. Here we provide more in-depth discussion about social computing and networking that occurs via Web forums like MySpace, Facebook, and YouTube as a basis for social learning, abusive attitudes, and behaviors. We also discuss insufficient discipline and accountability on the part of youth, parents, and officials who are responsible for providing supervision and safe environments for young people to interact in. We explain why youth are reluctant to report instances of bullying, and why some youth and parents take matters into their own hands through vigilantism.

## BULLIES AND THEIR VICTIMS

### PSYCHOLOGICAL TRAITS

Bullies have been shown to be aggressive toward their peers, and often to adults such as parents and teachers.[1] By aggression we mean behaviors that involve uncontrolled anger, violence involving property damage or physical injury, hostility including making threats or otherwise putting people in fear, and belligerence or antagonism toward parents or legitimate authority figures and the rules they establish. In a general sense, bullies have a more positive (i.e., apathetic) view about being aggressive than their peers. Consequently, despite social norms that discourage causing harm to other people, bullies derive satisfaction from acting out even if it causes emotional or physical pain to others. Researchers, psychologists, and guidance counselors have long known that bullies often lack empathy for their victims. It is by repeating and establishing patterns of behaviors that erode joy, trust, and hope in other people that distinguishes a bully from someone who infrequently gets upset or lashes out. Many, but not all bullies, are emotionally insecure, have anger management issues, and tend to take out their frustrations on other people.

With regard to school functioning, the attitudes, behaviors, and values of bullies have been shown to be at odds with the majority of students in school populations. When bullies become regarded as such they often receive less positive attention by teachers to facilitate their learning.[2] It is as if teachers subconsciously no longer wish to deal with bullies and perhaps reduce effective teaching of them as the result of disciplinary measures necessarily taken against them to ensure control of classrooms. Bullies may live in socio-economically deprived, abusive, or estranged home or neighborhood settings, though this is not always the case. Communities plagued with criminal youth gangs and crime problems may systematically produce and perpetuate bullying attitudes and behaviors as youth necessarily get tough in order to survive on the streets that they live, play, and hangout on.

Community environments in which tough street kids live is somewhat analogous to the "wild west" environments of cyberspace in which rules are not well-defined or enforced and cyber bullies languish. However, some bullies live in very comfortable settings, attend fine school districts, and have very loving parents who provide their every imaginable need even to the point of spoiling their kids into becoming selfish brats. After all, youth can only experience cyber bullying to the extent they are online, implying that they need information technology (IT) devices and Internet/cellular phone connections to become a cyber bully, a cyber-bullying victim, or both. Regardless of socioeconomic and school environments, bullying tends to decrease as children get older, but increases markedly at the beginning of secondary school (middle school) when students entering a new school building are vulnerable to being picked on by older students who are already familiar with settings, routines, and campus cultures.[3] This is akin to juvenile or adult offenders entering into a new institutional setting—they are very vulnerable to being abused in various ways by prisoners who already know whose who and what's what. Of course middle school years are also when most youth enter puberty and experience raging hormones, develop greater independence from parents, establish progressively more influential relationships with friends, and sometimes find themselves askew of status offenses such as drinking, smoking, and truancy. It is during middle school years when troublemakers such as bullies typically have their first encounters with law enforcement and school security officers.

It follows that victims of bullying are often younger and more passive than bullies, and may also lack close or supportive peer relationships at school.[4] Bullying victims are more likely to be depressed, anxious, have low self-esteem, perform poorly academically, and have suicidal thoughts.[5] Children who are bullied tend to be more socially isolated than other children.[6] These correlations do not necessarily mean causation. For example, children may be bullied because they are socially isolated, or become socially isolated because they are bullied, or both. For any number of reasons, victims often stand out and are easily recognized by bullies as potential targets (i.e., someone who is easy to pick on). Factors contributing to the onset of bullying victimization often worsen with repeated bullying, as when children who are already uncomfortable in new settings or never fully adjusted to these have difficulty learning and become intimidated and afraid. Sadly, many victims of bullying cannot learn effectively because they are distracted by the glares of bullies in a classroom or in hallways—they literally fear for their basic well-being—safety, security, and comfort. Have you ever been so preoccupied with something of concern that you cannot carry out your chores efficiently? This is how victims of bullying feel much of time, whenever they lose confidence in the system that should provide for them.

## AGE, GENDER, SEX, AND MATTERS OF JUVENILE JUSTICE

We now know that kids report being mean to each other online beginning around the 2nd grade when they are approximately a 7- or 8-year-old.[7] We also know on the basis of Rochester Institute of Technology's (RIT) "Survey of Internet and At-Risk Behaviors" that boys initiate mean online interactions earlier in life than girls do. However, by middle school age, girls are slightly more likely to engage in cyber bullying than are boys after which males are steadily more likely than females to engage in cyber bullying. We also know from other research that older teenage girls are more engaged in interpersonal communications and wider online topical information searching than similar aged boys. For example, older girls are more likely to communicate with friends using e-mail and text messaging. This is also true when comparing online activities of female teenagers with those of younger girls and boys. Older girls are also more likely to search for information about colleges, health, religion, and the latest scoop on their favorite stars.[8] They are generally more likely to use blogs, with more than one-third of all female teenagers being bloggers, though younger females aged 12–14 are currently believed to be blogging more than teenage boys.[9]

Boys, on the other hand, are more likely to watch and upload videos than are their female counterparts.[10] By nature, while females are inclined toward socially bonding with each other, male adolescents and young men are generally less so. When it comes to sexuality, males are naturally attracted to sexual images as they mature and consequently much more apt than female adolescents and young women to view pornography.[11] Research conducted by RIT involving 40,079 K–12th grade students found that younger males in high school and less frequently in middle school also viewed pornography, as did a lesser number of females in 7th–12th grades.[12] Of legal concern is the reality that youth are now widely known to make, request and exchange nude photos of each other while discussing sexual things online. When such pseudo child pornography occurs (by virtue of the creation, distribution, and/or archiving of sexual images of real minors) we may assume that state and federal crime laws have been violated.

In May 2008, a 12-year-old girl living and attending middle school in Westport, Connecticut allegedly took a nude snapshot of herself during a video chat session and distributed it to others online. Following school rumors and a police investigation she was referred to juvenile court on "a charge of second-degree breach of peace, which involves the distribution of offensive and indecent material."[13] In May 2007, a 17-year-old Wisconsin youth was arrested and charged with a felony for allegedly posting child pornography to his MySpace page consisting of a photo of his 16-year-old ex-girlfriend. He reportedly did so to get back at her.[14] Earlier that year, on March 26, 2007, a prosecutor in Douglas County, Colorado declined to prosecute 18 middle school students for exchanging nude pictures of themselves with cell phones (a.k.a. "sexting"). In that case at least one photo found its way onto the Internet with very embarrassing consequences for the youths involved.[15]

In May 2006 the badjocks.com Web site was found to contain numerous nude and sexually provocative photos of young men and women athletes from several prominent academic institutions.[16] Findings from RIT's "Survey of Internet and At-Risk Behaviors" confirms that taking, posting, sending, and receiving nude photos, experiencing sexual chat, receiving unwanted solicitations for sex, and viewing of pornography is now common among middle and high school students, and extends downward into primary school to involve 6th grade and even younger students. Sex-related text and images are so ingrained into social computing activities that exchanges of such content, though illegal, can no longer be considered deviant for many youths. More to the point, since sex-related issues matter a great deal to adolescents who are spending more time interacting online, it is not surprising the extent to which cyber bullying activities have to do with relationships, gender, and/or sex, and that posting or distributing nude photos is now a common aspect of cyber bullying.

Clearly, gender must be considered an important element in our thinking about cyber bullying especially in contexts of social networking activities among teens. Consider that most bullying, except for online cyber bullying in middle and high school, is done by males. Longstanding research on pre-Internet physical bullying has clearly substantiated that boys are generally bigger, stronger, rougher and tougher, and more naturally prone to mix it up physically (e.g., shoving, punching, kicking, fistfighting, and so forth). However, just because an individual is bigger and stronger than someone else does not mean they are necessarily more inclined to bully their peers.[17] Nonetheless, these attributes, when combined with aggression often result in physical bullying behaviors. Female bullies often are more subtle and/or cunning in their methods (e.g., spreading rumors and manipulating social relationships), which may help to explain why recent research shows that girls can dominate teenage cyber bullying.

From research we also believe that males are more likely to be bullied by other males, and females are bullied by both sexes.[18] Males are more likely to be physically bullied, while females are more likely to be victims of rumors and sexual comments.[19] RIT's "Survey of Internet and At-Risk Behaviors" of K–12th grade students also substantiates that gender factors into cyber bullying varies among age and grade levels. Some of these research findings, as shown in Figure 2.1, reveals that cyber bullying defined as someone being mean or being mean to someone begins in 2nd grade. At this grade level,

**Figure 2.1**
**Cyber Bullying in 2nd–12th Grades**

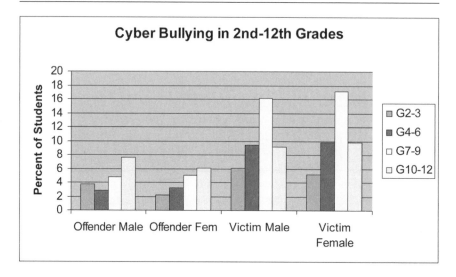

cyber bullying victimization is higher than cyber bullying offending, and boys more actively experience bullying as offenders and victims than do girls.

Beginning in the 4th grade and continuing through 12th grade, RIT's research consistently analyzes cyber bullying as a combination of being embarrassed, harassed, or receiving threats online. At the 4th–6th grade level, children are victimized much more than they commit cyber bullying, with little distinction between genders. This relationship continues at the 7th–9th grade levels, although rates of offending and victimization increase rather substantially. This supports other research findings that cyber bullying peaks in middle school, but RIT's "Survey of Internet and At-Risk Behaviors" involving more than 10,000 middle school student respondents clearly show the peak only pertains to victimization, not offending. As students age into high school, rates of offending by both boys and girls continue to increase as victimization declines. But it is interesting to note that the percentage of female victims is consistently higher than male victims from 4th grade through 12th grade. From other research, we also know that characteristics of both the bully and the victim predispose children to future violent behavior.[20] Without adult intervention, these children are more at risk for continued bullying, social rejection, and depression.

Whether a bully is male or female matters less than the reality that both genders now commonly engage in cyber bullying such as intentionally embarrassing others, harassment, intimidation, or making threats online. It is also important to note that most bullying continues to be verbal rather than physical in nature.[21] Since youth are increasingly communicating online, cyber bullying via e-mail, text messaging, posts to blogs, Web sites, and during electronic gaming sessions, our conceptions about bullying and its being limited to face-to-face encounters needs to change. Although words may not cause physical injury, they can result in emotional pain and suffering that far exceed physical pain, especially if a youth's whole world revolves around their being able to go online to connect and interact with their friends.

Sadly, many people bullied in their formative years grow up to become bullies in their own right as young adults and continue their abusive ways throughout their adult lives. Over time their own unresolved issues including substance abuse, anger or depression, impulsive or antisocial behaviors, combined with mean-spirited intentions, flare-up or resurface again and again, often with escalating harm caused in the lives of people with whom they interact. We see this in cases of domestic violence and child abuse, as well as in the workplace and public settings, and in systematically committed crimes such as those involving ongoing harassment or coercion. Broadly speaking, some level of bullying is prominent in many forms of organized and gang-related crimes, including, for example, human trafficking of youth for sexual or labor exploitation. In this book we focus on bullying by and among youth, such as that now commonly occurring online between kids in and out of school.

Readers should keep in mind that bullying tolerated in our society is an aspect of myriad other forms of abuse and crime. Indeed, regardless of age and gender, one of the more troubling aspects of bullying is that it is often associated with numerous other negative behaviors. For example, those who bully are more likely to get into physical fights, damage and steal property, drop out of school, and carry a weapon.[22] Also of significance, bullies are more likely to report owning guns that are used for intimidation.[23] In addition, bullies have also been associated with groups who systematically victimize specific groups of peers,[24] and boys identified as bullies are 4 times more likely to have a criminal conviction by age 24.[25] This brings us back to crime ridden communities in which youth often struggle to survive the dangers of real and cyber streets. Commonly held views about classical bullying in physical ways carry over into the paradigm of digital youth culture and social computing thereby confounding understanding of the new reality in which cyber bullying is an insidious extension of real world aggression and violence.

## THE TEN COMMONLY BELIEVED MYTHS
### ABOUT BULLYING

There are obviously many pieces to the complex puzzle of bullying, but developing a greater understanding of the issue provides a solid foundation to initiate meaningful and much needed change. Enduring myths about bullying however continue to be accepted as truths by adults as well as youth, who look to the adults for guidance on how to respond in bullying situations. The following myths must be debunked in order for additional progress to be made in reducing bullying behaviors, with the caveat that the "truths" offered below in response to each of the myths are not absolute. In reality, as we have emphasized, bullying is a complex social problem made worse by virtue of capabilities now provided as a result of the Internet and technological devices. No single myth or suggested truth is likely to sum up every bullying situation encountered by youth. Therefore, consider the following as a list of possibilities for intervention with no guarantees they will be effective in all or any particular case.

> *Myth #1:* Bullying helps victims "toughen up," and only makes them stronger in the long run.
> *Truth:* Bullying generally does not help victims toughen up—it causes substantial pain. Left unchecked continued bullying causes more pain.

In a face-to-face interview a 15-year-old male from western New York indicated that he was a victim of gay bashing via Web sites with comments such as "He walks like a girl," "Great big homo," and "He's a fag." The teenager was crushed, and now feels like he needs to leave the town he lives in when he is able. In the interim, he is quitting school as soon as he turns 16. Gay bashing is a common element in youth cyber bullying, because it has to do with relationships, gender, and issues of sexuality. In this case it left a boy feeling depressed and thinking bad thoughts about what he wants to do to the other kids. One alternative, which parents and other adults responsible for this boy's welfare may be tempted to consider, is simply telling him to tough the situation out. After all, perhaps you remember being bullied and necessarily outlasting the bullies, and in the process becoming thicker skinned and less naïve about people. Yet, more often people who are bullied don't get stronger—they experience sadness, depression, humiliation, and worse.

> *Myth #2:* Bullying is a "normal" part of childhood development. Get over it.
> *Truth:* Being repeatedly subjected to cruel and abusive treatment is not a normal part of childhood development or acceptable in civil societies as a matter of law.

A 15-year-old female from Munich, Germany recalled when her friends posted to a Web site that "she was a slut and would screw any guy at any time." They also started a petition on the Web site to comment on her sexual abilities, to which over 100 males responded and wrote sexual comments and claimed to have had sex with her. She told her parents that it was not true and that she was a virgin, but they did not believe her and sent her to live with her strict religious grandparents. Her life now exists with no computer, no dances, no television, no music, and no social life. She plans on running away to the United States when she turns 16 and her bags are already packed. Unfortunately, many children are exposed to cruel and abusive treatment by peers or even by their parents along with other adults who have influential roles in their lives. This case also reveals that cracking down on innocent youth amounts to another form of abuse known as blaming the victim.

> *Myth #3:* Bullying is sometimes just "playing or goofing around" so what's the big deal?
> *Truth:* Bullying is not playing around unless *everyone* involved is having a good time.

A 7th grade girl attending a Catholic school stated that her friends started a rumor in an online chat room that she had an abortion, although she had never had sex. She knew who was passing the rumors around because they were her friends, and she told them to stop. They told her that the rumors were intended as a joke and that it was funny. The girl was not amused, but she stated that there was no-way she would report the gossip even though it had been happening for over a year. When interviewed she said "my life is ruined" and that she also felt very depressed. In this case, the victim's so-called friends thought it was funny to spread a rumor about an abortion, which to a girl of faith who endears every person's right-to-life is especially denigrating. This joke led to the destruction of her joy, she became depressed, she lost friendships, and was led to a sense of hopelessness.

> *Myth #4:* When bullying becomes serious enough, kids will tell an adult.
> *Truth:* Youth rarely tell parents or other adults about being bullied. This is especially true if their friends are the bullies. Instead they live by a code of silence with "no snitching" allowed.

"There is no way I'm going to report it. I would be totally screwed and friendless" reported a 7th grade boy who, when interviewed, said he was being bullied online. Research has consistently shown that students, and also bystanders, are very reluctant to tell adults about bullying because they do not trust parents to understand or be empathetic with their problems. Nor do they believe that grownups who hold official positions can or will do anything about their situation. Unfortunately, they are often correct, as we indicate in several case stories revealed in this book. Moreover, from a child's perspective, one of the worst things in life is to be labeled a "snitch."

The code of silence that predominates as an aspect of digital youth culture is the risk or an expectation of cyber bullying, as well as other types of abusive and offending behaviors committed by people, who relatively speaking, are friends and/or strangers online. This reality is consistent with false hopes that regardless of the technology used to interface, people can actually know and trust each other *not* to abuse them, but in any case not to report incidents when they do occur. Hence, youth and young adult victims of bullying, including witnesses of bullying, rarely, if ever, tell adults in positions of supervision or authority. Fear that telling may make the bullying worse, and that telling brands someone as a snitch cannot be overemphasized. In addition, the fear among youth of having the technology or access to the Net taken away may be equally dissuading to report cyber bullying. Youth will not risk having their lifelines to their peers taken away, who they genuinely believe to be friends.

"Friending" as a process and goal is fundamental to contemporary digital youth culture, yet it creates interactive conditions ripe for mistrust in relationships leading to incivility via cyber bullying. Actual people physically interacted with and known as friends are periodically confused with online friends who may be the same people, or real people they have or have never met in person, or real people masquerading as someone who does not even exist. Specifying levels of friends in social networking environments may be of some help to victims of cyber bullying who would suffer the consequences of non-reporting rather than risk being labeled a snitch or give up their connections to the Internet and social networks that, for them, is a substantial part of their world. Consequently, for millions of connected youth, cyber bullying is simply the way life is.

> *Myth #5:* Parents of students who bully or are bullied, are usually aware of the problem and will intercede if they deem it necessary.
> *Truth:* Because bullying victims rarely tell parents or other adults what is happening in their online world, grownups are often unaware of the warning signs.

When asked in an interview for this book, a 15-year-old boy living in Brazil defined cyber bullying as "friends that ruin your life and think it's fun. Nobody reports cyber bullying because nobody does anything about it and they don't care. You might as well talk to the wall. Adults don't care. Kids can kill each other in front of a grownup and nothing will be done. My own parents don't care, why should anyone else?" Just as victims of bullying rarely tell grownups about their bullying problems, they also use technology in ways that are foreign to parents who then are not well positioned to intervene if they want to. This is especially true if parents do not understand ways in which computing and telecommunications devices are commonly used by youth, social computing, and key elements of digital youth culture such as the imperative for youth to interact with each other online in order to fit in and be liked. And since kids live online adhering to principles of the digital youth culture, and rarely tell adults details about what is really happening in the world of cyberspace they spend so much time in, parents often do not see warning signs of the bullying their child is experiencing.

> *Myth #6:* Most bullying occurs outside of school or on the way to and from school.
>
> *Truth:* Although schools usually provide for very safe computing environments, most physical and verbal bullying occurs within schools or in connection with school activities. Cyber bullying however, can occur at any time, while a victim is interacting with bullies online or not, and from any location in which portable computing devices make it possible for bullies and/or victims to connect to the Internet.

"Online is the only time I feel powerful. It's powerful, real powerful. A kid tripped me in school and he was real sorry that he ever did it. I smeared his name and face on every social chat site there is. I guarantee that he is toast—burnt toast." This 14-year-old boy lives in Cebu, Philippines. His counterstrike to the tripping incident was to trash his classmate online without the tripper initially realizing that bullying can occur online in real-time exchanges between a bully and a victim, and asynchronously, meaning that bullies can do their thing online in order to ambush their victims with content discovered afterward. More will be said about this in Chapter 3. For now, remember that while cyber bullying can take place on or off school grounds, regardless of where online attacks are launched from, symptoms and outcomes often spill into and out of school, living, recreational, and employment settings during or afterward. Therefore, bullying is a condition, not a single event nor is it a series of events. It prevails within cyber and physical environments occupied by youth. For youth who carry around portable devices and feel compelled to be online in order to interact with their friends, there may be no escape. In this case the tripping incident happened in school, but the counterattack occurred online. Nasty things were being posted online regardless of whether the victim chose to either read, view, respond to the content, or withdraw from the Internet and the socially interactive world of cyberspace in which his friends hang out.

*Myth #7:* Physical bullying is the most common form of bullying among boys and girls.
*Truth:* Verbal bullying is the most common form.

Research has shown that the most common form of bullying among boys and girls is verbal. Name calling, insults, false accusations, whispering rumors, or yelling threats are the easiest ways to bully requiring no money or technological skills. By extension, cyber bullying also involves written or spoken words most of the time, as when youth use group speak software applications to audibly talk rather than write messages to each other, or when they IM or text each other online respectively using computers or cell phones. One female college law student from New Orleans stated that a group of about 20 girls started to pick on her for some reason. It could have been anything—youth frequently report they do not understand what set their friends off against them. This is a common aspect of cyber bullying in which online written messages are frequently misinterpreted.

In this case, the online bullies would repeatedly send the law student text messages saying, "You're a bitch," "You're a loser," and "You're a fat pig," despite her weighing 120 pounds. When interviewed however, the student was baffled as to what started the bullying. If it keeps up, she is thinking about changing colleges. What may be equally troubling here, is that it did not automatically occur to the student to discover the root cause and resolve the conflict in person rather than online. Here again we see the power of years of conditioned responses to relying on IT devices and social computing as a significant augmentation if not a replacement for face-to-face communications. This is very common within digital youth culture that values rapid fire responses to messages often composed in shorthand, semicoded text called netspeak or leetspeak. We will discuss this in some detail in Chapter 3.

*Myth #8:* Bullies suffer from insecurity and low self-esteem.
*Truth:* While some bullies are insecure or have low self-esteem, many bullies are not suffering in these ways. For whatever other reason(s) they can be just mean!

Research has also shown that bullies often have average or above average self-esteem. Contrary to the image of a malcontent bully hiding in an alley waiting to jump out and attack a victim on their way home from school (as was Ralphie's bully in the movie *A Christmas Story*), bullies exist throughout society and may have various or no social, economic, or psychological problems such as intermittent explosive disorder that results in ordinarily controlled people blowing up in a rage for some inexplicable reason. Sometimes it is very hard even for professionals to diagnose what really causes a person to become violent or mean. So as untrained professionals, most people naturally hold up their hands, shake their heads, and resort to saying things like "Oh, he's just a jerk" or "She has a mean streak in her." Unfortunately, this often occurs among parents and other adults who are responsible for the actions and the well-being of youth.

Sudden anger, being mean, and other undesirable qualities in a person sometimes involves bullying as repeated actions intended to embarrass, harass, intimidate, or threaten. In any case, bullies are not always obvious troublemakers, which is part of our challenge. They can be popular, involved with sports, and be part of the "in" crowd. Bullies can believe in God and attend church, where incidentally, bullying can also occur. Bullies often feel pretty good about themselves, are prone to showing off or strutting their stuff on- or off-line, and feel even better when they can exert power over people they regard as being different or weaker in some way.

Within certain environments, bullying can even be a "cool" thing to do, as when sentiments or prejudices of a majority can be played upon. This happens a lot in gay bashing cases, and is worsened by the fact that so many kids are now mean or disrespectful to each other online. This was previously referred to as uncivil aspects of social computing and an element of digital youth culture. It relates to ways in which cyber bullying has advantages over physical bullying and why youth who would never engage in face-to-face bullying will cyber bully. As stated by a 14-year-old female from Reyes, France when asked about cyber bullying: "Yeah what about it? I can get away with anything on the computer. If I do it in person, I can get in a lot of trouble. It's cool and that's what kids do. Who's going to stop us? We can't be stopped, and we're not hurting anyone, so grownups should mind their own business." Her comments betray the reality that: (1) many youth today seem not to equate online activities and emotional harm in cyber bullying with physical actions and physical harm that occur in traditional bullying; and (2) often possess an arrogance having to do with the harmful elements of digital youth culture described in Chapter 1 and perceptions of invulnerability and anonymity as part of disinhibition mentioned earlier in this chapter.

*Myth #9:* Bullying and conflict mean the same thing.
*Truth:* Bullying involves a perpetrator holding power over and dominating a victim in some way usually over an extended period of time. Conflict however, involves mutual disagreements. Whereas two or more parties involved in conflicts may perceive themselves as being "the victim" who needs to stand up for their rights, bullies originate and perpetuate one-way aggression directed toward the victim(s).

A female from western New York described how her "high school was a hell because of cyber bullying." She explained that another student in her class began repeatedly picking on her in chat rooms for no apparent reason. She and her parents complained to the school, and also went to the police but nothing was done about it. She was told to ignore it. However, the damage had been done. No one seemed to like her anymore, and everyone seemed to be talking behind her back. Her hopes for the future were dashed and she no longer desires to attend college despite having good grades. In this case, the victim was not "fighting" with the other student or having a disagreement over something. The cyber bully was deliberately, repeatedly, and publicly exercising power over the victim. The sense of power was heightened *and shared* as other students piled on in the public shaming.

*Myth #10:* Bullying affects only a small number of students.
*Truth:* Bullying affects a large number of students as victims or witnesses in direct or indirect ways. Spin-off effects of bullying can disrupt families, school environments, neighborhoods, and even entire communities.

A teenager from St. Petersburg, Florida defined cyber bullying as "terrorizing kids in his class." Specifically, a 15-year-old boy made serious threats online to kill other students and teachers. In this era in which we live, following the massacres at Virginia Tech in 2007 and Columbine (Colorado) High School in 1999, death threats by students are taken more seriously than ever. Schools everywhere are instituting "no tolerance policies" to promote awareness about the seriousness of bullying and intervene swiftly when incidents occur. But when this does not happen, bullying can affect everyone in its surroundings in some way. Some students pile on as they determine bullying to be cool, expected, and risk free. Witnesses may be conflicted about reporting incidents while they and onlookers feel a chill as in, "I'm glad it's not me being picked on."

Children become increasingly callous over time whether they are bullies, victims, or witnesses; teachers and school administrators often feel their hands are tied as do law enforcement officers (for reasons later discussed in detail), and they too can become callous to bullying and its effects especially in locations haunted by youth crime and school violence. What they may not realize is that the causes of considerable youth aggression, crimes, and violence are connected with bullying. As victims of bullying become socially isolated, estranged family members or other sources of support groups of people as well as the individuals are negatively affected. Ultimately neighborhoods and communities must endure the costs and other consequences of unchecked bullying.

## ONLINE DECEIT AND INCIVILITY

Individuals communicate for a number of reasons such as developing identity; satisfying social needs related to companionship and affection, and as a means of achieving goals such as those related to employment, school and so forth. Whatever the reason, communication has traditionally taken place in person, on the phone, or through some written manner. With advances in computing and telecommunications technologies, communication processes have been drastically altered and enhanced in many ways, though not for the good in all instances. With face-to-face communication, participants have verbal and nonverbal cues, body language, and visual feedback that allow them to better assess how messages are being received, as well as the associated feelings. In the cyber world, the nonverbal cues and immediate feedback are not present. With digital communication, it can also be difficult to determine the intent and tone of written messages. Have you ever sent what you intended to be a humorous or sarcastic e-mail only to have it taken the wrong way? Absent the emoticon of a smiley face, or perhaps an exclamation point, it can very tricky to convey a humorous intent.

## DISINHIBITION

While online, some people will say, type, or do things they normally would not do in person. Youth often lose their sense of inhibition and self-control especially when not in structured settings or under close supervision by parents or other adults they respect (or fear). When it happens online Nancy Willard calls it the "disinhibition" effect.[26] Willard explains that disinhibition occurs when young people feel free to express themselves with relatively little or any reservations online, such as when youth reveal personal information without really considering what the outcomes may be. With decreased self-awareness comes decreased concern for how they are perceived or judged by others. Although untested in medical experiments or treatments, Willard's conception of disinhibition may logically be grounded in applications and extensions of dissociation theory "originally proposed in 1899 by the French psychologist and neurologist Pierre Janet (1859–1947) to explain automatism and in 1907 to explain hysteria."[27] After all, several known dissociative disorders link patient trauma to otherwise inexplicable behaviors involving social relationships and employment environments. We have already discussed various ways and the extent to which youth bully one another online and even go so far as to take nude photos of themselves with cell phones or post these online to exchange. If that's not disinhibition, what is?

Perhaps future research linking aggression and dissociation will advance construct validity for disinhibition to explain aspects of cyber bullying. For now we can reason and hypothesize that disassociation, dissociative disorders, and/or disinhibition may relate to and perhaps lead to behaviors that are deviant, uncivil, abusive, or even violating of crime laws. Conceivably disinhibition, if such a condition actually exists, may not always be negative or cause harm, as when opening channels of communication, introducing oneself or showing acts of kindness. However, in excess disinhibition and being naïve about dangers online can result in unsafe behaviors, such as posting too much personal information that can then be used against victims targeted for cyber bullying or cyber crime like identity theft. As one school principal reported when interviewed, "Students do not see their words and other comments as bullying—they write what they feel, are not connected to it in anyway and often, don't feel any responsibility for it as they didn't say anything in person."

The Internet and portable electronic devices now routinely carried and used by tweens and teens often with inadequate supervision and role modeling as to what is considered acceptable communication demeanor and content has clouded moral clarity for millions of youth. Lack of "online upbringing" combined with moral confusion about civility has decreased concern among youth for how their communication is being perceived or received by others. Without seeing a nod or a smile, a frown, or a look of complete boredom, youth and adults may not discern how they are coming across to others online. Simply put, if you can't see me and I can't see you, harmful things may be written or said and done with little awareness or empathy. As discussed in Chapter 1, alarming aspects of contemporary digital youth culture do not merely tolerate uncivil communications, but actually promotes these via social computing activities that tolerate and even espouse harmful and criminal behaviors. Consider the perceptions of a school principal as expressed in a recent cyber bullying survey:

"I am concerned that the anonymity of cyberbullying could tempt children, who would typically not bully f2f, [face-to-face] to engage in cyberbullying. Therefore, I can see the incidences of cyberbullying increasing in time. I am also concerned that many incidences of cyberbullying happen without any adult knowledge of it. As a middle school teacher, I taught an Internet safety class. I created a blogging environment for my students so that they could become familiar with blogging and practice netiquette. I observed that many of the conflicts that occurred f2f, would spill over into the class blog. There, the students spoke more freely and often the conflict would escalate and more students would join in to add their two cents. I found this was especially true with the girls. There were a few occasions where I had to step in and help the students work out their differences before the comments on the blog got out of hand. They were great teaching moments and also an indication of how quickly the real world and the virtual world can come together. In fact, for the students, there is no difference between the two worlds."

## REAL VERSUS CYBER WORLD PERCEPTIONS OF ANONYMITY

Dissociation and disinhibition may also contribute to illusions of online anonymity and invisibility.[28] Youth who engage in illicit online activities, whether fantasy as in electronic gaming, or via actual real life online interactions, often believe they cannot be found out especially if they do not use their real names. However, law enforcement computer forensics and investigation capabilities can usually determine who is responsible for online crimes. Nonetheless, feelings of anonymity and invisibility prevail among many youth who immerse themselves in electronic gaming and other social computing where characters degrade, assault, and kill each other virtually without actually causing harm to anyone. It is important to understand that just as youth assume the identities of gaming characters, many spend inordinate amounts of time achieving success vicariously through their characters in increasingly realistic digital environments. Many youth known by the authors have reflected on subtle ways in which their real personalities can become injected into gaming environments through their characters, while in their real lives they take on aspects of the games they play. This is accomplished through the language they use and by associating gaming characters and situations with people they actually live and interact with.

Findings from RIT's "Survey of Internet and At-Risk Behaviors" reveal statistically significant and large correlations between cyber bullying and electronic gaming behaviors for both male and female students in primary and secondary grade levels. This is not to suggest that gaming causes cyber bullying or other forms of aggressive behavior, merely that kids who play games online are more likely to be cyber bullies or victims of cyber bullying than kids who do not. And while most youth play electronic games, many do not play games that feature violence, sex, or belligerence toward authority figures such as law enforcement officers. However, other research has found that people communicating in the cyber world assume the role of unreal caricatures and perceive cyberspace as a great big game.[29] And why not? The most popular form of social computing and online interaction involves electronic gaming that can literally involve thousands of people from all over the world playing against each other in teams at the same time.

Millions of people now engage in online gaming and many are very serious about their character's roles, possessions, and success. Oftentimes gamers feel no responsibility for their online interactions as they might otherwise while playing a board game in person with other people. Further, why while playing intense combat shooter games should players *not* engage viciously? After all you don't win shooter games by being sympathetic or nice! Are players not intending to harm their opponents? Why should they not use foul or insulting words intended to ruin the concentration, insult or infuriate their enemy? In games rated for mature audiences destroying property, beating people up, sexually assaulting and killing other characters are the goals. Besides, it's only a game, right? We do not have a good answer for this, except to note that significant amounts of crimes, violence, sexual promiscuity, and disrespect are integral parts of many popular electronic games, and all this and more underscores incivility and aggression that plays out online within the digital youth culture.

## The Destruction of Joy, Trust, and Hope in a 14-Year-Old Girl

### "Online Deceit and Sexual Exploitation—How a Shy Girl was Manipulated, Raped, and Bullied into Silence"

I met a guy named John on MySpace who was 14. I never had a friend who was a boy. I've never had a boyfriend and no boy ever liked me or paid attention to me. I didn't exist as far as boys were concerned. All my other friends had associations with boys except me. I felt like the ugly kid on the block even though when I looked in the mirror, I saw pretty. I couldn't talk to my parents about boys because they were the forbidden fruit—they didn't even want me talking to them. To make matters worse, I am very shy. I love to talk on MySpace because even though I'm too shy to talk to people, the computer doesn't have eyes. I guess it's the eyes that make me nervous. And the computer isn't intimidating. I can say anything on the computer.

When I met John online I told him how shy I was and he said that he was the same way. I couldn't believe that everything I said that I was, he agreed and sympathized that he was too. We were twins except we weren't related. I counted the hours every day in school until I got home to talk to him. He was so nice and understanding and he always gave me compliments. I could tell him anything and he would listen. Even when it came to my parents, he said that they were wrong and I was right. He used to help me with my homework and lots of times he actually did my homework because we were in the same grade. He would always suggest that we should hang out, but I told him how strict my parents were and that would be hard. He used to tell me that it would be fun if I snuck behind my parents back and met him. He asked me if I had ever done anything that my parents didn't want me to and disobeyed them. I told him no.

After a while John said that it was about time that I grew up and that part of growing up is not doing everything our parents tell us to do especially when they are as ridiculous and nonunderstanding as my parents were. He kept on insisting that we meet at his parents' house after school. All I would have to do is to tell my parents that I had a project to work on after school. I slowly told him little bits and pieces about myself and my family, including my parents' schedule. I finally gave in. It was a Friday. I put my finger down my throat and told my parents that I must have eaten something that didn't agree with me at school because I didn't feel that well after I ate lunch. I gave John my address and told him that we could finally meet. I was all excited, happy, and anxious.

The doorbell rang and I answered it. There was this creepy, stinky, dirty, cruddy old guy—like in his 30s. I asked him if I could help him and he said that his car broke down and he wanted to use the phone. I let him in, and he started repeating the conversations that I had with John. He asked me what grade I got on my science test that I was so worried about, and did the teacher like the essay that he wrote for me? He went on and on. I asked him how he knew all of this information and he threw me down on the floor and raped me. As he was leaving, he said, "By the way. I'm John. And if you tell anyone, you're going to be in a lot of trouble with your parents!"

I haven't told anyone this. My grades are going down. I can't concentrate. I have nightmares; I have headaches, and I think I'm going insane sometimes. I cry at the littlest things and I really don't know what to do. I can't tell anybody, and I don't trust anybody, although they say that counselors are ruled by confidentiality. I trusted John with my life. I am terrified of my parents—I can't ever tell them. Who knows what they would do to me. According to them, when I disobey my parents, I disobey God. They drilled this into me my whole life. I will go to the grave with my secret. I feel like my life is over before it's hardly begun.

Feelings that fictitious online activities do not cause any real harm extend into and are reinforced by asynchronous communications like e-mail that often provide for time lags between the sending and receiving of messages. When participants are not communicating at the same point in time, response time to a message or posting can vary from minutes to months. This allows cyber bullies to plot and plan their next moves alone or with input from others over extended periods of time, or to engage immediately alone or with others in real-time written assaults that bombard victims targeted for attacks. Flexibility in using different technological means to carry out cyber bullying (discussed in Chapter 3) also results in victims being unable to intercede in stopping rumors and gossip, or otherwise to engage in damage control. This is because considerable online assaults can occur in silence, effectively behind their backs, in social computing environments that may be unknown.

Before a youth even knows what's being cooked up against them online, an entire student body can know something that is untrue or grossly exaggerated! It is a little easier to put something out there online, especially something negative, knowing that it won't be immediately responded to. In addition, communication online can be influenced by the notion that cyberspace equals the playing field. In other words, without knowing who or where you are, social status is not taken into account. Therefore, in a virtual world where people are seen on the same level, the perception of power or authority is minimized and can lead to misbehavior. Similarly, for teenagers, they may view communicating online as a form of game, especially when they create avatars or online personas. Thus, poor treatment of someone online can be attributed to an online character, with a teenager rationalizing that they were only doing what they were doing as a pretend character.

Think about this statistic: the majority of male teenagers, and about one-half of female teenagers have reported that their online profiles such as on a social networking site contain false or made-up information.[30] Research has also shown that eight percent of teenagers with online profiles stated that most or all of the information they posted online was made-up! In these instances, when done under the guise of a fabricated persona or information that is untrue, cyber bullying can be much easier to rationalize. It is also very simple for a cyber bully to create a fake online profile about their victim, complete with unflattering pictures and phony information. This can become even more problematic as a victim may not be aware of the profile, and may not know for some time even as untold numbers of other people view the content and pile on additional degrading information. Similarly, other dangers may exist as predators can easily take on a character to set up an attack in real life. Therefore, while teenage offenders may rationalize their actions in beliefs of anonymity, teenage victims often believe that communications and relationships are very real, and at times they may be. However, at other times they may not be, yet the price to pay can be tragic.

## CULTURAL AND MEDIA PERPETUATION

From a cultural perspective, the media can also have an impact on aggressive behaviors and on society's tolerance of bullying even though most people, at least ostensibly, condemn such behaviors. Sure, we know that some research has shown a positive correlation of physical aggression between watching violence on television, in movies, and while playing video games. The truth is that, taken on the whole, research of this kind varies in its quality, findings, and conclusions. For example, violence, crime, and sexual promiscuity featured in electronic games has not been proven to cause similar behaviors in youth, although recent research has shown this to be debatable. Besides, millions of law-abiding youth play aggressive shooter games and many other types of electronic games without apparent harm to themselves or anyone else. So what's all the fuss as suggested in the section title about cultural and media perpetuation of bullying and cyber bullying?

The authors believe having grown up in previous times and now serving in responsible positions that regularly involve interacting with youth on- and off-line that some aspects of digital youth culture and social computing are not only harmful to youth, but are fostered and tolerated by society in general. Notwithstanding the observations above about aggressive online gaming, just take a look around. The Internet, which is largely unregulated (and perhaps should remain so), along with IT devices carried around by adults as well as youth, are now integral to almost everything people in modernized societies do. As explained in Chapter 1, critical information infrastructure now depends on interconnected computer systems, and upon hundreds of millions of devices that connect to networks that make up the Internet. By the way, these include those used by traditional media such as newspapers, radio, and television.

Because we live in a high-tech society we press schools to use information technology in classrooms and promote the promise of computerization. Since the 1980s, colleges and universities have offered entire programs of study in computer science, software engineering, and/or network administration. Colleges and universities boast about being among the most "wired" in the country. And more and more jobs require basic or advanced computer skills. So be it. Meanwhile parents are increasingly struggling to provide for their children. Many family units have become estranged through divorce or abandonment by one or both parents. Many two-parent families struggle to make ends meet by working the equivalent of three or more jobs, thus having less time to supervise kids, much less interact routinely to promote their physical, psychological and social wellbeing. And everywhere in our free society consumerism is pushed via advertisements, a substantial proportion of which focus on youth who naturally cannot effectively discern between "wants" and "needs."

For better and worse, this is contemporary life in America and many other modernized countries that also have been subsumed by the allure of technological devices and the Internet. Note that modern computing and telecommunications technologies did not cause our culture to become fused with the very technology that made it possible, and on balance computers and IT devices are probably a good thing. Nonetheless, here we are, and it is inescapable that a considerable amount of traditional media including Hollywood films, along with newer media such as Web forums, chat rooms, blogs, and so on feature, tolerate, and even push aggression, bullying, and violence. We mention this in order to observe, along with numerous other authors, that contentious media content dates to at least the efforts of Postmaster General Anthony Comstock during the 1870s to regulate interstate mailing of obscene materials, and later sexuality, and violence portrayed in silent and then talking films of the 1920s.

Controversy over what constitutes appropriate content in electronic media continues today. Notwithstanding Federal Communications Commission (FCC) regulations governing broadcast (but not cable) content, First Amendment free speech coupled with public fiduciary responsibilities of a free and independent press have culminated to where the saying, "if it bleeds it leads" applies to considerable amounts of news media, online gaming, and other recreational content (e.g., adult entertainment). In this context we must consider whether societal role models in sports, entertainment, modeling, and politics, as well as in our neighborhood schools and service organizations are worthy of imitating by our youth. Do we even have to ask whether political character assassinations and smear campaigns launched by and against both Democratic and Republican contenders reflect values and messages our teenagers should emulate? What about popular reality television shows like *The Mole, Survivor, The Bachelor* and *The Bachelorette* that routinely broadcast participants and actors in mean, sexually suggestive ways, using foul language or judging to put each other down? Cable television such as MTV, designed specifically for youth and young adults, has its versions as well, including *True Life, The Real World,* and *Tila Tequila.* If celebrities demeaning aspiring singers is your thing, the popular show, *American Idol* has plenty of verbal denigration of teenagers and young adults by adult judges. Even *Parental Control,* which offers parents suggestions for discipline and tough love, features highly disrespectful juveniles and periodically inept parents that sadly reflect television that merits airing economically given the social appetites and tolerances for such content.

Models such as Paris Hilton who glamorize sexual promiscuity, sports heroes like NFL quarterback Michael Vick and Mike Tyson both arrested and convicted for felonies, news commentators like Don Imus, Geraldo Rivera, and Rush Limbaugh who have also indirectly endorsed incivility through their words and actions (e.g., respectively making repeated racist remarks on the air, physically fighting during broadcasting, or inciting disrespectful attitudes toward poor people or those having different political views). The public feud between celebrities Rosie O'Donnell and Donald Trump that was repeatedly broadcast by the media in 2007, among numerous other examples, demonstrates that name-calling and taunting are in vogue, earning media market share and that the public appetite for such behavior is insatiable. Is it any wonder that elements of contemporary digital youth culture have adopted abuse, bullying, and crime as a reflection of what really transpires in society? What are youth suppose to stand for amidst so much mass media in forms of electronic gaming, blogs, chat rooms, radio, television, and movies that condones if not promotes disrespectful behaviors?

Despite our apparent tone, we are not moralizing or disregarding the importance of free and dissenting speech, nor of artistic expression via digital content on the Net. Still, consider the infamous case in 2007 that involved a response to a question posed to Miss South Carolina, Lauren Caitlin Upton, in the Miss Teen USA pageant. When answering a question about why it is that recent polls showed that one-fifth of Americans cannot locate the United States on a world map, she stated: "I personally believe that U.S. Americans are unable to do so because uh, some people out there in our nation don't have maps, and I believe that education, like, such as in South Africa, and, uh the Iraq and everywhere like such as and I believe that they should our education over here in the U.S. should help the U.S. should help South Africa and should help the Iraq and the Asian countries so we will be able to build up our future for our children."[31]

Obviously, the answer was not as clear as Ms. Upton would have liked. On hearing or reading her response, even we raised our eyebrows and rolled our eyes . . . but did her answer deserve the media frenzy and public humiliation that followed? Media responsibilities to report news and First Amendment rights to free speech and an independent press notwithstanding, on what standards for civility and digital youth culture should we evaluate the following comments posted on YouTube in the aftermath of millions of people viewing Ms. Upton's embarrassing response?

> "This IDIOT was just on TYRA tryin to respond to this and looked even worse/lol."
>
> "Damn, so stupid. . ."
>
> "What is the IQ eater doing in her head? Answer: starving."
>
> "Dumb Blonde."
>
> "How can she be that stupid? This must be a joke."
>
> "what a stupid slut. i hope she does not reproduce. she should be ashamed of her own ignorance"
>
> "Perfect woman, dumb as a box of hammers and GORGEOUS!!!"
>
> "i think Americans have maps its just you're a f****** retard."[32]

Rather than responding with empathy, the majority of the responses such as those above were demeaning—over 12,000 mostly denigrating responses in total. How many people were even inclined much less dared speak out in her defense? Few—very, very few. Using an average of 10 words per response this amounts to approximately 1,395 words of condemnation for every clumsy word spoken by Ms. Upton. Talk about piling on! Why is it that making someone look bad is so entertaining, condoned, and even promoted in our society? When thinking about how the media has an influence on bullying, it is important to recognize that all forms of electronic media affect the attitudes of youth who take in broadcast or posted content. If marketing through words, images, and associations did not work, why else are hundreds of millions of dollars spent annually on marketing products to youth?

We cannot ignore the fact that children's lives are completely saturated by mass Internet media. Despite imperfect and inconclusive research studies about the effects media content has on youth, why would we not err on the side of caution? Just because something is legal does not make it right. As parents, educators, and adults responsible for supervising, mentoring, and role modeling of youth, we should remember this. We also need to remember that in the final analysis, bullying and cyber bullying is about ethical decision making. Youth are easily impressed, aroused, and stimulated. They can also become desensitized to violence, sexual images, and foul or obscene language over the long-term. Given that technology now enables our youth to access, create, and share all forms of content via social networking, what sort of society do we really want them and ourselves to live in? Rather than being passive consumers of mass Internet content, people everywhere should stand up not to banish protected content, rather to espouse responsible decision making that promotes civility in concert with respect for differences in genders, ethnicity, abilities, and so forth.

Finally, media emphasis on pedophilias that sexually prey on children online has heightened but may misplace appropriate levels of fear among parents. Several research studies discussed in Chapter 4, including both national Youth Internet Safety Studies and RIT's "Survey of Internet and At-Risk Behaviors" administered to more than 40,000 K–12th grade students clearly reveal that more than half of all *unwanted* sex-related interactions experienced by youth stem from other youth less than eighteen years of age. Classical images of adult sexual predators lurking everywhere online to groom, entice, and arrange encounters with youth are real. However in the broad scheme of cyber crimes, including credit card fraud and identity theft; pirating of music, movies, and software; academic dishonesty; computer hacking, password cracking, and data/file snooping; and cyber bullying in all its forms (e.g., intentional embarrassment, harassment, intimidation, or threats), unwanted sex-related encounters that occur online, or in person following online chats and exchange of content are comparatively rare. Put differently and in stark contrast, the number and associated harms of cyber bullying by and among youth far exceeds illegal incidences and prevalence of sexual contacts and relations promulgated by adults on juveniles. America in particular needs to come to grips with this reality even as it continues to enforce crime laws banning online sexual predation.

## OTHER THINGS THAT CONTRIBUTE TO BULLYING IN SOCIETY

Attempts to determine a singular cause of bullying are futile. There is no single factor that explains why cyber bullying occurs, and the "nature versus nurture" debate is alive and well when looking for answers. Since bullying is tantamount to abuse and may involve violations of law, criminologists specializing in juvenile crime issues have considered several well-established theories in their reasoning about what contributes to the onset and continuation of bullying behaviors. Chief among these are social process, social learning, and social structure theories. Taken together these theories claim that deviant, socially abusive, and criminal behaviors are influenced by things in society rather than by simple choices individuals make to commit crime in response to biological or psychological factors, or as the result of political beliefs and conflict. Most criminologists now also look to so-called integrated theories that combine all other major theoretical explanations of crime and crime victimization, and that draw from theoretical explanations of human behaviors.

As a result of theories of crime and why people behave as they do, we have come to understand that many factors, in addition to those indicated previously, can contribute to the onset and continuation of bullying or being the target of bullying. For example innate personality traits or inborn temperaments may be factors in bullying or bullying victimization. Influences including those found within homes or that are familial, peer, school, community, and economically or culturally related should also be considered with respect to environmental settings.[33] Lack of family cohesion, family violence, community violence, and inadequate parental supervision have also been shown to influence aggression and bullying.[34] Poor modeling of problem-solving skills, delinquent peers, and bystander behaviors also influence aggressive behaviors, especially during adolescence.

It is unknown whether individual or environmental factors also apply to cyber bullying, but it is reasonable to believe that they do. As we have said, cyber bullying is bullying but with a technological twist. We also know that bullying is sometimes caused by *individual factors* such as the need to show power over and dominate others by inflicting mental or physical injury. Research has shown that an individual's moral approval of bullying, which is whether an individual thinks it is morally acceptable or not, relates to whether they become involved in verbal, physical, and cyber bullying.[35] *Family factors* are also often associated with more bullying including homes that lack warmth and parental involvement and supervision.[36] *School factors* have also been shown to be related to verbal, physical, and cyber bullying (e.g., youth who felt more connected to the school and viewed school as trusting and fair are less likely to report engaging in bullying).[37] Similarly, *peer factors* have been shown to be related to reported bullying. For example, research has demonstrated that youth who feel that friends their age are trustworthy, caring, and helpful are less likely to report participation in verbal, physical, and cyber bullying.[38]

Despite the multitude of things that can contribute to bullying and cyber bullying, we must consider in some detail a few specific major factors that have not as yet been carefully considered in research studies.

## SOCIAL COMPUTING AND SOCIAL NETWORKING

Social networking Web sites like MySpace, Facebook, and YouTube are among a vast, growing, and probably unknowable number of Web forums intended for teenagers and young adults. It is important to understand that Web forums now:

> take the form of instant messaging clients, chat rooms, community message boards or forums, and blog style social networking sites. Often participating youth are able to exclude or include people of their choosing in these forums. Privacy controls are an essential part for identifying who can and cannot visit

a personal webpage or contact youth via a messenger service. Privacy controls often allow users to minimize or layer information they reveal about themselves online (i.e., their "appearance" or "digital footprint"). However, these controls are only as effective as the settings that the user knows about and chooses to enable, along with the type and amount of information that is shared with others online. Given potential flaws in computer coding, discovery of exploits have been found in the privacy settings of software, such as those used by social networking firms like MySpace and Facebook. When this happens, personal information posted by millions of youth participants can become known despite their efforts to keep certain information from becoming publicly known.[39]

Yet having a personal Web page on MySpace, Facebook, YouTube, or similar forum is part of what many young people consider cool if not necessary in order to be accepted by their online and/or in-person friends. For many participants of such forums, having a Web page dedicated to and revealing of their personal life enables outreaching to an invisible audience of peers who they may wish to interact with. In short, social networking provides a technological means through which to meet new people and make friends online . . . As a result, digital youth culture can be considered an important aspect of growing up in computerized societies as well as an extension of complex real-world (i.e., noncyber) social interactions. Said differently, for millions of youth there is no distinction between being on- or off-line, because they live simultaneously within the realm of cyberspace and physical place. This has complicated traditional social dynamics and challenged notions of what may be considered normal versus deviant behaviors, moral or ethical versus immoral or unethical behaviors, and legal versus criminal behaviors. In other words, youth who [are growing up] with computers, other IT devices, and the Internet may be developing different standards for behaving online as opposed to when they are not using the Internet."[40]

Since today's youth are interacting earlier, more often, and for more purposes via cyberspace where social standards of behaviors and sanctions are not clearly defined, what constitutes misbehaving in online forums is muddied. Young people learning to use online forums must often rely on inconsistent messages about what constitutes "flaming" in order to stay engaged with other youth. To this extent rules for engaging in such environments are not clearly specified, carefully monitored and enforced, misconduct among unsupervised youth will eventually thrive. And this is what has happened online since the Internet became commercialized in about 1993 and was effectively transformed into what is now widely known as the World Wide Web or simply the Net. Aggressive, abusive, and criminal behaviors facilitated via communications in Web forums are now commonplace. They are widely committed by and among youth and often involve cyber bullying. If you have a child who goes online, chances are they have been the victim of cyber bullying, or a bully online, or both. Again, RIT's 2007–2008 "Survey of Internet and At-Risk Behaviors" reveals statistically significant and large correlations between cyber bullying and victimization.

Even so—and despite numerous tragic cases discussed in this book—we must be careful *not* to overstate or sensationalize the amount or problematic effects of cyber bullying, which despite a growing number of research studies, currently are mainly known through snippets of information revealed in media stories or through personal experiences. While cyber bullying has been shown to exist rather extensively among youth populations, increasingly involve younger ages, and involve dreadful consequences in numerous instances, it is not an epidemic that has turned all tweens and teenagers into faceless cyber tormentors. Millions of great kids use the Net every day for constructive purposes. Further, even though new communication technologies have enabled youth to connect in new ways, the technology itself does not cause bullying. As we will continue to emphasize, bullying is an ethical issue subject to interpretation of events and circumstances in social settings and cultural contexts.

The Internet and IT devices used and relied on by youth and adults alike should not be demonized, nor should Web forums that create the backbone for the digital youth culture be universally condemned. After all, there are positive aspects of evolving digital youth culture and the online activities that youth engage in (e.g., enhanced education through use of various purpose software, ability to interact and empathize with people of different cultures and regions of the world, learning new technical skills some of which can be related to future employment, alternative methods of entertainment, and quicker sharing and acquisition of information as part of learning how to approach and solve problems, etc.). Let's face it: today's youth are using computers and other IT devices as part of their preparation for assuming responsible adult roles in societies that depend on critical information systems and infrastructures.

## INSUFFICIENT DISCIPLINE AND ACCOUNTABILITY

When bullies are allowed to get away with bullying, they learn to bully more effectively. Some learn from their mistakes and successes and through hearing about and experimenting with new means to annoy and hurt people that are within their own capabilities and warped sense of justice. Like juvenile and adult criminals who develop preferred ways of committing certain types of crime (which police refer to as their "modus operandi" or simply their "M.O."), bullies also develop and refine their favorite methods and types of victims they feel confident in preying upon. Consequently, when left unchecked, bullies learn to bully better over time and when they do, the harm they cause may also spread to involve other people and worsen in its effects across time and distance. Like a malignant tumor in the body of our society, bullying can spread and pop up in new places like untreated cancer. Only in the worst cases, and too often only after significant harm is done, are

### THE DESTRUCTION OF JOY, TRUST, AND HOPE

**"How a High School Boy Was Harassed and Resorted to Technology and Physical Attacks to Exact Revenge and Even the Score"**

Mike was a senior high school boy who was being harassed by a group of freshman boys because while they were members of the school Junior Varsity Lacrosse Team, "Mikey" as he was called when being taunted, participated in the Audiovisual (AV) Club and was considered to be a geek. Mike did a great job filming the Lacrosse Team events, but he was not a jock . . . For months and especially during Lacrosse season the younger boys publicly yelled his name "Mikey" in obnoxious ways, threw food at him in the school cafeteria and hallways and stuck "Mikey" name tags all over lockers, classroom ceilings, and bathroom urinals so his name could be peed on. As the bullying escalated there was one occasion on which Mike had expensive school AV equipment intentionally knocked out of his hands. After he told school officials what happened in order to avoid blame for the damage, the freshmen bullies "bologna-ed" Mike's car with lunchmeat that stripped the paint.

Mike complained and sought help from the Lacrosse Team coach who did not want to bench the players; from the guidance counselor who said it was up to the coach to take disciplinary action; and from the Assistant Principal who told him to "get over it." Infuriated by the nonsupport, Mike resorted to retaliation by organizing a band of fellow AV Club members to spy on the Lacrosse Team freshmen, document their movements, and then plan and execute paintball/pepperball gun ambushes with military precision that included: (1) ordering supplies from third-party vendors and having these shipped to P.O. boxes in anonymous names to nearby towns; (2) conducting dry-runs to scope out vehicle and pedestrian traffic at prospective ambush sites, and (3) renting a conversion van using false ID as an escape vehicle.

These were not trivial assaults, but several singular attacks on individuals, two of whom were hospitalized with lung injuries that prevented their competing in lacrosse events for the remainder of the season. Not satisfied, Mike also arranged for varsity football players to "swirlee" four particular Lacrosse Team members, a process which involved dunking their heads into the swirling water of a flushing toilet. Before stopping in his vigilante rampage, Mike also spray painted epithets and sexual graffiti on the houses of his enemies. This incident reveals that young individuals who would never engage in such outlandish and criminal behavior, when bullied sufficiently, can snap in unpredictable ways.

human tumors—the worst of bullies—able to be surgically removed from the mainstream of society and imprisoned for their crimes.

The problem here is that bullying and cyber bullying take many forms and occur in myriad circumstances only a few of which clearly violate crime laws. When behaviors are not clearly illegal, society necessarily relies on people to use sound judgment, exercise discipline, and be accountable. Oh, if only this were universally possible! When it comes to youth exercising sound judgment, this is often considered a contradiction in terms. Child development experts have long known that human brains governing decision making and risk taking are not fully developed until people are about 25 years of age. So as the old saying goes, "youth are not (and cannot be completely) responsible for their actions" even though we wish they could be and were. We also know that youth are inconsistently self-disciplined to do what is expected of them, and the same goes for accountability. Even the best behaved children and adolescents make mistakes, sometimes repeatedly for the same sorts of things. Obviously this is all part of growing up.

What is more complicated for our societal bullying and cyber bullying problem is that adults are often lax in these areas. Many parents and other adults in positions of trust and authority are perfectly willing to allow their children to use IT devices and the Internet while believing they only need be concerned about adult sexual predators and inappropriate sexual content. Too often parents do not take the time to understand the purposes and ways in which their kids use technology, or reflect on fundamental realities such as digital youth culture and risks associated with social computing in all its forms. In fairness, these issues have not been well articulated through research and writings, until now. Consequently, just as adults fail to discipline themselves to pay attention, to learn, and become actively involved in the online lives of their children, they sometimes fail or incorrectly discipline their children when they behave inappropriately or make mistakes.

The same often holds true for other adults including school and juvenile justice officials who, though legally bound to intervene when appropriate or required, fail to do so, not necessarily because they are negligent (though this is sometimes true), but for similar reasons as parents—they do not understand what youth are capable of and what these youth are doing online. And even if they do, they work within juvenile education and justice systems with dozens and even thousands of other adult professionals who do not. More will be said about these things in Chapters 5 and 6. For now, let's just admit that bullying and cyber bullying comprise a complex societal problem that in the end must be solved by adults exercising discipline and being accountable for what they need to do. Let us not however, sit back and think to ourselves, "well this is just the way it is" or delude ourselves that because our children are (seemingly) not involved or affected that bullying is not our problem. That has gone on far too long and invariably contributes to bullying left unchecked.

## The Destruction of Joy, Trust, and Hope

### "A Father who Reportedly Had Enough . . . and a Mother who Doesn't Want to Know What Happened"

Yeah, I heard about that Ryan Halligan, and it's really too bad. My son had the same type of situation except my son is gay and we have always sort of known it. My husband's sister, cousin, and uncle are gay. I guess it's in the genes, but my husband and I really don't care as long as our son is healthy, happy, and a good person. You couldn't ask for more of a perfect kid. He even gets upset when kids purposely hurt an animal for the heck of it. We love him and we wouldn't change a thing about him. He wants to find a cure for AIDS when he grows up by either becoming a scientist or a doctor. He is extremely intelligent and a straight A student. My husband and I used to comment that, "God help anyone that ever tried to hurt him."

Not too long after the Ryan Halligan case, different kids started getting targeted about being homosexual. Our son was one of them. It was stated on a Web page that our son would give anyone a blowjob in the school bathroom for $2. In the same text, they wrote, wear a facemask, because if you breathe the same air, you'll get AIDS. When I saw this I immediately went to the school and demanded that something be done. I made it clear that I was not going to have my son be another statistic. I also told them that my husband is a quick-tempered man who doesn't always think of the consequences of his actions. His kids are his life. He would kill for his kids to protect them and this is no laughing matter.

The school said that they would try to get to the bottom of who was putting all the stuff on the chat rooms, but it went on for months. Our son's happy-go-lucky self became quiet and withdrawn. My husband couldn't take it anymore. He took matters into his own hands. The crap on the chat lines stopped immediately. It was a few months later when police officers were investigating physical assaults on kids who claimed my husband had assaulted them. I told them that he never left the house. He was here with me all night in bed. I don't know what he did, and I don't want to know, but there's an old saying: "In Caesar's world, you play Caesar's game!"

## NONREPORTING AND VIGILANTISM

Another societal level cause of bullying and cyber bullying is nonreporting of abuses that do occur, and vigilantism that occurs when people decide to take matters into their own hands. People decline to report cyber bullying because in its initial phases the bullying does not seem that severe. After all, we're all told from the time we are little that "sticks and stones can break my bones but words can never hurt me." Since most bullying and cyber bullying respectively consists of words or text, most victims carry on as best they can realizing that it's not the end of their world. As bullying escalates in numbers of incidents, methods used including physical attacks as well as verbal and written attacks, and in intensity as more kids become aware of smearing made public and then engage in bullying of their own, victims progressively become more and more isolated. In the process, they exhibit symptoms including being sad, grumpy, lashing out at friends not involved or family members for seemingly no reason, and so forth. All the while compelling aspects of digital youth culture haunts their emotions and confuses their minds about what if anything can or should be done when they are bullied.

Most youth elect not to report bullying for all the reasons we have discussed. Parents also generally do not complain about bullying to school or law enforcement except in extreme cases, either because they are not aware of the problems their children are facing or they think it is no big deal. The gross irony is, they may be right or not, simply depending on the circumstances. The tragedy is that cyber bullying affects youth in ways not readily appreciated by parents or other adults who did not grow up with the technology used by kids of today. So even though adults use the same technology, even for the same kinds of things to varying extents, the significance of IT devices and content sent and received by them does not register in the same way. In their disbelief or fear that no one will understand and stand up for them, some youth and even some parents, resort to vigilantism.

**3**

# Technological Means and Methods of Cyber Bullying

*Attention everyone!! I'd like to announce that I'm gay, I play with myself, and I'm proud!!!!*
          *—Message posted by a cyber bully pretending to be someone else*
                    *(victim's name was used in actual post)*

By now you may be thinking to yourself, "OK, I get it. Over time the Internet, IT devices, and now social computing have enabled a lot of kids to misbehave online. But how is this actually accomplished? What are the digital nuts and bolts of cyber bullying?" In this chapter we focus on technology. In the first section we explain, from a theoretical and historical standpoint, why cyber bullying is bullying with technological twists. This lays the foundation for the second section where we explain the online language of cyber bullying commonly known as netspeak or leetspeak that youth use to snap together rapid-fire text messages and encode what they are saying so parents and other adults who supervise their activities cannot decipher the content.

In the third section e-mail, instant messaging, text messaging, Web sites, message boards, blogs, chat rooms, online gaming, and social networking sites are described with respect to their technological implications for cyber bullying. We conclude the chapter in the fourth section by addressing digital tactics that are used by cyber bullies to torment their victims. These include embarrassing victims often by "outing" their innermost secrets, casting insults and denigrating slurs, harassment, intimidation, and making threats. We also describe ingenious lengths that some bullies will go to using their creativity to combine these tactics and technological means along with their imagination to make life a living hell for victims on the receiving end of cyber bullying.

## CYBER BULLYING IS BULLYING WITH TECHNOLOGICAL TWISTS

Nearly everything people *know* about bullying is based on their individual experiences as youth growing up. When the authors grew up as children in the 1950s, 1960s, and 1970s the concept of personal computers was well beyond the collective imagination of ordinary people. In those time periods, rotary home telephones and coin-operated public phone booths with hinged folding doors were technologies of the day. In those days, mean things may have been said by kids to each other over telephones, but most bullying occurred face-to-face. Obviously these antiques have now been replaced with personal laptop and mini computing devices along with cell phones, all of which can interconnect over the Internet. Technology and therefore people change over time. Consequently, as we have already stressed, cyber bullying committed by youth today is an extension of classical physical in-person bullying but with new technological twists.

In other writings, author Samuel McQuade has developed what he calls the "Theory of Technology-Enabled Crime, Policing and Security." According to his theory, new forms of abuse and crime emerge with technologies that make them possible. When "new crimes" first occur, people and the media are often astonished and it is not uncommon for a new crime term to be coined like "hijacking," "cyber crime," or for that matter, "cyber bullying." Sensational terms for what are usually new forms of old crimes are latched onto and driven by media coverage, but only until the new forms of abuse or crime become more common and no longer make news. Over time people find ways to improve upon abusive and criminal methods by using technology in increasingly clever ways. As this happens there is typically public outcry and new crime laws may be passed to enable police and prosecutors to increasingly crack down on deviant offenders. Eventually what was once radical, surprising, and innovative abuse or crime is considered ordinary crime simply because it is no longer unusual and law enforcement routinely responds, investigates, and prosecutes violations. But the theory and its implications are not quite that simple. McQuade further posits that means of preventing and managing levels of abusive and criminal behaviors in society become more complicated as methods used in their commission come to rely on increasingly complex technologies. In other words, technology and crime coevolve, become more complex, and thereby more difficult for society to grapple with.

In the late 1950s, the first computers were developed during World War II to guide rocket propelled munitions and then missiles. About 10 years later, a computer was first used in a Minneapolis bank to skim transaction account rounding errors worth less than a penny each into a secluded account controlled by the perpetrator who was a bank employee. Now known as "salami slicing" this early form of computer abuse and embezzlement has been repeated many times by bank insiders who possess computer programming skills of their own, or who can collude with others who do. Since that time society has experienced many new forms of computer-enabled abuse and crime (e.g., hacking into systems, writing and releasing malicious code like viruses onto the Internet, and more recently the development of "bots" (i.e., home or business computers remotely taken over and controlled to carry out illicit and illegal activities online). In such instances society does not initially have laws that explicitly criminalize new forms of using technology in illicit ways. As a result, society is continually updating its crime laws with new legislation that addresses technological tools, methods, and systems used to carry out harmful activities (i.e., with new technological twists!).

Not many years ago there were no laws in the United States banning "spam" (i.e., e-mail advertisements for unwanted products and services). Now the federal government and certain states ban spam unless it meets certain criteria, such as giving people a means to opt out of receiving future messages like advertisements for the latest sex enhancement drug. The new crime of identify theft is actually not new to all, rather good old-fashioned bank and credit card fraud that has existed for decades along with criminals assuming the identities of other people whether they are alive or dead. However, even credit cards could not be used prior to the early 1980s to commit bank fraud because credit, debit, smart, and gift cards, along with ATM (automatic teller machine) and purchasing swipe machines did not exist. Cyber bullying is akin to many other forms of abuse and crime in society that has and continues to evolve technologically. As this book is being written new laws prohibiting cyber bullying are being proposed within the federal and state-level governments. "Megan's Law" was prompted as the result of 13-year-old Megan Meier (described in Chapter 1) committing suicide after she was deceived, betrayed, and bullied online. Two years after Megan's death, the primary culprit in that case, Lori Drew, was convicted in federal court on three misdemeanor counts of accessing computers without authorization rather than on the potentially[1] applicable felony crimes with which she was originally charged.[1] The case exemplified how technology is periodically adopted for activities that are eventually criminalized when society determines that a new crime law is needed.

There are many examples in history of abuse and crime becoming more difficult to manage due to emergent technological conditions in society. This is especially evident during what McQuade calls, "technological shifts" that occur as the result of major inventions such as the telegraph, repeating and automatic weapons, telephone, automobiles, computers, and the Internet. Cheats, fraudsters, and other kinds of criminals have always been among the first to adopt such technologies for their illicit purposes. The challenge for society at this point in history is to understand technological twists in bullying that has resulted in the new phenomenon of cyber bullying.

Although what we know about traditional classical in-person bullying is useful in providing insight into cyber bullying, technological differences between the two creates difficulty in understanding and managing all kinds of bullying in our increasingly high-tech world. For example, cyber bullying may not involve an imbalance of power and physical domination as in classic face-to-face bullying. With cyber bullying, a power imbalance may exist as the result of technological proficiency rather than face-to face power imbalances due to body size, popularity, or dominant personality. In cyberspace stereotypical geeks rule regardless of their gender or how big their bodies are, and unpopular students who are frequently picked on have technological means to cyber bully literally at their fingertips. At the end of Chapter 2 we presented a case of vigilantism in which a geek of sorts being bullied by a group of athletes exacted revenge by innovatively and aggressively using technology to carry out physical attacks resulting in serious injuries to those responsible for his harassment.

## THE DESTRUCTION OF JOY, TRUST, AND HOPE
### ANONYMOUSLY ONLINE

**An Experiment that Revealed Just How Technologically Skilled and Cruel Youth Can Be When Social Computing**

In an ABC news primetime special in 2006, three Brigham Young University psychologists with expertise in childhood development conducted an experiment on females and cyber bullying that showed some surprising results. In the experiment, 11 girls between the ages of 13 and 17 who did not know each other were sequestered for a weekend away from their friends and families. Most of the girls were academically successful honor students, including a national merit scholar being courted by Ivy League colleges. Several were active members of their church youth groups, and one girl had been homeschooled for a year. The girls were divided into groups of younger, older, and more popular individuals. They were then separated into three rooms and were provided with computers connected to the Internet equipped with e-mail and Webcams. They were also issued cell phones. In other rooms there were older college-age males who were identified to the girls only as "the popular group of males." For this experiment the girls were instructed to role-play using the technology to communicate in order to gain acceptance into the popular group (consisting only of male college students). The girls were also told they could use fake names and personalities and do whatever they wished online or while using their phones.

Researchers observed the youth on screens located in a completely separate room and here is what they observed: The girls began by sending greetings and viewing personal Web pages with pictures that they had quickly created. One Web profile included a picture with a fake name, screen name, state, country, birth date, gender, and interests. Rivalries formed in a short amount of time with nasty text messages sent among the groups. Although the girls appeared calm and collected, the text showed a more cruel side to participants of the experiment. Participants later commented that the line between what was real and not real was not clear, even though they knew they were role-playing. Younger girls verbally attacked the older girls and vice versa. These included comments about physical appearance and clothing, name-calling using terms such as "slut" and "bitches." Digital pictures of participants were altered in negative ways. Nasty comments were taken very personally by some of the girls. Even in a controlled experimental setting, the harm caused by the comments were real for the girls involved.

Researchers also reported that after the experiment began, the older males were startled by the technological proficiency of the younger females. The males commented that the younger girls were doing things with the technology that they have never seen before, and that they themselves did not know how to do. It revealed a technological knowledge gap between teens and very young adults who were not that much older. It also revealed to the males just how vicious and cruel young girls can be. Whether male or female, one researcher described how even seemingly nice people can be nasty when under the cloak of secrecy. Simply put, people will often say and do what they would not normally do when they feel they are anonymous, or because they cannot see the reactions from the receivers of messages. A young female participant in the experiment echoed this sentiment when describing how she did not think about how the comments would be taken on the receiving end.

From *Primetime Live: Cyberbullying*. DVD. ABC News Productions. First aired on September 14, 2006.

Cyber bullying occurs relatively invisibly—there is no shoving on school grounds to observe, which handicaps and complicates what school officials can do. Also, in traditional bullying situations, the victim nearly always knows the attacker because they have periodic face-to-face encounters. This may not be the case when bullying happens online, because youth as we have learned can assume fake identities. Using the Internet to bully also enables more youth to "pile on" as aggressors using real or fake identities. Possibilities for this are worsened by the reality that, as indicated above, cyber bullying can happen anytime from anywhere. For youth who carry around IT devices everywhere they go, and feel a need to be continually online in order to be cool and interact with friends, there may be no escape. Further, abusive content can be quickly and widely disseminated anonymously, unless or until police become involved and initiate an investigation.

These things combined with inadequate supervision of youth computing activities by adults may also result in intensified bullying. Hatred inspired by one youth can be infectious among impressionable friends all trying to fit in and potentially outdo each other to compete for status in the digital youth culture. It is easy to imagine how relatively innocuous bullying online can quickly escalate and become out of control via social computing interactions that are not understood and carefully monitored by adults. As indicated by the 14-year-old female from Reyes, France previously mentioned, who is going to stop them? Besides, as indicated in the opening chapter quote, once parents and other responsible adults figure out how online bullying is done youth who realize this and who remain intent on cyber bullying will find new ways to do it.

Cyber bullies adapt to changing environments and adopting new methods just as criminals do. And because technology within society is always changing and affecting the interactive environments in which people live, we must regard cyber bullying as ethical, attitudinal, and behavioral problems, not primarily a technological problem. In short, *cyber bullying is bullying with a new twist!* Although bullying in the Digital Age is more technologically complex, it is much easier to accomplish and potentially more effective for most kids adept at using IT devices. They don't have to be big or strong, have a car or lots of money for gasoline through which to be popular or mobile, or even access to weapons with which to inflict injuries. All they need are fixed or mobile IT devices and a connection to the Internet. (Remember, cellular phones also connect to the Internet via satellite and land-based telecommunication systems and switches, just as computers and other types of IT devices do.)

Despite technological differences between classical bullying and cyber bullying, fundamental elements remain the same: repeated aggressions deliberately intended to cause harm to one or more individuals. When these are carried out using technology such as computers and cell phones this constitutes cyber bullying. One can debate whether the idea of repetition is needed to constitute bullying or cyber bullying, but this misses the point. One single act can cause enough harm to constitute cyber bullying as we have seen with the "Star Wars Kid." Practically speaking however, the Internet and social computing involving interactions among dozens or more youths in online forms and forums mean that insults, threats, or a victim's fear of these being repeated once they begin exacerbates cyber bullying situations. Ongoing fear of being bullied again or repeatedly can be even worse than original insults and threats even if these never recur. In time cyber bullying "products" such as the Star Wars Kid video can take on a ridiculing life of their own, perpetuating fear of embarrassment or physical harm. In other words, repeated harm occurs in the mind of victims, not just through the actions of bullies. When demeaning or threatening content is posted online, it can be months, years, or forever just depending on how many people keep it alive as content on the Web sites they control. Bullying in any manner should be considered serious on the basis of the intent and the level of harm caused in the short-term as well as by its potential to cause long-term harm to victims and their reputations rather than by how many times it occurs

## DIGITAL SHORTHAND FOR
## COMMUNICATING ONLINE

A significant challenge facing adults who are interested in intervening in cyber bullying involves the language of online communication. The language on the Internet used by youth has evolved along with computing and tele-communications devices and the ways in which people use these online. It has been said that adolescents are actually in the middle of a "language evolution."[2] Many researchers now refer to the written language used by kids and adults in their online communications as "netspeak." Some researchers argue that the language is creating a generation technology gap that prevents parents and educators from understanding the language of the Internet. Some also advocate that cyber bullying policies should be created with an understanding of ways in which youth express themselves through Im-ing, texting, e-mail, and when posting to social networking sites and so on. For their part, youth more often refer to netspeak as "leetspeak" or simply "leet" (written online as l33t).

According to author, security researcher, and research assistant for this book Neel Sampat:

> "[Leetspeak] . . . is a text-based communication method primarily used on the Internet which uses combinations of ASCII characters to replace traditional western style Latin letters. The term is derived from the word "elite" reduced to "Leet" (written online as l33t) to initiate this specialized form of symbolic writing. There are several different dialects of Leet found on various Internet forums and message boards, but the basic syntax remains the same allowing the intended meaning of words and phrases to be understood by users who communicate in this manner. Originally the word Leet was used as an adjective to describe the behavior or accomplishment of people who practiced this form of communication. In effect, they were considered elite Internet users because they could communicate online using symbolic syntax. Being able to communicate in Leetspeak is a badge of honor similar to the online status someone who possesses excellent electronic gaming or computer hacking abilities. In other words, the ability to communicate in Leet is a technical skill that merits status depending on one's creative and expressive abilities using ASCII characters . . . Leet may also be utilized as a substitution cipher for personal communications or those related to illicit activities. Leetspeak styles of expression vary significantly among Internet users. Like slang terms used in other

languages, Leet consists of odd expressions that may have particular meaning only among certain groups of Internet users. Loose grammar, just like loose spelling, encodes some level of emphasis, ironic or otherwise. A reader must rely more on intuitive parsing of Leet to determine the meaning of a sentence rather than the actual sentence structure. "In particular, speakers of Leet are fond of turning verbs into nouns and back again as forms of emphasis."[3]

Netspeak or "l33t" are advantageous because they allow users to more quickly construct messages using abbreviations and acronyms. The coding that invariably results is difficult to understand until you get use to it. Parents and other adults rarely have a clue what kids are writing as their thumbs tap away on miniature cell phone key pads. Here are some examples of what youth mean with typing the following:

U = you

LOL = laugh/laughing out loud

BTW = by the way

CYA = see you later

OMG = Oh my God

OUT = reveal (as in "he outed me being gay")

P911 = parent emergency (as in, parents are coming!)

PAW = parents are watching

PAL = parents are listening

PIR = parent in room

POS = parent over shoulder

OM = old man (as in father)

OL = old lady (as in mother)

KPC = keeping parents clueless

NIFOC = nude in front of computer

IPN = I'm posing naked

LMIRL = let's meet in real life

ASL = age, sex, location?

In the above examples we equate leet using all capital letters. In actuality leet is written in combinations of upper and lower case letters, along with numbers and other keyboard symbols just depending on how something needs to be expressed in customary ways of the people engaged. Most people understand THAT USING ALL CAPS is an expression of anger, shouting or "in your face" (i.e., the sender would literally be standing up in your face if they could). In addition, not using proper punctuation like periods and question marks are common, but using them in excess (e.g., several question marks in sequence "???????") conveys emphasis as in "i'm REALLY x-cited!!!!" or "R u DENSE???????."

These examples are fairly simplistic. As kids spend more time learning and becoming proficient in writing (and in some instances actually speaking) with netspeak terms, they also will use increasingly cleaver digital shorthand that is harder and harder to decipher unless of course you understand the language. Leetspeak may be considered an important and complex aspect of technology-enabled cyber bullying. The result is that cyber bullying can occur silently right under the watchful eyes of naïve adults. Parents and other adults need to stay current on emerging and evolving netspeak in order to provide adequate supervision of their children's social computing activities and civility. Numerous Web sites are now available to aid in this and help decipher online language used by youth, including: www.netsmartz411.com and www.cyberbullying.us.org.

## DIGITAL TACTICS FOR TORMENTING OTHERS ONLINE

As indicted earlier, we define cyber bullying as intentionally using computers or other electronic devices to harass, threaten, intimidate, embarrass, or otherwise cause harm to another or others. Cyber bullying can be done in a number of ways, and can vary in degree of seriousness. As in the physical world, victims of cyber bullying can be harassed online about their physical appearance, social status, race, age, sex, gender, religion, academic performance, or disability. Victims are often youth, but adults such as teachers and school administrators have also reported being victims of cyber bullying by youth.

In a recent survey of school building administrators from a large county in upstate New York, 32 percent of 107 administrators indicated that faculty and staff in their school had been victims of cyber bullying.[4] In reality anyone can be bullied, threatened, or harassed online. The possibilities are endless, and the reasons and ways in which cyber bullying is taking place are constantly evolving. The bullying can take place through sending harassing e-mails and instant messages, or posting harmful material or images using the Internet or cellular phones. It can also be accomplished via social networking sites, blogs, and even through online gaming. Each method merits a little explanation with regard to how it is used to cyber bully.

## E-MAIL

E-mails and instant messages have been considered a primary means in which cyber bullying takes place. Cyber bullying can be done through e-mail by the direct sending of annoying, cruel, insulting, or threatening messages to another. It can range in degree of seriousness from fairly benign (somewhat annoying, cruel or insulting) to very serious (threatening, or extremely cruel). In addition, flame mail (provoking e-mails) and hate mail (hate speech directed at minorities or marginal groups) are other ways to electronically cause harm to others. Depending on the facts and circumstances, the cyber bullying may be considered a form of simple harassment, or could even rise to the level of stalking. E-mail can also be used to transmit unflattering or embarrassing digital photos, or to spread rumors about another or others. Also, the forwarding of a private e-mail to others who were not intended to see the message is becoming much more common. This can cause extreme harm and discomfort, especially if the information was very personal in nature, or involved comments about others. E-mail has long been considered the old standby of electronic communication. However, there seems to be an emerging preference by teenagers for instant messaging (IM). For example, teenagers have expressed that they use IM most often when communicating with friends, with some viewing e-mail as a means to converse with "old people."[5]

## INSTANT MESSAGING

Instant messaging involves using a computer to send text messages in real time over a network such as the Internet. Instant messaging services such as AOL Instant Messenger, MSN, and Yahoo! Messenger are a few examples that allow individuals, especially teenagers, to instant-response written conversations provided they are online at the same time. Open source software also makes instant messaging possible without paying for a subscription service as long as users can find a way to get online (e.g., home, community WiFi, or school connection).

Typically instant messaging software and services allow users to create buddy lists that allow youth to see who is already online. In this way they can simply click on the names or nicknames of users to establish two-way, three-way, or more-way conversations in real time. Newer applications also allow exchanging of voice messages, photos, music, video, and links to Web sites or articles. In a recent court case, a federal appellate court with jurisdiction over New York State dealt with an 8th grade student who shared with his friends, via instant message, a small drawing that suggested that one of his teachers should be shot. The picture depicted a gun pointed at a person's head with dots of blood splatter nearby. Beneath the drawing was the teacher's name and the word "kill."

Through instant messaging, individuals can be bullied by their friends or by peers with anonymous screen names through the direct sending of harmful information. Also, using features such as "buddy profiles" enable others to insert harmful or embarrassing information or images for others to read or see. Another example of cyber bullying involves the exclusion of others from participating in their conversations (blocking from a buddy list), or also using instant messages to quickly spread malicious rumors about others. The following real-life example of instant messages sent via Yahoo! mail between two teens demonstrates how the online communication can be harassing, and sexually harassing in nature (screen names and real names have been changed). Note the communication style, and that the two participants obviously know each other:

Boy: wat up doe? u thought about what we talk'd about n clas the other day?

Girl: and!!!! ????

Boy: so did u think about it

Girl: think about wat?

Boy: wat john asked u for

Girl: JOHN ASKED ME 4 HEAD AND I SAID NO WAT ABOUT IT

Boy: but u told me u waz gon think about it so waz good cuz I want some

Girl: IF I SAID NO 2 JOHN THEN IM GONNA SAY NO TO U AND DON'T OUT WORDS IN MY MOUTH LITTLE BOY YOU DON'T KNOW ME AND JOHN WAS WRONG 4 ASKIN ME THAT BUT YOUR EVEN MORE WRONG BECAUSE YOU R 17 YEARS OLD AND IM 15 YEARS OLD COME ON BE REAL

Boy: how do u sound cuz aint noth'n wrong wit talk'n 2 gurls thats 15 cuz itz only a 2 year difference and u talk'n it way overboard itz just a ? and all u had to say was no and I aint John so u could try dat again and I kno some gurls that a give me some and not John just like he probably got some gurls that would do him and not me.

Girl: OKAY BUT MY PROBLEM WITH THAT IS U ASKED ME BEFORE AND I SAID NO SO Y WOULD U ASK ME AGAIN? U NO I HAVE A BOYFRIEND SO Y ASK ME CAUSE YOU NO THE ANSWER SO IF YOU HAVE GIRLS THAT WOULD GIVE YOU HEAD WHAT WAS A POINT OF ASKING ME COMMON SENCE AND ASK ME AGAIN I WILL TAKE YOU OFF MY FRIENDS LIST AND BLOCK YOU SO U CANT WRITE ME ANY MORE THINK IM PLAYIN AND WE WILL SEE HOWS PLAYIN.

Boy: I don't giva fuck bitch and I aint never ask u 4 no head so u can knock it off 4 u get dat ask spanked on 2morrow by 1 of my little shorties true story how u like dat1 and plus dis was the only time I ever asked for some head so waz really good wit chu I kno u feel'n sick right now so fall back.

Girl: YOU JUST SAID YOU DIDN'T ASK ME FOR HEAD THEN YOU SAID THIS WAS THE FIRST TIME YOU ASKED FOR IT AND DON'T THREATEN ME CAUSE I DIDNT DO NOTHIN TO YOU DINT SAY NO AND I CAN TELL THE POLICE THAT YOU ARE HARASSING ME AND YOU WILL GO TO JAIL SO STOP WHILE YOU ARE AHEAD OKAY. . . . OKAY THANK YOU!!!!!!!!!!

Boy: I noe u feel sick cuz u cant tell the police noth'n lol but i got something 4 dat ass 2morrow 4 try'na play me

Girl: NO I CANT TELL THE POLICE NOTHIN BUT I CAN SHOW THEM THIS E-MAIL OR I WILL SHOW MY PRINCIPAL AND YOU DONT GOT NOTHIN 4 MY BUT OH AND IM NOT A BITCH EITHER OH THANK YOU CAUSE NOW I CAN TELL THEM YOU THREATEN ME AND IF THEY DON'T BELIEVE ME THEN I CAN SHOW THEM THIS PAPER SO I WILL SEE YOU

2 MORROW GOOD NIGHT SLEEP TIGHT DONT LET THE BED
BUMPS BITE BYE
Boy: do it den BITCH BYE

## TEXT MESSAGING

Despite the increasing ownership and use of cell phones by teenagers, the use of text messaging is often left out of the conversation about cyber bullying. This is a mistake, because texting via cell phone and other mobile text messengers has become another popular means to cyber bully others. With increased availability of affordable and miniaturized "do-it-all" IT devices now being used, texting represents a new challenge in preventing cyber bullying. The mobile nature of texting devices is what makes them dangerous: cyber bullying in the palm of one's hand anytime from anywhere! Parents concerned about Internet use have always known to locate a home computer in a public place like the kitchen, den, or family room. Keep it out of a child's bedroom and everything will be OK, right? WRONG! We already mentioned that some kids are now text messaging after family members go to sleep, or from private places other than bedrooms.

Texting devices now allow uploading, downloading, sending, or receiving media files such as photos, videos, or links that can be used as cyber weaponry. Recent research has indicated that 13 percent of teenagers reported being a victim of cyber bullying by receiving a threatening or aggressive e-mail, instant message, or text message.[6] Clearly, direct threats or cruel messages in the form of text are not the only ways to cyber bully. Embedded content within messages, attachments to messages or links to Web content can be just as or more effective than words. Forwarding private communications, spreading rumors, outing secrets, excluding individuals from conversations, or sending embarrassing or doctored images are the cyber equivalent to an arsenal of potential assault weapons.

The self-esteem and reputation of an unsuspecting victim can be forever changed with just a few clicks of a bully's mouse or taps of a cell phone keypad. As a principal in a 2008 interview about cyber bullying said, "While in this position for five years, I have seen an increase in cyber bullying (cb) incidents mainly over the past two years. Currently, I am less concerned with the use of school computers to commit cb incidents as I am with the use of cell phones. The issues I've dealt with mainly have involved students using cell phones in cb incidents."[7] Similarly, another school principal in the same interviewing process stated: "I am most concerned about the use of cell phones and the photographs and videos shared. Many young people are losing their moral compass and sending photos that will embarrass them in the near future."

Another concern about small, lightweight and easily concealed IT devices is the possibility of their being lost or stolen. When this happens, unencrypted devices containing incredible amounts of personal data can fall into the hands of bullies or cyber criminals. Even a perception that devices such as cell phones are being used for illicit purposes can lead to abuse by others. Consider the following narrative taken from an actual violent and disruptive incident report that was documented in a school district:

> John was within a stall in the boy's bathroom in the main hallway. Another unknown student entered the bathroom and began to use the stall next to John. The unknown student mistakenly believed John was using his cell phone to take pictures of him. John stated that he was merely texting a friend with the phone. The unknown student became angry and pounded on the stall door. Being unable to enter, the student exited the bathroom and returned with friends. This group of unknown students harassed John. In response to this, John called 911 for assistance. The group of students fled when they were told the police were on the way. The police arrived and completed a report of the incident. The suspects have not been identified.

## WEB SITES AND MESSAGE BOARDS

Web sites and message boards can provide additional means to cyber bully others. For example, a Web site can be created for the specific purpose of demeaning or bullying someone or a group of individuals. These sites can also encourage others to join in as the word spreads and creates a snowball effect. Web sites that rapidly become popular are referred to by youth as being "hot," which means they receive many hits or visits in a short amount of time. Through Web sites, many types of lists can be posted that invite users to digitally pile onto cyber bullying in progress.

Consider the Web site schoolscandals.com, which fortunately as of this writing no longer exists. On this site, a person could choose from a large list of schools located within the United States to view postings about many different topics. A "thread" is a series of posts in a conversation about something in particular. On schoolscandals.com dozens of threads focused on someone rather than something, and included extremely derogatory and insulting comments. The opening comment of one thread titled "Amanda" said: "Hey guys do you know Amanda (real last name was actually used)? O My God she's such a loser. She is always hooking up with guys and no-one likes her and everyone hates her-even the people who hang out with her are just pretending to like her. I hear she slept with 3 guys while she was going out with her boyfriend."[8]

How would you feel if *you* were Amanda, or if she was your sister or daughter? Remember, the comment launched a thread naming a person in a particular school. Amanda is not that common of a name, so chances are everyone who participated in the thread actually knew Amanda (remember her last name was actually used in the first thread post). Since the Web site was not configured to disallow posts made by nonstudents of the school, anyone in the world could pile on with their own false yet persuasive insults. Although this Web site was no longer active, the contents could still be viewed years later. (The quote above was retrieved online in late 2007 even though the

Web site was discontinued in April 2003.) This is another example of how online content, and therefore the effects of cyber bullying, can be enduring or permanent, and inspire and reinforce fears that derogative online content may haunt victims forever. The prospect of information posted onto the Web remaining online and available forever is disconcerting to say the least and helps to explain why Internet savvy people periodically google themselves just to see what is being posted about them online. College-age adults, and even younger youth, who allow themselves to be photographed or otherwise portrayed in compromising situations may never be able to run for political office, get a good job, or marry the partner of their dreams. Colleges and universities now routinely google applicants in the process of making student admissions and scholarship decisions. Information posted online about anyone, even in the course of malicious cyber bullying, may at a minimum raise doubts about their suitability for any kind of a position, approval, or relationship. Notwithstanding the questionable ethics of so-called googling for names of prospective job or promotion candidates without their prior knowledge or approval, which is often done for personal safety and nonemployment security purposes (e.g., to see if someone is suitable to date, or whether the new next door neighbor is a convicted sex predator), maybe organizations should consider using such open source information to screen for and hold cyber bullies accountable! The problem with this of course, is that our juvenile justice systems are generally setup to protect the identities and reputations of people who engage in illicit activities when they are young; and few organizations have formal human resources policies, procedures, or training governing googling for any purpose, much less with regard to using company computers!

Now let's think about online polling Web sites used by people to rank or score just about anything imaginable, from the popularity of someone to whether they look hot or not. What are the Net effects of ranking someone in ways they may not even know about much less approve of? Similarly posting of online hit lists also appears to be gaining in popularity and is potentially very harmful to people when targeted. In case you don't know, a Web list can be something civil, wholesome, and therefore positive such as creating a list of favorite movies, songs, or bands. However, when Web sites list the ugliest, stupidest, fattest, least athletic students, most hated teachers, or explicit things someone would say to another person, the effects can be devastating because they are made public and express opinions in un-vetted ways. It's one thing to speak your mind at a public meeting or shout in anger at someone who upsets you. It is quite another to orchestrate a public bashing process especially when youth victims incapable of defending themselves very well are targeted.

In a 2006 edition of *SAANYS Journal* it was reported that Long Island's *Newsday* had a "Who do you hate?" question that allegedly appeared on a MySpace blog followed by this message: ". . . I want everyone to take a moment and really think about who you hate in our school, then choose the one you have the most disdain for and write in here for all to see. This may cause violence . . . aggression and death. But iam [*sic*] willing to look past that for the better of the cause, so let's hear it."⁹ There were 240 responses to the question, a perfect case of what is known as "*trolling*." The intention of trolling (like a combination of the fishing method and folklore portraying small, repulsive, and mischievous creatures known as trolls) is to disrupt an online discussion and entice others to respond in a negative way. As you can see, trolling amounts to another variation of online incivility that can be used to cyber bully.

The good news for college-age trollers, cyber bullies or other uncivil netizens of cyberspace is that schoolscandals.com has been replaced with Juicy Campus.com! This is the latest Web forum in which college students can identify with particular academic institutions to overtly or indirectly slime each other by taking up an issue and inviting others to participate. Very similar to the classic trolling described above, original posts in JuicyCampus.com (as the URL name suggests) are designed to elicit gossip, snide remarks, and insults in response to straight forward questions, comments, or invitations to discuss an issue. For example, one post from University of California–Los Angeles (UCLA) simply stated a person's name followed by: "Everyone seems to know him. Discuss." This posting resulted in the following responses:

"Tool."

"fag."

"Really big jerk. treats girls like crap."

"omg his ego already enormous and he is a man whore"

"HAHAHAHAHAHAAH OMG I was waiting for a post about this dude on here this made my day haha"

"he's such a man whore and thinks he's legit. Fuck that. what a tool."

"most obnoxious person I have EVER met EVER EVER EVER"

"he definitely thinks he's the shit. Bigheaded and egotistical"

*People* magazine did a story on JuicyCampus in their April 14, 2008 edition that discussed the controversy over the types of comments stated on the Web site. The article described a freshman female at Duke University who reported breaking down and missing classes for three weeks after she saw false statements about her on the Web site including a statement that she once attempted suicide. While some people view the JuicyCampus as a source of entertainment consisting of harmless jokes along with opinions and true statements, other people, including campus administrators, faculty members, and lawyers, view such statements as inappropriate and potentially slanderous and libel. Counterarguments also include posts made by people who know each other even as genuine friends and that what is written is not much different than talking out loud in a public place like a school cafeteria.

OK, fair enough. Considering again that cyber bullying is an ethical rather than technological problem, what do you think about these posts: "Who is the sluttiest girl??????," "Biggest slut at Baylor?," and "Sexiest man at vandy?" Each were responded to repeatedly. Students written about in the responses reported being totally humiliated, at times by someone they had considered a close friend. Do you think these examples constitute intentional embarrassment, harassment, intimidation, or threats—which is our definition of cyber bullying? Perhaps yes, perhaps no, but these and *thousands* of other examples from various Web sites represent a form of cruelty in society that is currently unregulated and causing varying levels of harm to *millions* of people. Live stream sites such as Justin.tv, which hosted the November 19, 2008 suicide of Abraham Biggs, a 19-year-old Floridian who overdosed while thousands of Web viewers watched and some reportedly egged him on, dramatizes and underscores new alarming aspects of contemporary digital youth culture and cyber bullying enabled by information technology.[10]

When not monitored for abuse, online forums in which youth engage will often digress to denigrate certain students, teachers, coaches, school building administrators and so forth. Frequently Web sites and social networking forums created specially for bullying purposes or that effectively digress into *bullying forums* are not policed even as required by written policies that put users on notice as to what the rules are. As a practical matter, popular Web forums with millions of users can hardly be expected to be monitored for every single thread and post. Besides, our First Amendment right to free speech protects even hate speech in the United States. Still, with millions of users and presumably commensurate advertising revenue maybe Webmasters and owners of social networking forums should try harder. As an alternative, people and organizations can boycott or ban access to certain forums deemed to have inappropriate content. RateMYTeachers.com claims its Web site has been blocked by over 900 American school districts, which are now listed on its "wall of shame," which youth can readily still access from home or while mobile computing.

Since banning hate speech is not possible despite being civilly inappropriate, and Web sites cannot or will not regulate themselves, and neither Internet filtering or blocking software used by schools or parents will actually prevent determined youth from accessing controversial content, what are we left with? Even more ways to cyber bully!

## BLOGS AND CHAT ROOMS

Web blogs, which have come to be known simply as blogs, have become hugely popular on the Internet. Blogs are journals or diaries that can be instantly published online. They are interactive and allow readers to comment on and add to already published information including on so-called bashboards. Alternatively cyber bullies can visit a blog that a person they wish to target is known to post messages. There they can gather intelligence about their intended victim and when the time is right either post defamatory remarks to the blog itself or on another forum known to be read by the victim's friends. Since blogs can be quite popular and known by adolescents in a particular community, cyber bullying that happens in blogs can be visible to many in a community, or even worldwide. The implications are quite different than comparatively limited effects caused in traditional bullying, in which relatively few people can witness an event or spread rumors within a school.

Indeed the "blogosphere" as it is called, is a force multiplier for cyber bullying. Blogs are often used on social networking sites (which will be discussed shortly), which raises the question as to which blogs are more popular among youth? A more sinister question is what makes for a popular blog with respect to hurtful activities promulgated by contemporary digital youth culture? The Web site www.hitsusa.com discusses ways to increase blog traffic: "Be controversial—Be opinionated. Take a stand on issues you and your readers care about. Don't be afraid to go against the grain or take a negative slant on things. Controversy stirs people up and makes them want to find out more. Plus, your blog's comments will increase exponentially." How true, challenging, and sad this advice is, a variation of the mass television and newspaper mantra: "if it bleeds it leads." Broadcasting or posting descriptive, albeit painful, accounts of tragedies and issues that require reflection and confrontation by society is one thing. But exploiting individuals to profit or with the intention of stirring up embarrassment, harassment, intimidation, or threats toward them crosses boundaries defining civility in civil societies.

Chat rooms constitute another important way of sharing information, and thus another means to cyber bully. Development of peer-to-peer (p2p) file sharing software now commonly used by youth to pirate music, movie, and software has also enabled youth to share photos and videos created with digital cameras and Webcams. Consequently, bullying in the Digital Age can now include still photos and action clips that target individuals or groups for defamation. If indiscriminate youth have allowed themselves to be photographed or videotaped in compromising situations or poses, and such content finds its way onto the Web, all the more potential grist for the cyber bullying mill because these can then be used after the fact to embarrass them!

Research has shown that chat rooms are now commonly used in cyber bullying incidents, as evidenced from the following case interview: In Eldorado, Texas, a 17-year-old male stated that his friend started calling him a queer in chat rooms that they visited. Another friend joined in, and despite saying they were only kidding, kept doing it because other youth began believing that he was homosexual. He reported the cyber bullying, which was happening at home and at school, to the principal but felt that nothing was done about it. The cyber bullying got worse. His life turned into a complete mess. He stopped participating in sports and school activities, including running a successful fund-raiser for cerebral palsy. Even his parents experienced problems as the result of the cyber bullying. His father began getting comments at work and his parents began fighting with each other. At the conclusion of the interview the teen stated that "there has to be a law against cyber bullying, because it ruins lives."

## ONLINE GAMING

We have already discussed online gaming on a general level in Chapter 2 as the most popular form of social computing engaged in among youth, and how many young gamers seem focused on aggression, violence, and sex. Here we delve into the topic from a more technological perspective to further relate this form of entertainment to cyber bullying. As previously indicated, the Rochester Institute of Technology's "Survey of Internet and At-Risk Behaviors" established that online gaming begins in kindergarten when children are 4- or 5-year-olds if not earlier in life. This research also established that online gaming, cyber bullying, and being cyber bullied correlate with statistical significance and at high levels. Other research also substantiates that a majority of tweens and teenagers play games online, with the numbers growing significantly since the year 2000.[11] As Internet connection speeds have gotten much faster, more sophisticated multiplayer online games have emerged.

> Massively multiplayer online role playing games (MMORPGs) that may have as many as several thousand simultaneous players. *Everquest, World of Warcraft,* and *Final Fantasy XI* are examples of MMORPGs. With the 2007 release of the sci-fi action-adventure first-person shooter game *Halo 3,* the electronic gaming industry passed a financial earnings milestone by its creator Bungie Studios of Microsoft Corporation making over $175 million dollars in a single day! This tops the largest box office earnings for a movie shown in a conventional theater (e.g., *Spider-Man 3* also released in 2007, which earned $148 million in ticket sales within its opening weekend). This serves as a stark illustration of the commercial value of electronic gaming, and industry currently valued at approximately $20-billion dollars.[12]

The overall number and types of games are too extensive to cover here, but it is safe to say that the opportunities to play games online appear endless. One popular game online reportedly has over 10 million subscribers, half of these subscribers are under the age of 25. Unfortunately, as we have indicated, online gaming is not immune from hate, vulgarity, aggression, violence, and cyber bullying. Gaming bullies, also known as "griefers" or "snerts," can harass fellow players in a number of ways. For example, beginners can be subjected to online taunting as they are learning the game. Further, harassment can manifest itself in the form of obscene language and cheating, and can even involve a number of griefers forming online gangs. Griefers often seem less interested in the game and more interested in creating disruptions and getting attention. They may look for someone who has responded to their online misdoings, and continue to harass and annoy their target out of convenience or spite. They can also easily portray themselves as someone else, such as through impersonation or expressing statements that are not true. Unfortunately in the gaming world, there are few mechanisms for reporting wrongdoings such as those more common and under scrutiny with social networking forums.

## SOCIAL NETWORKING SITES

Social networking sites, including but not limited to Facebook, MySpace, and YouTube, represent a confluence of technology-enabled cyber bullying. It is on these sites where all forms of cyber bullying effectively converge, because it is here where all other forums are talked about and can be accessed through. An advertisement for social networking sites could read, "Live, uncensored, unmonitored, and uninhibited action at your fingertips." What teen would not be tempted to click on this ad, which could take them into a gaming environment, blog or chat room, or any other type of Web forum in which youth can find some "action"? The hook is always stimulating interactivity consistent with elements of contemporary digital youth culture.

Through the years, the biggest change in Internet use has been the increased ability to share, connect, create, and interact. Year after year youth continue to better understand, embrace and help expand upon this reality. In its infancy, the Internet was basically a means to read and view information. Today the Web attracts and is used by bullies to ensnare their victims flying and fluttering around cyberspace! Research shows that over half of all teenagers that are between the ages of 12 and 17 have created a profile on a social networking site.[13] Numbers of youth with these capabilities will surely increase while ages at which they begin capably using IT devices and the Net for more things will undoubtedly decline.

MySpace, Facebook, and YouTube get a lot of negative attention because they were among the earliest and are now among the most famous and largest social networking forums accessed by youth. MySpace has been repeatedly taking a hit due to safety concerns and accusations that they are not doing enough to protect young online consumers. In 2008 numerous State Attorney Generals took collective legal action against MySpace leading to an agreement for greater abuse prevention efforts by the firm. Nonetheless, parents, teachers, and police continue to express serious concerns over the safety social networking sites provide.

In truth, *hundreds* of other popular social networking sites now exist, being hosted by firms and individuals who are located in countries all over world in which laws and regulations governing cyber content vary considerably. How many social networking sites can you name? Some forums you may not heard of are: Friendster, Xanga, and Bebo along with Backwash, Breedster, Broadcaster, BuddyBridge, Chia Friend, ChosenNet, Christianster, Classmates, Click2Friends, easeek, eFriendsnet, enCentra, everyonesconnected, Friend Fan.com, Friendity, Friend Map, Friendoo, friendsbay.de, Friends of Friends,

Friend Surfer, Friendzy, Gruuve, HeiYou, hi5, hipster, Huminity, Hum-mingBoard, The Impersonals, iSocialite, Korea Data House, LDS Linkup, LianQu, linkyourfriends, Living Directory, Metails, mrNeighborhood, Net-Friendships, Neurofriends, orkut, Paljunction, peeps nation, qpengyou, Ringo, saywhatz, sconex, stickam, Tickle by Emode, ticqle, Tribe.net, twit-ter, UUFriends, Wallop, WiW, Wordshine, Yeeyoo, YOYO, zenetwork, and Zerodegrees. This is by no means an exhaustive list as the number of sites continues to grow and appear at a greater rate than they disappear. Inter-estingly enough, to sign up, all a child has to do usually is provide their real—or a false—age. This may explain why in RIT's "Survey of Internet and At-Risk Behaviors," 24 percent of over 10,000 middle school students surveyed reported they lied about their age online within the previous year (in 2006–2007).

The number of social networking sites in the future will likely expand to thousands if not ten-of-thousands as *billions* of relatively young people con-nect online. Also increasing are the numbers of teenagers who are considered "content creators" defined as "online teens that have created or worked on a blog or webpage, shared original creative content, or remixed content they found online into a new creation."[14] Content creators often use social net-working sites to share their work and many youth are validated within con-temporary digital youth culture for doing so. In the process, many intense Internet users will likely become victims of cyber bullying.[15] Simple logic suggests that the use of social networking sites will continue to increase, meaning that incidents of cyber bullying will also rise. The problem is very likely to get worse before it gets better.

## CREATIVITY GONE AWRY: OTHER WAYS TO CYBER BULLY

Although content creation can be very positive, the creativity can also have a dark side. Teenagers are constantly finding new ways to express themselves and some youth use the technology to cyber bully others. As said earlier, cell phones and PDAs must not be omitted from the discussion on cyber bully-ing. This is especially important given the reality is that some cell phones may now be used for texting and to upload and download Web content. In addi-tion to direct threats and insults communicated via phone calls and texting, these devices can also be used to record people without their knowledge or take their picture and then facilitate posting such content online as a basis of cyber bullying. Consider the following story from an interview conducted with an 11th grade female: "We were at a pajama party fooling around and we lifted up our shirts, and one of the girls took a picture on her cell phone. I didn't know about it, but she put it on the computer and told everyone that I am a slut. My parents don't believe it, but it is the truth."

Phones can be used to record after baiting someone into saying something inappropriate, or can simply be left on to record anything than can be used against them. Photos, either online or from a cell phone, can also be easily doctored (e.g., photoshopped) showing a person doing something they were not really doing, or show an embarrassing moment (such as someone drinking alcohol or using drugs, or a picture made extremely unflattering through digital manipulation). Another emerging phenomenon, happy slapping, which seems to have originated in the United Kingdom, involves a stranger being physically attacked while other members of the group take pictures on their camera phones or video cameras. The pictures are often circulated via cell phones, or posted on the Internet. The increasing creativity and technological means to cause harm has created venues for cyber bullying behavior that are constantly evolving.

Finally, text bombing is another way to cyber bully, which involves sending high numbers of text messages via cell phone to another cell phone. Given the fee per number of messages that are a part of many cell phone plans, the harm, in addition to the annoyance, can also be financial. Obviously there are many ways to cyber bully. Today's adolescents must grapple with the increasing ways they can be harmed by people armed with technology, and with questions about who they can trust and what constitutes civil versus abusive or criminal behaviors Unfortunately more and more teenagers who become victims of cyber bullying resort to not trusting anyone, whether online or in person. Many such young people having already been burned are compromised when it comes to establishing and building relationships, while many others remain naïve about inherent limitations to creating genuine, lasting, and trusting relationships when limited only to online interactions with people.

# Cyber Bullying Research, Surveys, and Studies

*I always minded my own business, but they started pushing me in school and tripping me. I said nasty things about them in the chat room because I was mad, and they beat me up 3 days later. I lost my front tooth, and they gave me a black eye and bloody nose. I didn't start anything.*

*—8th grader*

When you think of research, thoughts of excessive academic jargon and boring statistics may come to mind. However, for society to recognize and accept that cyber bullying is an important societal issue, it is important to consider research surveys and other types of studies that shed light on the problem. We have already referred to several important research works about bullying and cyber bullying, and these have prompted even more research on bullying in the Digital Age—what it is, how it occurs, how often it occurs, who is most impacted and in what ways, and what can be done about it. Many researchers are now taking up these and several other questions about cyber bullying to build what scholars call a "body of research" to help unlock its many mysteries.

This chapter provides an overview of primary surveys and studies that have focused on or substantially relate to cyber bullying. Our discussion is generally organized from early to more recent research, and in each instance we have used the name of the sponsoring organization, principal investigators, and/or the name of the study as published or commonly referred to by scholars. Collectively this research explains much of what we know about cyber bullying and what needs additional exploration. Our discussion entails detailed analysis and interpretation of findings having to do with incidence, prevalence, age-group, and gender among other characteristics of offenders and victims, and insights into harm experienced and possible prevention and invention strategies.

Unfortunately the extensive set of projects discussed does not lend itself to being logically categorized in groups, nor does the organizing structure of our book permit studies, surveys, and other types of research projects to be separately identified in the table of contents. We conclude the chapter by tying it all together to discuss what it all means for parents, educators, and juvenile justice officials who must invariably intercede with the resources they have to prevent and stop cyber bullying. This will lead into Chapter 5 that describes legal precedence for dealing with cyber bullying.

## PIONEERING STUDIES, SURVEYS, AND RESEARCH PROJECTS

Early research that shed light on cyber bullying were actually more general purpose studies that explored what youth do and experience when they go online. For example, the first national Youth Internet Safety Survey (YISS 1), on Internet victimization focused in part on the ways and extent to which children were sexually exploited online.[1] The study was of a nationally representative sample of 1,501 10- to 17-year-olds who were contacted by telephone in 1999 and 2000. The study was funded by the U.S. Congress and awarded by the National Center for Missing & Exploited Children to researchers of the Crimes against Children Research Center at the University of New Hampshire.

Results indicated that 19 percent of young Internet users were involved in online aggression. Specifically, 12 percent reported being aggressors while online, 4 percent reported being targets only, and 3 percent reported being both aggressors and targets. The percentages of youth identified as aggressors were based on two questions: (1) making rude or nasty comments to someone while on the Internet, and (2) using the Internet to harass or embarrass someone with whom the youth was mad. Victims were identified based on answers to: (1) whether anyone had used the Internet in the previous year to threaten or embarrass the respondent by posting or sending messages about that person for other people to see; and (2) whether they ever felt worried or threatened because someone was bothering or harassing them while online.

Of youth surveyed, 6 percent had experienced online harassment.[2] Additional results from the study indicated that 31 percent of victims knew the harasser, and that online aggression was repeated in many instances. Specifically, 55 percent of Internet targets reported being harassed more than once by the same individual. Of importance, the study also found that 48 percent of all unwanted solicitations for sex received by youth were conveyed by other youth. These findings underscore the reality that cyber bullying often occurs among youth who know and may be sexually interested in each other. Further, youth who report being an aggressor or target of cyber bullying often have serious psychological or social challenges such as depression and low commitment to school.

In another survey conducted in 2001 in Canada, researchers found that 25 percent of young Internet users reported receiving messages that involved hateful things being said about other people.[3] Additional surveys have shown similar results.[4] In 2002, researchers from the National Children's Home in Great Britain surveyed a number of 11- to 19-year-olds. Results indicated that the most prevalent type of cyber bullying at the time was via cell phone text messaging (16%), followed by Internet chat rooms (7%), and e-mail (4%).[5] In 2005, a survey of 770 11- to 19-year-olds conducted by the National Children's Home and Tesco Mobile found that 20 percent of participants reported being victims of cyber bullying.[6]

## EMERGING RISKS OF VIOLENCE IN THE DIGITAL AGE

In 2002, pioneering researchers Ilene Berson, Michael Berson, and John Ferron used an online survey designed to obtain information regarding risks for adolescent girls online.[7] In this study, 10,800 12- to 18-year-old girls completed an online questionnaire that consisted of 19 multiple-choice and open-ended questions. Results were categorized into three areas, including: (1) online habits, (2) supervision of online activities, and (3) patterns of interaction online. Nearly 25 percent of girls surveyed reported being online for 6 to 9 hours per day, with 12 percent spending 10 to 12 hours online per day. Of these girls surveyed, 92 percent stated that the home computer was their primary access site. This survey also reported that 58 percent spent their online time instant messaging or e-mailing friends, 20 percent were surfing the Web, and 16 percent spent time in chat rooms. Regarding supervision, 70 percent of participants reported that their parents had discussed online safety with them, with 35 percent reporting that teachers discussed cyber safety. While online, 50 percent of participants reported being supervised at least occasionally by parents or teachers, with supervision defined as sitting with them or periodically checking the screen. Regarding, interaction patterns, 60 percent of respondents reported giving out personal information while online. Also, 15 percent reported receiving "disturbing communication" online, with 3 percent stating they had initiated threatening or sexually explicit messages.

This study was designed to assess online risks to female adolescents that may be associated with threatening behavior. Results confirmed that a significant number of adolescent girls were engaging in risky online activities such as releasing personal information. The data also indicated a gap in preventative action to maintain awareness and safety for young individuals. Of importance, only 35 percent of respondents indicated that teachers discussed cyber safety with them, and the study was not able to specify or differentiate what those discussions entailed, how frequently they occurred, how long they lasted, or their impacts on youth learning, knowledge retention, or computing behaviors. Rather, 30 percent of respondents indicated that teachers, parents, and caregivers only engaged in periodic communication with them about their experiences online. Further, researchers did note that as adolescent girls spent more time online, they were more likely to participate in destructive or dangerous acts. Hence, this study provided an early framework for better understanding youth cyber activities, aspects of online decision making, and the potential for being victimized.

## i-SAFE Surveys

In 2004, a national foundation that specializes in Internet safety, i-SAFE America, Inc. conducted a nationwide survey of 1,566 4th to 8th grade students.[8] Among students surveyed, 57 percent reported that someone had said hurtful things to them online, and 53 percent admitted saying mean or hurtful things to others online. Of the students, 42 percent reported being bullied online, with 7 percent stating that it happens quite often. The survey also said 35 percent of students reported being threatened online, and 20 percent stated that they have received mean or threatening e-mails. An additional survey by i-SAFE of 12,000 5th to 12th grade students conducted in 2005–2006 found that 22 percent of students knew someone who had been bullied online, with 19 percent saying that they themselves said something hurtful to others online. The i-SAFE surveys also shed light on a significant issue: that a gap existed between what parents were saying about their children's online activities and what the children were saying. Specifically, the surveys found that 93 percent of parents stated that they established rules for their child's Internet activity. On the other hand, 37 percent of children reported being given no rules from their parents on using the Internet. Similarly, 95 percent of parents stated that they knew some or a lot about their children's Internet activities, while 41 percent of children stated that they do not share information about online activities with their parents. It appears as though parents are overconfident in their abilities to supervise online activities.

## A Closer Look at the Youth Internet Safety Survey

In 2004, using data from the first national Youth Internet Safety Survey (YISS 1) researchers Michele Ybarra and Kimberly Mitchell conducted another study that focused on youth engaging in aggressive behavior while online.[9] Specifically, they examined psychosocial characteristics of online aggressors and associations with parent-child relationships, substance use, and delinquency. Results indicated that 44 percent of Internet harassers reported a poor caregiver-child emotional bond, while only 19 percent of nonharassers reported poor bonds with caregivers. Further, 32 percent of Internet harassers, versus 10 percent of nonharassers reported frequent substance use. Results also revealed that victims of traditional bullying are more likely to engage in online harassment. For example, 51 percent of Internet harassers, versus 30 percent of nonharassers, reported being a victim of traditional face-to-face bullying, whereas 20 percent of Internet harassers also reported being harassed online, while only 4 percent of nonharassers reported being victimized online. In short, Internet harassers were found to have psychosocial issues and weak emotional relationships with caregivers (among other issues), and are more likely to experience harassment before or after they themselves harass.

## The Second Youth Internet Safety Survey

Researchers Janis Wolak, Kimberly Mitchell, and David Finkelhor also of the Crimes Against Children Research Center at the University of New Hampshire conducted a repeat national Youth Internet Safety Study (YISS 2). This too was funded by Congress and awarded by a grant from the National Center for Missing and Exploited Children. As in the first YISS, it focused on ways in which youth are victimized online and what contributes to this. In this second round, 1,500 Internet users between the ages of 10 and 17 were contacted by telephone.[10] Results indicated that 9 percent of Internet users in the previous year were targets of online harassment, and 32 percent of harassment victims reported being hassled online more than 3 times in the previous year. Results also indicated that 45 percent reported knowing the harasser prior to the incident, again supporting the assertion that cyber bullying can be anonymous, but that it is also associated with in-person knowledge of offenders and social networking activities. Approximately 50 percent of known harassers were male while only 28 percent were female, and 58 percent of the harassers were other youth.

The study also found that 38 percent of harassed youth were distressed over cyber bullying. Those significantly more likely to experience distress included youth who were: (1) targeted by adults, (2) asked to send a picture of themselves, (3) received an aggressive off-line contact (e.g., a phone call or in-person visit), or (4) were preadolescents. Also, youth who visited chat rooms were found less likely to report distress due to the cyber bullying. Findings reveal that cyber bullying can cause serious distress for some youth and that cyber bullying increased substantially from 2000 to 2005.

## New Bottle But Old Wine

Another study conducted in 2005 by Canadian researcher Qing Li of the University of Calgary explored the nature and scope of adolescent experiences with cyber bullying by surveying 177 7th grade students who were randomly selected from 2 middle schools in an urban city.[11] Results showed that 54 percent of the students reported being a victim of traditional bullying, and 24.9 percent reported being a victim of cyber bullying. Nearly

15 percent of students reported cyber bullying others, and almost 33 percent reported bullying others in traditional face-to-face ways. Regarding gender differences, 60 percent of the victims of cyber bullying were females, and 52 percent were males. In addition, similar to traditional bullying, the majority of cyber bullying victims and bystanders failed to notify adults. A significant implication from the research is that bullies, cyber bullies, and their victims often knew each other. Nearly 30 percent of traditional bullies also reported that they were cyber bullies, approximately the same percentage of bullying victims were also reportedly cyber bullying victims, and 1 in 6 bullying victims, or about 17 percent reported cyber bullying others before and/or after being bullied online.

## RESEARCH ON GENDER DIFFERENCES

The following year, in 2006, Qing Li further explored cyber bullying by focusing on gender differences and examining whether cyber bullying victims and bystanders reported incidents to adults.[12] A survey of 264 junior high school students (7th–9th grades) from 3 urban schools was conducted. The participants were randomly selected from these schools. Results indicated that nearly 50 percent of the students were victims of bullying, and 25 percent had been cyber bullied. In addition, over half of the students knew someone who had been cyber bullied, while 1 in 6 admitted to cyber bullying others.

When considering gender, no differences were found in relation to victimization. However, more males were found to be cyber bullies than were females. This was not consistent with other research, which found that females were more likely to engage in cyber bullying.[13] However, given the small sample sizes that Qing Li was able to survey, results may not be representative of youth generally. Still, this research provided findings consistent with other studies, including the fact that victims and witnesses of cyber bullying often chose not to report it to adults. It was also reported by students that over 33 percent did not believe the adults tried to stop cyber bullying even when informed.

## CYBER BULLYING AMONG MIDDLE SCHOOL STUDENTS

In 2007, researchers Robin Kowalski and Susan Limber from Clemson University, South Carolina, also focused their attention on cyber bullying among middle school students.[14] Their research questions considered both traditional and cyber bullying incidents that occurred within two months prior to the survey being taken. For this study, 3,767 students, 6th to 8th grade, from 6 elementary and middle schools throughout the southeastern and northwestern United States were surveyed. Results indicated that 11 percent of these students reported being bullied online at least once in the past 2 months; 7 percent reported that they had been cyber bullied and bullied someone online; and 4 percent of respondents said they bullied someone on at least 1 occasion in the past 2 months. Results also showed that the most common methods of cyber bullying involve, in this order, using instant messaging, chat rooms, e-mail, and on a Web site. Also, overall data indicated that girls generally outnumbered the boys at the middle school level in terms of frequency of cyber bullying.

## BULLIES MOVE BEYOND THE SCHOOLYARD

Another study by Justin Patchin from the University of Wisconsin–Eau Claire and Sameer Hinduja from Florida Atlantic University was published in 2006. The purpose of their study was to explore the scope and nuances of cyber bullying.[15] The study assessed perceptions about and experiences of youth with cyber bullying. The survey methodology involved a questionnaire that was linked to the official Web site of a popular music artist during May 2004. A total of 571 responses to the online survey were made, though it is not known what controls were in place to ensure that responses were made by separate people who did not know or confer with each other in formulating their responses to questions.

Nonetheless, results were generally consistent with larger and random sample surveys like YISS 1 and YISS 2. Of those surveyed, 30 percent reported being a victim of online bullying defined as: being ignored, disrespected, called names, threatened, picked on, or having rumors spread by others. Specifically, 60 percent reported being ignored by others online, 50 percent were disrespected, 30 percent were called names, and 21 percent were threatened by others. Regarding negative effects of cyber bullying, 42 percent of victims reported feeling frustrated, 40 percent were angry, and 27 percent felt sad. Also of interest is the fact that about one-third of participants reported that being bullied online affected them at school, even though the bullying may not have occurred during school hours. An important limitation of the study is that it did not describe *how* students were affected in school.

## OFF-LINE CONSEQUENCES AND ONLINE VICTIMIZATION

In 2004–2005, researchers Justin Patchin and Sammer Hinduja also explored the emotional and behavioral effects of cyber bullying by applying what is known as General Strain Theory.[16] Essentially this theory states that people abuse and commit crimes against each other because of other stresses in their lives. Data collected in an online survey of 1,338 adolescent Internet users confirmed that cyber bullying can be related to stress youth experience from unresolved school or delinquency problems. For the survey, an online methodology was used to survey 6,800 respondents that were linked to numerous Web sites that targeted adolescents. However, an overwhelming percentage of females (82%) responded, which presented a possible response bias.

To create a more proportionate number of females to males, a random number of females was drawn to equalize the number of both sexes. Data showed that over 32 percent of males and 36 percent of females reported being victims of cyber bullying, most commonly in chat rooms and via computer text messages. Over 30 percent of cyber bullying victims reported feeling angry and 34 percent reported frustration. Notably, 35 percent reported that the cyber bullying experiences did not bother them. The study found that cyber bullies experience off-line problems and stress, and they tend to be older; and that victims of cyber bullying may be at risk for school violence and delinquency. The following story dramatizes the potential harmful effects in a way that often stale research cannot. As reported by a paramedic who saved a 12-year-old girl's life:

MySpace, YouTube, Photoshop, anything and everything to do with the computer are the works of the devil. Our tweens and teenagers are dropping like flies and nobody gets it. I just want to play God for one day and take the world and shake it and shake it and shake it, until people wake up. It's horrendous! Internet, Web sites, chat rooms, instant messaging, cell phones should all be outlawed. They're not allowed in my house anymore—no way, no how. Parents have no idea how evil and deadly these sites are. I have been a paramedic for over 40 years and I have never seen anything like this. You can't measure or see the damage it does until it's too late. I have talked to my coworkers, friends, my pastor, and other parents about the chat rooms but nobody knows how to handle the kids. They go into a hissy fit if the mention of their computer is brought up. The computer is their world, their whole world. If it sounds like I'm bitter, I am and I have reason to be. If you saw what I see because of MySpace, the chat lines and everything else on the computer, and the damaging effects, anybody would be bitter.

Two weeks ago, a mother called 911 and said that her baby girl was dying in her bed. We went to a house in upper class Suburbia. It was an attempted suicide by a 12-year-old girl. When we arrived, the mother, father, sisters, and brothers were hysterical. Please, Oh God please save our little baby girl's life. The parents and siblings directed us to her little girl, pink, fluffy, teddy bear, poster-filled room. It was neat, clean, and organized. It looked like every tween's dream room. That is until I saw the most sickening sight. It was awful. Unbelievably awful. There laid on a neatly made bed, a fragile, beautiful, fair-skinned, freckled face, long red curly haired little girl who looked like "Annie" in the play. Her blood was spattered everyplace. Her dainty little dress, the bed, the wall, carpet, and her teddy bear lying next to her side were all covered with blood. Her wrist was still profusely dripping blood.

Being a paramedic, I have seen everything and anything but this one was different. I felt dizzy, disoriented, and wanted to vomit. I kept on asking God why? She didn't deserve this, her parents didn't deserve this, her siblings didn't deserve this, her friends didn't deserve this, I didn't deserve this, nobody deserved this. What could be so wrong that a young, beautiful, loved child with the whole world ahead of her, would want to end her life? And why this way? As we loaded her comatose body into the ambulance, I prayed like I never prayed before. We took her to the hospital and she was in surgery for hours, which seemed like days. While she was in the operating room, I decided to stay with the parents. I usually don't stay with the parents but I wanted to comfort them.

My shift had ended and for some reason, I had to console my mind and my soul by finding out what happened. I felt a connection to this family.

As I sat with the family, I found them to be a God loving, sweet, warm, nice family. We started casually talking in the waiting room at the hospital. They told me how their little girl, Suzie, had beat cancer two years prior. She was their miracle baby because the doctors didn't think that she would live when she was born. She was born premature and had a bad heart with several other health problems. She has always defied medical statistics. Suzie had a strong will to live with zest for life. This made matters worse in my head.

The parents explained the type of cancer that little Suzie had and how everybody loved her in the children's cancer ward. Suzie was such a trooper and would always support the other kids when they were going to cancer treatment. She would talk to them like she was an adult. She would tell them that it was going to be OK and it wouldn't be long until they got better and wouldn't have anymore pain. Suzie promised to be their friend forever. She never complained. The doctors and nurses said that she was remarkable. Suzie was a true soldier and the pain that she went through with the treatment was excruciating. People would take her presents and she would give them away to the other kids that were having a rough, painful day.

After hearing this, I really felt like crap. I started asking myself even more, why, why? Here was a beautiful little girl, inside and out who had gone through tremendous trials at a young age and survived. But, now she wanted to kill herself. I asked what happened to the suicide note and her mother said that she threw the evil paper in the trash. Suzie's brother spoke up and said that he had it. He retrieved it from the garbage. I asked the parents if they minded that I read the note. With their approval, I anxiously read the attempted suicide note:

Dear Mom and Dad, and (brothers and sisters) I love you more than anything but I don't want to be a burden to you anymore. You say I haven't been but my friend's told me differently. My friends don't want to be friends with me anymore and I have had hundreds of e-mails and instant messages for a couple of months now saying that nobody likes me and nobody is ever going to like me. They said that I don't have the guts to kill myself because I'm too much of a sissy. I'm going to show them that I'm not a sissy. They said that I am a big burden to my family and I would be doing my family a big favor if I wasn't alive. I would be doing the world a favor. I am so sorry for being such a burden to everyone. I always knew I was a burden even though you said differently. I love you more than anything and I promise that I will see you in heaven. I tried to find out why my friends didn't like me anymore and my friends said that they never liked me to begin with and were only pretending to be my friends. They said that a person like me will never have any friends because I'm such a burden to everyone. I am going to miss you Mom and Dad and (brothers and sisters). I'm going to miss you a lot. I love you . . . Suzie.

I had to excuse myself quickly. I rushed to the men's room and cried like a 2-year-old. My eyes were like a running faucet. I tried to stop being so emotional but I couldn't. There was just some type of attachment to this little girl. As I was wiping my face, her father rushed in and gave me a big hug. You saved our baby girl's life. She's going to make it. How can we ever repay you? You are our guardian angel. You are a hero. All these words that were said to me didn't mean anything. I had too much rage in me over this whole incident. I wanted to know if I could see little Suzie and the doctors said no. Only family was allowed. The family said they would call me. A couple of days later, I got a call from the family saying that it was alright to see Suzie, and besides, she wanted to meet the man who saved her life. I walked into the hospital room with overwhelming anticipation and anxiety that I never experienced before. A timid little voice greeted me as I entered the room. "Thank you for saving my life before. I really don't want to die," she said.

An investigation was started immediately by the police department. After extensive interviews with Suzie's friends, neighbors, teachers, and acquaintances the conclusive evidence was "her friends were only fooling around," they were only kidding around and therefore no charges were to be filed. But there should be charges. Lives are devastated in the name of fun. Lives are changed, people are hurt, and sometimes they die as the result of online bullying. Yes, I am bitter and I now hate computers, because I see how they can be used. If it wasn't for computers, Web sites, chat rooms, and e-mails wouldn't exist. I view the computer as a demonic mother who gives birth to deadly "in the name of fun" sites. Suzie's story is just one of many that my colleagues see on a regular basis. Something must be done! Laws must be made and enforced. Like I said, our youth are dropping like flies.

## VICTIMIZATION OF ADOLESCENT GIRLS

Further research by Patchin and Hinduja, along with Amanda Burgess-Proctor, examined cyber bullying and online harassment by exploring victimization experienced by adolescent girls.[17] The researchers were interested in the emotional and physical consequences of these girls. Their online survey of 3,141 girls included questions about the scope, extent, and frequency of cyber bullying victimization. Open-ended questions allowed girls to describe their cyber bullying experiences. Results indicated that 38 percent of the girls surveyed had been bullied online at some time in their lives. Specifically, 46 percent reported being ignored, 43 percent reported being disrespected, and 11 percent were threatened online. Responses to open-ended questions revealed that name-calling and spreading rumors were common, though being ignored was not emphasized.

## FIGHT CRIME STUDIES

Surveys conducted for Pre-Teen Caravan in the summer of 2006 involved 503 U.S. pre-teens between the ages of 6 and 11.[18] In this study, the Opinion Research Corporation used a random-digit-dial to sample households. Results showed that 17 percent reported being cyber bullied in the past year, with 4 percent saying that it happened more than 5 times. The survey also showed 79 percent reported that within the past year, they had never had any mean, threatening, or embarrassing things said about them through e-mail, instant messages, text messages, chat rooms or social networking sites. Of those pre-teens who reported being cyber bullied, the most common (37% reporting this) things being said to them had to do with their appearance such as their clothes, hair, height, or weight. Of the victims, 23 percent stated that they were cyber bullied by e-mail, 19 percent from comments on a Web site, 18 percent in a chat room, 12 percent from an instant message, 11 percent from an embarrassing photo being e-mailed or posted on a Web site, and 7 percent from a text message. Also, somewhat surprisingly, 45 percent of the victims stated that they received the messages at school, 44 percent at home, and 34 percent while at a friend's house. Of those surveyed, 45 percent reported that they did not know who sent the message, and 44 percent reported that they did know who sent the message. Slightly more than half of the victims reported telling their parents about the cyber bullying, 44 percent reported telling a friend, and 27 percent reported telling a teacher. Finally, 17 percent of the pre-teens stated they were worried that they would be bullied online or in some other way as they headed back to school later in the year.

Another survey conducted for Teen Caravan in the summer of 2006 involved 512 U.S. teenagers between the ages of 12 and 17.[19] In this study the Opinion Research Corporation used systemic sampling to generate a random-digit-dial sample. Results showed greater frequency of cyber bullying than the pre-teens with 36 percent of teenagers reporting being cyber bullied within the past year, and 6 percent saying that it happened more than 5 times. Also a lower number of teens versus pre-teens reported that they had never been cyber bullied in the past year (64%). Of those cyber bullied, 59 percent stated that the things said about them had to do with their dating life, or interest in a girl or boy, or someone who likes them. Of these, 38 percent reported that the cyber bullying messages had to do with their appearance such as clothes, hair, height, or weight.

Of the teenage victims surveyed in the Teen Caravan study, 44 percent stated that it happened via an instant message, 34 percent via an e-mail, 30 percent via comments on a Web site, 19 percent via a text message, 14 percent in a chat room, and 13 percent from an embarrassing photo e-mailed around or posted on a Web site. More teens than pre-teens (70%) stated that they received the messages at home, 30 percent stated they received the messages at school, and 25 percent stated they received the messages while at a friend's house. Also, more teens than pre-teens reported that they knew who sent the messages with 72 percent reporting that they knew the attacker, and 26 percent reported that they did not know. Also, a fewer number of teens than pre-teens reported telling their parents (35%) or a teacher (9%), while a greater number (72%) did report telling a friend. Finally, 10 percent reported that they had been threatened with physical harm while online, 8 percent reported that someone had pretended to be them online in a way that was harmful or embarrassing, and 10 percent reported that they had sent mean, threatening, or hurtful messages to others while online.

## CYBER BULLYING IN DATING RELATIONSHIPS

Empirical research has also been conducted regarding cyber bullying and technological abuse among teenagers in dating relationships.[20] In 2005 and 2006, Liz Claiborne, Inc. commissioned TRU (Teenage Research Unlimited) to conduct online surveys among 615 13- to 18-year-olds, and among 414 parents with teens within that age range. Results of the study indicated that cyber bullying among teenagers in dating relationships is problematic, with 25 percent of teenagers reporting that their boyfriend or girlfriend harassed, put-down or called them names online. In addition, 19 percent of teenagers reported that their partner spread rumors about them via the Internet or cellular phone, and 18 percent reported being harassed by their partner via a networking site. Fully 11 percent of victims reported that their partner shared private or embarrassing images or videos of them with others, and 10 percent reported that they were threatened with physical harm by their partner through Internet messages. From 70 to 82 percent of teenage cyber bullying victims did not tell their parents, depending on the nature of the harassment involved. This study confirms that parents are seldom told by their kids what happens online. For every type of cyber bullying behavior reported by teens, parents reported that it occurs less often than teens reported as a group.

## PREVALENCE AND PREDICTORS OF INTERNET BULLYING

The Colorado Multi-site Evaluation Study, led by Kirk Williams and Nancy Guerra from University of California–Riverside, was part of an ongoing bullying prevention initiative in 2005–2006. This study involved over 3,000 youth in 5th, 8th, and 11th grades taking surveys in 2005, plus 2,293 youth from the original sample in 2005 participating in a follow-up survey in 2006.[21] The focus of these surveys was to contrast the prevalence of cyber bullying with physical and verbal bullying, and to explore whether specific predictors of physical and verbal bullying also predict cyber bullying.

Results from the first year of the study indicated that 21 percent of youth reported being cyber bullied at some point in their lives, and 18 percent reported having cyber bullied others. Data from the follow-up survey indicated that just over 9 percent of youth reported engaging in cyber bullying, with a fairly small percentage of 5th graders saying that they cyber bullied, and the highest percentage of cyber bulling reported by the 8th graders. Incidences of reported verbal bullying exceeded physical bullying, which exceeded cyber bullying. Verbal bullying peaked in 8th grade, and remained high in 11th grade. Both physical and cyber bullying peaked in 8th grade and declined by 11th grade. The study concluded that three things were found to affect cyber bullying: whether a person thinks cyber bullying is wrong (moral approval), whether a person feels the school climate as being trusting, fair, and pleasant (perceived school climate), and whether a person feels that friends their age are trustworthy, caring, and helpful (perceived peer influences).

## OVERLAPS IN INTERNET HARASSMENT AND IN-SCHOOL BULLYING

The "Growing Up with Media Survey" was a national cross sectional survey of over 1,500 10- to 15-year-olds conducted in 2007 by Michele Ybarra (Internet Solutions for Kids, Inc.), Marie Diener-West and Phillip Leaf (both from the Johns Hopkins Bloomberg School of Public Health).[22] One purpose of the research was to examine overlap between cyber bullying and traditional in-school bullying, and to explore the relationship between cyber bullying and other school discipline problems. Results showed that almost 35 percent of youth surveyed reported being a victim of cyber bullying, with 8 percent reporting being targeted monthly or more often. A significant finding in this study was that 64 percent of those cyber bullied reported that they had not been bullied at school. However, a relationship does appear to exist between being a victim of cyber bullying and school behavior problems such as skipping school and carrying a weapon. Further, cyber bullying victims also reported more frequent discipline at school including detentions and suspensions.

## ADOLESCENT INVOLVEMENT IN TRADITIONAL AND CYBER BULLYING

Another study by Juliana Raskauskas and Ann Stolz in 2007 also examined the relationship between traditional and cyber bullying, but was not focused on in-school incidents.[23] This study of 84 13- to 18-year-olds, completed a questionnaire regarding their involvement in both types of bullying. Results indicated that 48 percent of participants reported being a victim of cyber bullying, and 21 percent reported being a perpetrator of cyber bullying. In this study, most cyber bullying was reportedly committed via cell phone text messaging. Results also showed a large percentage of overlap between offending and victimization. Specifically, the analyses showed that most cyber bullies are also traditional bullies, and most cyber bullying victims were also victims of traditional bullying. Another interesting finding from this research

---

### THE DESTRUCTION OF JOY, TRUST, AND HOPE

**"They call me a 'Sissy-queer-fag'"**

As related by a 14-year-old boy:

I used to be a friendly kid. My mother told me that I would go up to strangers and ask them what their name was, and after they told me their name, which was generally returned with a smile, I told them my name. I would follow with a statement that I was going to be a surgeon like my grandfather when I grew up. Sometimes people would give me a dollar to put toward my college education. I was always popular and got along with everyone especially kids my own age. I received many awards from Cub Scouts and Boy Scouts. I liked to help the elderly and disadvantaged kids. They used to call me a mommy's boy because I was close to my mom. I could always talk to my mom. She was a registered nurse, and I wanted to know everything about the medical field. I used to be a straight-A student. I loved school, and medical school is very hard to get into if you don't have good marks.

My father and my brothers like to wrestle, box, and fight. My dad used to be a boxing champion and wanted me and my brothers to walk in his footsteps. I don't like to fight or play rough and never have. I don't see any sense in it, and all you do is get hurt in the end. I like to read, study nature, astronomy, and build projects. I like to use my mind—my three brothers and my father like to use their fists. My father and my older brothers always try to get me to fight with them but I just walk away. Besides not wanting to fight, a surgeon can't do a good job if his hands are messed up. I have seen my father and brothers with lots of hand injuries. My father said that's what makes a man, and I'm not doing a very good job at becoming a man. I think my grandfather is a man and he's not a fighter.

My brothers hang with tough guys at school who always like to "have fun." One day, my brother was kidding around with his friends outside of school. He told me to give his friend a punch because his friend called me a sissy-queer-fag. I started to walk away, and my brother's friend said that I really was a sissy-queer-fag. Then all of my brother's friends started calling me that. I went home and told my mom what happened. Her response was the usual "just ignore them and they'll go away." My mother said that my brothers were rednecks just like my father and used their hands for brains.

After the incident, my brother went home and told my dad that he wasn't going to associate or admit that I was his brother, because all of his friends think that I'm a "sissy-queer-fag," and I should be wearing a pink, lacy dress instead of boys' clothes. My father sided in with my brothers and said that he was not going to have his son humiliate and shame the family. He decided that he was going to enroll me in boxing classes, because he refused to have the family's reputation and name ruined by having a son that everyone thought was a "sissy-queer-fag."

My first boxing lesson was a disaster. I told the instructor that I didn't want to box or fight because I didn't want to hurt my hands. The other kids started laughing and said that it was true, that I was a sissy-queer-fag. The next day, a rumor spread through school like a field of hay on fire. My friends said that they couldn't be friends with me anymore because I was a sissy-queer-fag.

Even kids I didn't know in school started calling me the same. I used to like to communicate in the chat room every night with my friends until they started telling me the same thing that my friends told me in school. They couldn't chat with me anymore because I was a sissy-queer-fag. Sissy-queer-fag was the buzz in every chat room, being talked about as if I wasn't on this planet, like I didn't exist. When I was in school, I could almost ignore them. But I thought that I was safe in my room, on my computer, like I had been for years. But now my enemies were telling the world that I am a sissy-queer-fag. They started imposing my face on girls' underwear, thongs, bikinis, dresses—you name it. They started printing out pictures and pasting them on lockers, bathrooms, and all over the school.

The administration wanted me to make a formal complaint. I was called into the office many times to talk to the counselor, psychologist, nurse, vice-principal, principal, school administrator, and other parents of kids who were getting bullied, on- and off-line. But I couldn't tell people what was happening to me. I was warned ahead of time, that if I tried to retaliate or SNITCH, my life would really be hell. Everybody was only having fun. Everyone was really my friend. This gets done to everyone. I had to learn how to take a joke and stop being so serious.

Even my best friends were in on it. My mother said to ignore them and they would eventually stop, but they didn't. They started pushing me into the locker, one at a time, and then two, three, four, and sometimes five kids. They tripped me and I fell. A few times I had to go to the doctor, because I thought I had a broken arm. I started carrying a wet washcloth in my hand to wipe off the spit on my face from the kids. Another one of their jokes was to give me a nice packaged present saying that they were sorry for what I was going through and wanted to be my friends. I would have a big smile on my face and they would take pictures of me with their cell phone, lots of pictures (before I opened the package). As I opened the present, they took more pictures with the cell phones as I held training bras, lacy underpants, a dress, female nighties and sex toys and then they would start laughing. If I didn't open the present, they would punch me in the head. Sometimes, I would get a bad headache from the punches.

My name was in every conversation in every chat room that is known to kids. I don't know why everybody is trying to hurt me. I have always been a gentle, kind person, and I am not a queer or a sissy. I like girls not boys. I like boys as friends but not in any other way. I'm even getting it at church. Our pastor was talking about homosexuality, and it seems like the whole church turned around and looked at me and started smirking. I used to always be early for class and church and any functions. Now

I am purposely late, because I just can't take the ridicule anymore. Maybe this world is too far gone. I use to see a lot of hope for this world, but I don't see much hope now.

If I go to counseling, my father will kill me. My mother suggested it to my father and he said that only sissy-queer-fags get counseling and that real men fight their own battles. My mother doesn't go against my father. Sometimes, I think that she's kinda afraid of him like I guess that I am. I don't care about my grades anymore, and I don't know if I want to become a surgeon. What's the use if the world is against me? I just can't win. I'm not a friendly kid anymore. I dropped out of the school clubs, and I don't talk in the chat rooms anymore. After a year, they're still calling me a sissy-queer-fag. My mom and my sister are the only ones I really talk to. Now, I just stay to myself. I don't know what's going to happen with my life. It looks really dim right now.

is that cyber bullying victims are likely to be involved as bullies in school that included physical bullying, teasing, rumor-spreading, and exclusion. Results associated cyber bullying with experiences in school and at school functions, and concluded that cyber bullying should not be addressed by school officials independent of traditional bullying.

## PEW AMERICAN LIFE SURVEY

Research conducted by the Pew Internet and American Life Project in 2007 explored cyber bullying and online teens by surveying 935 teenagers.[24] Results showed that 32 percent of teens that use the Internet reported being a victim of cyber bullying. Specifically, 15 percent reported that someone took a private e-mail, IM, or text message that was sent to them and forwarded it to someone else, or posted it where others could see it. It was also shown that 13 percent reported that someone spread a rumor about them online, and 13 percent reported that someone had sent them an aggressive or threatening e-mail, IM, or text message. Among teenagers surveyed, 6 percent reported that someone had posted an embarrassing picture of them online without their permission. Of those reporting receiving threats, older teens, particularly 15- to 17-year-old girls, were the most frequent victims.

Concerning gender, girls (38%) are more likely to report being a victim of cyber bullying than boys (26%). Also, teens that use social networking sites are more likely to report being cyber bullied (39% versus 22% of those who do not use social networking sites). Similarly, content creators (those who create blogs, upload photos, share information and art, etc.), were also more likely to report being cyber bullied than their peers. Finally, a majority of all teens surveyed (67%) reported that the bullying they experienced occurred more often off-line than online.

## ROCHESTER INSTITUTE OF TECHNOLOGY SURVEY OF COLLEGE STUDENT COMPUTER USE AND ETHICS

In 2004, Samuel McQuade, Tom Castellano, and student research assistants surveyed 873 randomly selected students at RIT. The survey asked first through fourth-year college students questions about the types of information technology devices they used and for what purposes they were used. Survey questions also asked students about their attitudes toward, perceptions of, and personal levels of engagement in 20 different forms of IT-enabled abuse and crime, including online embarrassment or harassment, making threats, and cyberstalking. Results showed that within the year prior to the survey being administered, 17 percent of students were embarrassed or harassed online, 8 percent were threatened online, and 6 percent were cyberstalked. Within these categories of cyber bullying: (1) *victims of harassment* were comprised of 56 percent males and 44 percent females, which constituted a statistically significant difference, meaning that college student males in universities like RIT are more likely be victims of harassment than are females; (2) *victims of threats* were comprised of 61 percent males and 39 percent females, with no statistically significant difference between genders; and (3) victims of cyberstalking were comprised of 40 percent males and 60 percent females, with results showing that females are statistically more likely than males to experience this type of cyber bullying or crime.

The study also showed that among the 33 of 732 students (4%) who admitted to harassing someone online (defined as using a computer to harass, embarrass, or pick on someone), 69 percent were male and 31 percent were female. Similarly among only six students that admitted threatening someone online, five were males and one was female. Obviously the low numbers of reported offending did not enable analysis of meaningful gender differences among college-aged cyber bullies. However, researchers were able to conduct a factor analysis that demonstrated with statistical significance that male and females college students combined clustered into five distinct groups of offenders, including pirates, academic cheats, hackers, "data snoops," and *harassers.*

## ROCHESTER INSTITUTE OF TECHNOLOGY-SURVEY OF INTERNET AND AT-RISK BEHAVIORS

In 2007–2008 Samuel McQuade, Nathan Fisk, Elizabeth Fisk, and Neel Sampat, with assistance from several other colleagues associated with the Rochester Institute of Technology, completed the "Survey of Internet and At-Risk Behaviors." As already mentioned, this involved survey responses from 40,079 K–12th grade students, plus responses from hundreds of parents and teachers in 14 upstate New York school districts. The purpose of this enormous survey was to:

> Measure the nature and extent of online victimization and offending experiences of K–12th grade students;
>
> Determine types and levels of supervision and role modeling employed by parents pertaining to the use of computers and portable electronic devices by their children; and
>
> Obtain information from teachers about their perceptions of school-related cyber abuse and crime, along with the potential need and challenges associated with implementing cyber safety and ethics instruction.

The survey project was the initial basis for establishing a partnership among RIT and approximately 30 school districts from throughout the Greater Rochester, New York area, along with 3 prominent national organizations, including: (1) the National Center for Missing and Exploited Children (NCMEC), (2) the Information Systems Security Association (ISSA), and (3) Rochester InfraGard Member Alliance. InfraGard is an information sharing and analysis effort serving the interests and combining the knowledge base of a wide range of members.

These organizations initially joined forces in August of 2006 and eventually, with involvement of 30 Monroe County, New York area school districts, formed the Rochester Regional Cyber Safety and Ethics Initiative (RRCSEI). It was under the auspices of the RRCSEI, now simply known as The Cyber Safety and Ethics Initiative, that RIT's online survey was administered. You may learn more about this research and see full results reported to school districts online at www.cybersafe.org. Since several findings from this study that relate specifically to cyber bullying are mentioned throughout this book, the only general conclusion repeated here is that children being mean to each other begins in the 2nd grade; and that by 4th grade when researchers defined cyber bullying as a combination of being intentionally embarrassed, harassed, intimidated. or threatened online, students bully and are victimized throughout their primary school years into high school, though at varying rates depending on age and gender (see Chapter 2, Figure 2.1).

## WHAT DOES ALL THIS RESEARCH MEAN?

How are we to make sense of this jumble of studies and statistics? If you are like most people, statistical research findings can be boring as well as confusing. Here at the conclusion of this chapter, we'll attempt to interpret what we think we now know as a society about cyber bullying and victimization by and among youth based on this limited number of available studies on the subject.

Collectively, the studies, surveys, and research described above offer an important initial examination of online bullying. They begin to define cyber bullying in ways consistent with the message of this book: that cyber bullying begins earlier and earlier in life, and that it occurs in several different ways in and out of school by youth who use computers and other types of IT devices to embarrass, harass, intimidate, or threaten. Boys and girls are involved as both offenders and victims, though rates of engagement appear to vary among school learning and community living environments. Troubled youth and those having difficulty in school or in the community with respect to juvenile delinquency appear more prone to engage in cyber bullying. Youth who are victims of cyber bullying also appear more likely to commit cyber bullying. Classical in-person forms of bullying, such as verbal abuse, shoving, kicking, hitting, and spitting frequently combine with cyber bullying inclusive of but not limited to writing abusive or threatening messages, posting of personal or embarrassing information, and sharing of data that has been manipulated to incite furor among groups of youth participating in social networking activities. Research also reveals that IT devices such as cell phones are now being used along with computers to cyber bully.

Research now also shows that cyber bullying commonly includes making rude or nasty comments online, and that many youth who bully online are mad at someone or something in their lives. Poor relationships with parents or caregivers can contribute to cyber bullying (a matter further explored in Chapter 6). Kids in general do not tell adults when they are bullied, and report not being closely supervised by their parents when using the Internet. Teens who are victims are especially unlikely to report cyber bullying they experience or witness. However, parents often feel that they are appropriately supervising online activities. (This contradiction will also be explored further in Chapter 6.) Research also reveals a gap in preventative actions and programming to maintain awareness and safety for young individuals, as indicated by reports that only small numbers of teachers discuss cyber safety with their students. We know this is not universally true, as many school districts are now using a variety of online instructional resources to teach Internet safety and cyber ethics. However, the large percentages of youth who admit to cyber bullying and/or report they experience bullying online indicates that not enough schools are doing so, or they are terribly ineffective.

Our conclusion despite the limited amount of scholarship on cyber bullying is that evidence indicates it is happening all too frequently. Consequences for victims include distress, frustration, sadness, anger, and embarrassment. In other words, it has destroyed a sense of joy, trust, and hope in the lives of real kids. Cyber bullying now represents a condition and trend of alarming proportions for boys and girls involved both as perpetrators and as victims, and it occurs across grade levels. The best current evidence shows that cyber bullying peaks in middle school possibly only for females, but remains high with males dominating as offenders throughout high school and into college.

Younger kids have reported being cyber bullied because of their appearance while middle school and older teens experience sex-related bullying. Cyber bullying can happen by a stranger, but is often if not usually done by someone known to the victim online and/or in person. Victims often consider people who bully them to be friends, even a boyfriend or girlfriend, and there are clear indications that some bullying has to do with dating relationships.

Cyber bullies are often also traditional bullies, and most cyber bullying victims are also victims of traditional bullying. This reinforces our belief that as a matter of theory and mounting data that bullying is bullying regardless of technological means and methods used; and that bullies are bullies no matter what the means, though individuals may well slide into or out of behavioral patterns of bullying. Longitudinal studies that track traditional and cyber offending and victimization patterns among youth are not currently available, although Rochester Institute's survey of at-risk behaviors has been designed to support longitudinal as well as household analysis (i.e., comparing how youth change over time and what they report versus what parents say their online activities consist of). Finally, it appears that large amounts of bullying still happen face-to-face but in combination with cyber bullying. For everyone involved, bullying in all its forms remains a complex social problem.

5

# Legal Issues—What Can Be Done about Cyber Bullying?

*Cyber bullying is costing administrators tons of time and even the police at times are at a loss about what to do.*

*—A school principal*

In the grand scheme of juvenile mischief, delinquency and crime instances of bullying and especially cyber bullying are seldom clear violations of law. Bullying in any form, using any technological means, is in general not against state or federal crime laws unless it involves specific types of actions in concert with a required level of mental intent and resulting harm. All these things must be clearly defined in writing and prohibited in advance for bullying to be considered a violation of law. Wishing something was against the law, or thinking, "There ought to be a law against *X*" (fill in the blank) doesn't make it so! Obviously wishing cyber bullying was illegal may also be futile, although our country is now wrestling with whether it ought to be.

For now bullying and cyber bullying are terms usually recognized *but seldom aggressively responded to* by professionals who have a legal responsibility to ensure health, safety, and welfare of children and adolescents. As we have learned, there are several understandable (though frustrating!) explanations for this, including that: (1) most bullying does not initially involve serious visible injury or emotional trauma; (2) youth don't report bullying until, or even after, it results in repeated or serious harm, if ever; (3) school administrators and police are already busy with matters that demand immediate attention (after all, they reason if it were serious why wasn't the bullying reported sooner?); (4) by the time things get out of control and become known, initial offenders may have been retaliated against causing hesitation about who the real bully or bullies are; and (5) since bullying in the grand scheme of juvenile troublemaking, delinquency, and crime rarely amounts to a violation of a crime law able to be prosecuted, parents are expected to step up and control their kids.

All these things combined with facts, circumstances, and personalities of people involved can easily blur that which is actionable by law versus incidental or ongoing "harassment among kids and youth" requiring only periodic attention. The seriousness of bullying is often unclear even to concerned and trained professionals like school guidance counselors, school principals, and law enforcement officers. Day-to-day, week-to-week, and year-after-year officials in charge of youth must determine what circumstances call for their intervention versus careful monitoring and consultation with parents; or some combination of these; and ultimately, formal investigation, arrest, and prosecution when warranted. It would be convenient if every school, home, and community center were connected to a giant bullying radar screen on which we could track stormy conditions building among youth. In that way authorities could at least know about danger signs when they emerge and possibly intervene sooner. Experienced teachers, counselors, school staff members, and building administrators in touch with their school populations know to watch and listen for signs of brewing trouble between students. However, research data such as that presented in Chapter 4, clearly indicates that cyber bullying is extending and transforming classical bullying problems out of sight and beyond their reach. What now begins off school grounds on the Internet with home computers or mobile information technology (IT) devices continues during school hours in classical and clandestine ways. Like tidal waves building offshore, too often the full effects of cyber bullying can only be seen when waves of youth chaos come crashing into the shores of their homes, schools, and neighborhoods.

It has often been claimed that very few states have laws against cyber bullying. This is *not* true when considering the reality that all forms, technological means, and methods of bullying can potentially be prosecuted under existing state level crime laws that already ban assault, making threats, harassment, stalking, using electronic communications to cause harm and so forth. It is also true that decisions to investigate bullying rest upon the discretion of parents, school officials, law enforcement officers, and normally a willingness of victim(s) to press charges. Prosecutors at the local, state, or federal levels of government must also agree that charges are warranted when considering elements of crime laws, community standards, case precedents, and political issues of concern in a given jurisdiction.

Repeated intentional hitting, pushing, kicking, or shoving along with verbal name-calling, teasing, taunting, and shouting threats are relatively easy cases to investigate and prosecute because they demonstrate behavior patterns, intentions, and over time tend to result in tangible harm to victims. However, whether such aggression qualifies as assault or threats will depend on definitions and nuances of existing statutory and case law in relation to circumstances of individual cases. Further complicating this matter is the fact that in many states assault and threats are codified in laws that specify varying levels of harm and/or mental intent (e.g., simple versus aggravated assault, or third, second, and first degree assault); and that making threats that place a person in fear of immediate injury or property damage may even be a required element of assault. It can be very confusing.

These legal realities, along with the confusion and frustration that can be involved for everyone affected by bullying and cyber bullying, is why we decided to include a chapter devoted to legal issues. The fact that bullying is a complex social problem that may include online activities that are not explicitly illegal confounds understanding about what can legally be done to curb cyber bullying. For example, exclusion and rejection of children from a group may cause them emotional pain, but people have a right to choose and change their friends—parents know this happens periodically, often as the result of kids feeling picked on. However traumatic, this is not a police or a school matter, or is it? What if a child's constitutional right to learn in a public school setting is so compromised by online activities (that they have a right to engage in also) that they can no longer effectively learn? When are statements protected by American's right to freedom of speech? Do schools have the right to discipline students for speech that occurs off campus via computers or mobile IT devices? At what point does bullying, cyber bullying, or harassment become a violation of crime law meriting prosecution? At what point can bullying in any form be considered a cause of action for civil damages?

This chapter addresses these and other questions from the standpoint of Constitutional, criminal, and civil laws, and legal underpinnings as determined by an emerging body of case law rulings that bear on cyber bullying. We begin by discussing the right to freedom of speech with a focus on online communications. Next, legal implications for schools regarding free speech will be explored, as well as a review of case law involving school responses to cyber bullying that occurred off school grounds. Finally, applicable federal and state criminal laws will be reviewed, along with civil laws pertaining to cyber bullying. Along the way, we use legal case histories along with examples of comments and stories about bullying and cyber bullying to help explain items of importance.

## CONSTITUTIONAL ISSUES RELATED TO ONLINE COMMUNICATIONS

Americans strongly value their right to communicate orally and in writing, to do so openly and in free association with people of their choosing. This expectation is grounded in the First Amendment to the U.S. Constitution. It provides that "Congress shall make no law respecting the establishment of religion, or prohibiting the free exercise thereof; or abridging the freedom of speech, or of the press, or the right of the people peaceably to assemble, and to petition the Government for a redress of grievances." For over 200 years, this exceptional addition to the Constitution has guided courts in protecting speech and other forms of expression, even when these are troubling to individuals and groups to whom hurtful things are directed. But although the First Amendment protects against the federal government in restricting free speech and the Fourteenth Amendment extends this restriction to state governments, people are not free to say whatever they want whenever they want, and to whomever they decide.

People are not free to yell "Fire!" in a crowded theater because an ensuing stampede might endanger moviegoers. Teachers are others in society that are not allowed to use *obscene language* that is inherently offensive to local community standards. Adults and minors cannot create, possess, or share *child pornography,* as youth being prosecuted throughout America for exchanging nude pictures are quickly learning. And so-called *fighting words* are banned in nearly all legal jurisdictions because they may cause people to begin physically fighting and this is not the way that people in civil societies are suppose to behave. Said differently, if people on the whole did not voluntarily obey the laws, regulations, and customs of society, civility and ultimately civilization itself would crumble. *Defamation, libel, and slander* are also excluded from the protection of the First Amendment, because these generally involve expressing things that are not true that jeopardizes a person's reputation or standing in a community. Finally, *threats* in the legally prohibited sense are communications that are so unequivocal, unconditional, immediate, and specific that it places a person in fear. In other words, to be a victim of threats, a person must genuinely be afraid that threats made against them are imminent (i.e., could be carried out at anytime). What does bullying and cyber bullying mean legally? What it comes down to is *what a child believes is likely to happen to them in the short-term*. But even this is subject to interpretation by adults who must ultimately make informed decisions about whether and how best to intervene on a case by case basis.

## LEGAL CONSIDERATIONS FOR STUDENT CYBER BULLYING OFF SCHOOL GROUNDS

In general, speech that is communicated over the Internet is also protected by the First Amendment. When considering cyber bullying, online communications outside freedom of speech protection may be fighting words, creation of content that presents a clear and present danger to persons or property, defamation, and threats that victims believe bullies to be capable of carrying out imminently. Online fighting words may also be illegal if content is likely to provoke a violent response from recipients such as racially charged messages or those pertaining to sexual preference. As we have already explained, many cyber bullying cases center on sexual preferences and relationships. In the future, as case law involving cyber bullying becomes more established, it will be interesting to see the extent to which fighting words and the so-called clear and present danger doctrine are applied by courts.

If specific directions on how to break into a school building or hack into a school district's computer system are posted online from off school grounds, perhaps this would constitute a clear and present danger sufficient for school or law enforcement officials to act to prevent such physical or cyberattacks. Perhaps not, as what constitutes a clear and present danger in publicly broadcasted messages is subject to many assumptions that fly in the face of rights to free expression and association. Similar legal challenges and reasoning will factor into fighting words expressed online that spill over onto school buses, grounds, and campuses during school hours. Mobile computing among youth make such possibilities more likely even if school districts seek to control or ban possession or use of IT devices on school property. After all, just because youth communicate spiteful things online doesn't mean they are actually looking for or trying to incite a physical confrontation, or that the receiver of the message is likely or will be sufficiently angered to act out of anger or fear. Besides, mere possession of IT devices that can be used for all kinds of responsible purposes in and out of school is not the same as unethical decisions of abuse by someone online when teachers or other adults are looking the other way.

## LEGAL IMPLICATIONS FOR SCHOOLS

A significant challenge facing schools today involves the role of the school in disciplining students for cyber bullying behavior. Parents often look to schools to assist with problems related to cyber bullying, but schools have very limited authority to discipline students for off-campus conduct. School districts also remain constrained in their abilities to limit Constitutionally guaranteed free speech on school grounds. Fortunately courts are increasingly providing guidance to schools that involve cyber bullying. For example, in famous cases such as the "Triumvirate" of *Tinker v. Des Moines Independent Community School District* (1969), *Bethel School District No. 403 v. Frasern* (1986), and *Hazelwood School District v. Kuhlmeier* (1988) several important legal precedents now provide school officials with important pieces to what would otherwise be a completely unassembled jigsaw puzzle!

The *Tinker* case was ultimately decided by the United States Supreme Court, which held that student speech is not protected if it "materially and substantially disrupts the educational process of the school environment." In this case, students were suspended by their school after wearing black armbands to protest the Vietnam War. In rendering its decision, the Court asserted that while students do not shed their constitutional rights to freedom of speech or expression at the schoolhouse gate, schools do have the authority to regulate student expression if it substantially interferes with the work of the school, or impinges on the rights of other students (e.g., to learn). In this case disruption in school caused by students wearing armbands was not proven, meaning that the students had been inappropriately suspended.

In *Bethel,* the Supreme Court upheld the power of schools to censor lewd and vulgar speech that did not rise to a level of being legally obscene. In this case, a student was suspended for giving a speech during a school assembly that was filled with sexually suggestive statements. In emphasizing the role of the school in promoting civility and citizenship, the Court upheld the suspension. The Court also asserted the notion that the rights of students in schools are not automatically as protected nor as extensive as those of adults in different settings.

In *Hazelwood,* a school principal censored student articles about teen pregnancy and divorce from the school newspaper due to concerns that three pregnant students could be identified and due to inappropriate content. In upholding the censorship, the reviewing court held that school authorities have the right to use discretion and delete objectionable articles from school publications. Specifically, the Court asserted that the content of a school-sponsored newspaper could be regulated by school officials who must oversee matters involving privacy and defamation.

The applicability of these three cases to instances of cyber bullying, though not explicit, is not too hard to imagine. For example, information that is posted or sent on the Internet by a student while on or off campus, as discussed in *Tinker,* has the potential to cause substantial disruptions at school. Further, students while in school can easily use their own devices or school computers to transmit lewd or vulgar speech, which was addressed in *Bethel.* And since the Internet can be school sponsored or part of a school's curriculum, meaning that content may be subject to school regulation as decided in *Hazelwood,* schools may be able to extend their regulation of student speech to content they author in interactive cyber realms designated for official instructional purposes and student learning. So what have the courts actually decided in actual cases involving cyber bullying?

## CASE LAW PERTAINING TO CYBER BULLYING

Many of the lawsuits that have been brought forth through the years have involved the online harassment of teachers or school officials, and a consequence imposed by a school district. The following cases provide examples of how adults can be victims of cyber bullying by students, and how courts have interpreted the issue of free speech versus school authority. *Kim v. Bellevue School District-Newport High School* (1995) involved a senior honor student in the state of Washington who created a Web site that discussed his friends and their obsessions with sex and football. After calling the Web site his school's unofficial home page and creating links on the site to pornographic

Web sites, the school rescinded recommendations that had been sent on his behalf to colleges where Kim had applied and also revoked his National Merit Scholarship. After a lawsuit, the case was settled out of court. The district paid him $2,000, apologized, and sought to have him reinstated as a National Merit finalist. Although this case did not establish any legal precedent, it did pave the way for more discussion about the free speech rights of students when using the Internet away from school but in ways involving school interests and reputation.

In *O'Brien v. Westlake City School Board of Education* (1998), an Ohio student received a 10-day suspension for creating a Web site while off campus that included a photo and insulting statements about the school's band teacher. A federal court ruled that the suspension violated the student's right to free speech and expression, reversed the suspension, and ordered the district to write an apology letter. Also in 1998, in *Buessink v. Woodland R-IV School District,* a Missouri student had created a personal Web site using vulgar language while off campus that criticized teachers and the principal. The student in this case had a record of problem behavior and was previously banned from using library computers after being violent and disrespectful toward a staff member. The school imposed a suspension, which was later overturned by the reviewing court because of a lack of evidence of any disturbance or material disruption in the school environment.

Two years later, in *Beidler v. North Thurston School District No. 3* (2000), a Washington high school student created a Web site while at home that showed doctored pictures of his assistant principal doing such things as book burning, drinking alcohol, and making graffiti. As a result, the school temporarily expelled the student for one month and then allowed him to enroll in an alternative school. After a lawsuit was filed by his parents citing violation of the First Amendment, the reviewing court citing *Hazelwood* and *Tinker* (described above), found that the Web site was not school sponsored or disruptive. It was therefore decided that the school had no authority to police off-campus speech. The student was subsequently allowed back to school and was paid $62,000 in damages and legal fees by the school district.

A similar decision was made in *Emmett v. Kent School District No. 425* (2000), which involved another high school senior from Washington who, while at home, posted obituaries and a "who would die next" list on a Web page. The student had written a disclaimer on the site detailing that the content was for entertainment purposes only. After court intervention, the expulsion of the student was reduced to a short suspension given that the court felt that there was no evidence that the speech constituted a true threat or a substantial disruption at the school. Also, in *Killion v. Franklin Regional School District* (2001), a student from Pennsylvania was suspended for creating and posting online—while outside of school—a "top ten" list about a school employee that included statements about the employee's physical appearance. The court held that the speech was not threatening, and that there was a lack of evidence of an actual disruption at school. At this point, the emerging legal standard involved determining whether the speech constituted a true threat as explained above, and whether there was a substantial disruption to the educational process.

Yet, a more recent court decision upheld school disciplinary action that was related to cyber bullying off school grounds. In *J.S. v. Bethlehem Area School District* (2002), a court reviewed a case in which a student was suspended and later expelled for creating a Web site that solicited donations to help pay for a hit man, and also discussed having a teacher killed. The site showed a picture of the teacher with her head severed, then changing into an image of Adolph Hitler. The teacher was unable to return to the school due to fear and stress. In this case, the Pennsylvania Supreme Court upheld the expulsion agreeing that the incident caused an actual and substantial disruption of the work environment.

A significant case involving cyber bullying of students by other students was *Coy v. B.O.E. of the North Canton City Schools* (2002). In this case, a student from Ohio, along with several friends, created a Web site from a home computer that included a section called "Losers." The Web site contained insulting comments and photos about three other students from the same school. An investigation directed by the school principal determined that the students had accessed the Web site during class time from a school computer lab. The student was suspended initially for 4 days, and the school board later unanimously voted to uphold an 80-day expulsion. The court decided in favor of the school, stating that the school had the right to discipline the student for accessing the Web site during the day. However, this case most likely would have been decided the other way if the site had not been accessed during school hours and from a school owned information system.

In *Mahaffey v. Aldrich* (2002), a student from Michigan was suspended after posting to an existing Web site a list of names of "people I wish would die." The student was later suspended indefinitely for threats and intimidation, despite a psychiatric evaluation determining that the student was not a threat to himself or others, and the recommendation by the evaluators that he be allowed back in school. After filing a lawsuit, a court found in favor of the student stating that the student was off campus when he posted the content to the Web site. The court also found that specific and credible threats were not made, nor did the content disrupt school learning or as a place of work. Also, in *Flaherty v. Keystone Oaks School District* (2003), a student from Pennsylvania was kicked off the school volleyball team, prohibited from attending after school activities, and banned from using school computers after posting critical comments on an Internet message board about the mother of an opposing team member. The court found no disruption of the educational process that warranted suppressing his right to free speech.

In *Muss-Jacobs v. Beaverton School District* (2003), a 13-year-old student from Oregon was suspended and later expelled from school after creating a Web site while at home that included derogatory racial and sexual statements aimed at students and teachers from the same school. After the student claimed being denied admission to the school after attempting to return the following school year, the American Civil Liberties Union (ACLU) intervened and filed suit on behalf of the student and his mother. The ACLU claimed that the Web site did not result in any criminal violations or disruptions to the school. The school agreed to settle the case out of court and paid the student and mother $20,000.

In *Goldsmith v. Gwinnett County School District #1* (2003), two senior honor students from Georgia with no prior discipline records created a Web site asking visitors to discuss concerns they had about their school and its teachers. The two students made aggressive and explicit comments regarding how certain teachers should be killed. Both students received suspensions for making threatening statements, and the families of both responded with separate lawsuits. A court found in favor of the students, stating that no actual threats were made on the Web site, and no disruption at school occurred. They were awarded $95,000 in damages and legal fees, and the court ordered that their disciplinary records be expunged.

In *Dwyer v. Amato and Oceanport School District, et al.* (2005), an 8th grade student from New Jersey created a Web site from home that was critical of his school district, and invited others to post complaints. Visitors then posted some comments that were deemed by the school as crude and offensive: content included photos of the principal with his head flipped upside down, and a picture of a school building with an X over it. As a result, the student was suspended for a week, suspended from the baseball team for one month, and banned from a class trip. After his parents filed suit, a court ruled in favor of the student indicating that the comments in question were written by visitors to the site, and not the student. In making its decision, the court also determined that no threats were made and no disruption at school occurred.

In *Neal et al. v. Efurd and Greenwood School District* (2005), two high school students from Arkansas created Web sites while off campus that contained insulting messages about other students and the school, as well as some violent illustrations. The two students, along with two others, were suspended for making threatening statements posted on these Web sites. In this case the school alleged that a disruption occurred at school—that "buzz" occurred in the district after word got out about the suspensions. This court also ruled in favor of the students, citing the decision to suspend the students caused the disruption, not the Web content that lead to the suspensions. The court also found no substantial disruption in this case.

In 2007, the United States Supreme Court decided what could be a very influential case in the areas of freedom of speech and the authority of schools to discipline for off-campus conduct. In *Morse v. Frederick 555 U.S.* (2007), a student was suspended for 10 days after unfurling a banner containing the message "Bong hits 4 Jesus" during a parade held during the school day. Students had been released during the school day to attend the parade, and the student was standing across the street from the school when he displayed the banner. The school took the position that controversy surrounding the banner held up by the student in close proximity to the school and to students attending the parade was disruptive to what was in effect a school event. The trial court agreed. However, the Ninth Circuit Court of Appeals reversed the lower court's decision. In citing *Tinker* (described above) the appellate court stated that school authorities can only suppress student speech if they can reasonably predict a substantial disruption or material interference with school activities, which did not happen in this case. Therefore, the Court stated that the student was punished for the message, rather than for any disturbance. As of this writing, it is not known whether this case has been appealed to the U.S. Supreme Court, nor obviously if the High Court would agree to review it.

In a different case however, the U.S. Supreme Court, by a 5 to 4 vote, reversed the Ninth Circuit ruling that school officials can suppress student speech that promotes illegal drug use. The court reasoned that the message itself is (merely but not necessarily) *interpreted* as encouraging or promoting drug use, not actually doing so. In a concurring opinion, one Justice stressed that the decision applied only to promotional drug messages, and not for more general political speech. The effect of this decision was to rekindle debate over what may be considered free speech by students. Two additional case decisions underscore fears that free speech rights of students may be threatened, or not adequately curtailed.

To illustrate, in *Layshock v. Hermitage School District* (2006), a student while at home on MySpace.com, created a parody of a high school principal described as an alcoholic who also used illegal drugs. In this case, the parody was accessed by so many students in the school that the district prohibited student use of its computer system for six days. Afterward, the reviewing court upheld the suspension of the student based on the school disruption argument. However, in reviewing this case, a federal court, citing *Tinker, Bethel,* and *Hazelwood* cases stated that schools must have a "well-founded expectation of disruption." The judge in this case, defined evidence of substantial disruption as violence, widespread canceling of classes, disorder that prevents teachers from controlling their classes, or disciplinary action against many students. The court in this case felt that disruptions caused by the Web content were not substantial enough.

However, in New York State, a federal appellate court took a different position. In *Wisniewski v. Board of Education of Weedsport CSD* (2007), an 8th grade student was suspended for an entire semester after creating a drawing suggesting that a teacher be shot and killed, and sharing the drawing with 15 friends, including some classmates, via instant messages from a home computer. The police were also contacted in this case, and officers concluded that the drawing posed no real threat to the teacher or school. After the parents sued the school board and superintendent in federal court, a federal district court ruled against the parents finding that the drawing was reasonably understood as a true threat. In effect, the federal district court disagreed with the opinion of investigating law enforcement officers. On appeal, the U.S. Court of Appeals for the Second Circuit, again citing *Tinker* and *Morse,* also ruled against the parents holding that it was reasonably foreseeable that the teacher and school officials would find out about the drawing, and that it would create a substantial disruption within the school.

## PUTTING IT TOGETHER: OUR SUMMARY OF CURRENT CASE LAW

As the result of seemingly contradictory decisions in *Layshock* and *Wisniewski,* students, parents, school officials, law enforcement officers, attorneys, and judges are currently in a state of limbo about cyber bullying threats. So what? This is to be expected as the result of technologically evolving abuse and crime in society that we discussed in Chapter 2! The good news is that through our justice system and court processes society is slowly coming to agreement about what should and should not be permitted by youth using the Internet, at least when it affects *school* learning environments, school-sponsored activities, use of computers in school, school publications, or schools as places of employment. That's not bad for a little over 10 years since widespread use of the World Wide Web. It is also not surprising that a body of case law is developing around school issues, because public schools are de facto agencies of government that must be especially cautious in matters affecting civil rights.

The collection of cases described above clearly show that courts have often favored oral, written, and posted speech rights of students over the authority of schools to impose discipline for off-campus and on-campus conduct. Like the timeless debate between freedom of speech versus societal safety and security, school districts must now tread lightly because, unlike the federal government, they cannot resort to claims that national security hangs in the balance if they do not crack down on insolent students (i.e., those who are disrespectful, uncivil, insulting, contemptuously impertinent, etc.). In effect, courts have ruled that it is not the job of schools to police uncivil aspects of digital youth culture. What youth post online is not the business of schools unless it disrupts school learning environments.

Case law also shows that whether or not schools can reasonably predict a substantial disruption remains open to interpretation. It can be very difficult to demonstrate a reasonable basis to anticipate a disruption at school. For incidents that are on school grounds, free speech cases that involve safety and security of are less concern: authority of schools to maintain order, safety, and security is not debatable. For cases then involving cyber bullying that was accessed or displayed at school or using school technology, schools can also take actions deemed reasonable and necessary to ensure order, safety, and security for students, staff, and other people who may lawfully occupy campus facilities. For off-campus incidents, an important burden for schools is to establish a clear nexus between a cyber bullying incident and substantial disruption of school environments, which as we have seen, is not always easy to do.

Cyber bullying often begins anonymously in cyberspace, but it can have a significant impact on people in the schools. Thus, the common sense, or reasonableness standard, should apply for dealing with off-campus incidents. Courts have created some confusion over when a school can impose discipline, but this often misses a larger point. Rather than focusing on whether the school can punish, the attention should be on the school's *legal responsibility to protect students*. If cyber bullying has a connection to school, or a "school nexus," even if it does not meet the substantial disruption requirement focused on in so many of the cases above, schools may still have a legal responsibility to ensure safety and security of students who ride a school bus, attend class, or participate in extracurricular activities. Remember, the interplay between classical physical bullying and cyber bullying is inextricable—they are two sides of the same abusive coin! And mobile computing coupled with social computing changes everything from the standpoint of potential safety and security threats, as well as disruptions to learning and workplace environments.

Another as of yet unsatisfactorily resolved issue is "substantial disruption" *for how many students?* It befuddles logic to think that classical bullying and/ or cyber bullying that places even a single child in fear, or substantially disrupts their ability to learn effectively according to their own desires and attributes, should not have equal legal standing with educational desires of several bullying students who may not give a damn about school! After all, learning through middle school is a legal and civil right of every American child, arguably as important as free speech. We do not envy courts that will invariably weigh in on behalf of individuals, groups of people, and all society to resolve these complicated issues. Until they do, however, a considerable and increasing amount of embarrassing, harassing, intimidating, and threatening content created and posted by youth online will need to be contended with by youth and adults alike.

## FOURTH AMENDMENT AND PRIVACY ISSUES

Schools dealing with cyber bullying are also concerned about issues related to privacy and unlawful searching of property. An investigation of cyber bullying may necessitate searching a school computer that a student has been using, or potentially their own IT device such as a laptop computer, cell phone, or PDA. The Supreme Court case of *New Jersey v. T.L.O.* (1985) held that the Fourth Amendment's prohibition against unreasonable searches and seizures applies to searches conducted by public school officials. In this case, the High Court upheld a search of a 14-year-old student's purse after the student was discovered to be smoking in a school restroom. An administrator searched the purse and found cigarettes and cigarette rolling papers, but also found marijuana and drug paraphernalia. In the decision, the Court ruled that the search of a student and their property depends on reasonableness under what lawyers call "the totality of circumstances."

Reasonableness of a search hinges on whether it was: (1) justified at its inception, and (2) reasonably related in scope to the circumstances that justified initiating an investigation. Another legal term, "reasonable suspicion" means facts and circumstances that would lead a law enforcement officer to believe—or have reason to believe—a crime has been or is about to be committed, and that the person stopped and investigated is somehow involved. This case set the reasonable suspicion standard for searches of students and their property conducted by school officials. Cyber bullying cases being investigated by school officials require reasonable suspicion based on objective facts indicating criminal activity or a violation of school rules. Reasonable suspicion can also be considered more than a hunch, but less than "probable cause," which in legal parlance means facts and circumstances that would lead a law enforcement officer to believe—or have reason to believe—a crime has been committed, and that the person is arrested who committed the crime. Search incident to an arrest by a police officer is legal, but this standard does not apply to school officials. Since probable cause is encompassing of reasonable suspicion, and since school officials do not have powers of arrest, probable cause is mute. In other words, school officials may search any student, for their own safety as well as the safety of other students, whenever they have reasonable suspicion that they will find evidence of a violation of school rules or a crime law.

Therefore, if a school official can articulate a reasonable suspicion that the content that exists on an IT device is either illegal or in violation of school rules, a search would be justified. Courts have also held that lockers and desks do not have an expectation of privacy because they are owned by the school, and therefore can be searched without suspicion. It is reasonable to assume that the same standard applies when considering the use of school computers and the Internet. For example, if a student is suspected of using a school computer to access a prohibited social networking site, schools may investigate to determine who was responsible. By extension, schools may monitor Internet browsing history and exact discipline when warranted.

Consider this scenario: A teacher is informed by a student that another student in class just sent a threatening cell phone text message to her. The teacher asks the suspected student about the message, to which the student states that he was only kidding. The student's cell phone is then seized by the teacher and checked by an administrator. (Note: making threats is a violation of school policy even if the contents of a message do not rise to the level constituting a violation of state or federal crime laws.) The administrator examines the cell phone text message history and the threatening message that was sent from the phone during class time. Now *two* adults have witnessed the message. Is this search legal? In applying the reasonable suspicion standard, the answer appears to be yes. But what if the cell phone had been confiscated for mere possession in violation of school rules, rather than the content sent *or seen* on the IT device that was suspected of violating school rules or a crime law? Based on current legal standards, a search of the device's contents would not be justified.

Regardless of search legalities, school officials will need to contend with political and parental realities when seizing and searching student-owned portable devices. In 2007, a school principal related how during routine hallway monitoring between classes he found himself standing at the shoulder of a middle school student looking at what was obviously pornography on his cell phone. The principal seized the phone, escorted the student to his office, and proceeded to search the Web browsing history. He discovered lots of porn, and that sexually explicit photos had apparently been sent to and received from other students in his school during school hours. The principal began by calling parents and then conferring with police about what to do. In the end, parents were upset with him for seizing and looking at the cell phone content and police declined to treat the matter as a violation of child pornography laws. If that incident happened today, our guess is the students involved would be suspended and prosecuted for "pseudo-child pornography."

## Legal Standards and Internet Service Providers

In 1996, Congress passed federal legislation, 47 United States Code 230, called the Communications Decency Act (CDA) of 1996. In passing the legislation, Congress granted broad immunity to Internet Service Providers (ISP) from legal responsibility for behaviors that include cyber bullying, harassment, defamation, and stalking online. Although portions of the law having to do with obscene Web content readily available to minors was struck down by the U.S. Supreme Court (see *ACLU v. Reno 1997*), Section 230 (2) of the CDA pertaining to civil liability, states that: "No provider or user of an interactive computer service shall be held liable on account of: (A) any action voluntarily taken in good faith to restrict access to or availability of material that the provider or user considers to be obscene, lewd, lascivious, filthy, excessively violent, harassing, or otherwise objectionable, whether or not such material is constitutionally protected; or (B) any action taken to enable or make available to information content providers or others the technical means to restrict access to material described in paragraph (1)."

The landmark case, *Zeran v. America Online, Inc.* (1997), resulted in a ruling that Section 230 of the CDA provided immunity for AOL regardless of defamatory material being transmitted through AOL's message boards. In this case, an individual filed suit against AOL after a perpetrator posted a series of anonymous messages that were offensive in nature and referred to the Oklahoma City bombings in 1995. In granting immunity to AOL, the court reinforced the status of Internet service providers as distributors and rather than publishers of information who may actively edit or monitor online content. Social networking services however, are not currently granted ISP status and are increasingly pressured to monitor and restrict abusive and illegal content posted on forums they own or manage.

## Criminal Laws Pertaining to Cyber Bullying

Online threats of a specific and credible nature, along with harassment and stalking are considered criminal offenses in most states. As indicated at the beginning of the chapter, states are already equipped to curb cyber bullying of a serious nature. On the federal level however, the laws pertaining to cyber bullying and online harassment are more limited. The 18 U.S.C. Chapter 110A addresses stalking and domestic violence, and 18 U.S.C. 875 makes it illegal to transmit any communication in interstate or foreign commerce containing threats to injure another.[1] Further, federal law 47 U.S.C. 223 prohibits online harassment that involves a direct communication between stalker and victim. Historically, federal law has not been used to intervene in cyber bullying cases. However, the feds did take action in the case involving the suicide of Megan Meier in which an adult was convicted of using a computer connected to the Internet (an interstate telecommunications system) to torment a minor (see Chapter 1).

Regardless of existing statutory law and emerging case law, the continual challenge for society is applying laws to evolving technology-enabled abuses for which "there should be a law against it!" States continually enact laws to fill gaps in federal legislation, and also imitate laws passed by other states when public pressure to curb illicit conduct mounts. We have already mentioned how specific laws have been passed banning hijacking, computer hacking, and e-mail spamming. During the 2007–2008 Congressional session, three data security bills were favorably reported out of U.S. Senate committees that would require firms that amass digital records on individuals to report breaches of information systems. This action follows a series of incidents in recent years in which cyber criminals have socially engineered and hacked their way into computer systems that store massive amounts of personal data.

The point here is that laws evolve with technologies that enable abuse and crime to occur. Cyber bullying is no different: legal forces are now at work to address this problem in ways appropriate to our legal traditions and civil rights. Sometimes the courts "get it right" according to our personal political views on issues, and sometimes they do not. In the meantime, we muddle through with our best understanding and judgment about laws that do exist. Absent specific rulings on specific issues, "test cases" provide new opportunities to expand upon legal methods of prevention, investigation, and corrective actions. According to the National Conference of State Legislatures, there are now 45 states that have laws that explicitly include electronic forms of communication in their harassment and stalking laws. As of this writing, only five states including, Arkansas, Idaho, Iowa, South Carolina, and Washington specifically address *bullying* in laws governing electronic communications.[2]

## STATE LISTING OF CRIME LAWS PERTAINING TO CYBER BULLYING

As previously indicated, although specific language about cyber bullying is not included state crime laws, many aspects of cyber bullying are nonetheless already addressed. For example the New York State Penal Law includes a statute that could be interpreted to include cases of cyber bullying. According to this law (§ 240.30): "A person is guilty of Aggravated Harassment in the Second Degree when, with intent to harass, annoy, or alarm another person, he or she: Communicates, or causes a communication to be initiated by mechanical or electronic means or otherwise, with a person, anonymously or otherwise, by telephone, or by telegraph, mail, or any other form of written communication, in a manner likely to cause annoyance or alarm. Aggravated harassment in the second degree is a Class A misdemeanor punishable by 15 days to 1 year incarceration."

What do your state laws say about harassment, threats, or cyber bullying? Do you think they adequately cover emerging cyber bullying issues? The authors all live in New York State, so for purposes of this book we jumped online and in a matter of minutes uncovered the following additional information about laws that could apply to cyber bullying:

§ 240.25 Harassment in the First Degree. A person is guilty of harassment in the first degree when he or she intentionally and repeatedly harasses another person by following such person in or about a public place or places or by engaging in a course of conduct or by repeatedly committing acts which places such person in reasonable fear of physical injury. Harassment in the first degree is a class B misdemeanor.

§ 240.26 Harassment in the Second Degree. A person is guilty of harassment in the second degree when, with intent to harass, annoy or alarm another person: He or she engages in a course of conduct or repeatedly commits acts which alarm or seriously annoy such other person and which serve no legitimate purpose. Harassment in the second degree is a violation.

§ 120.45 Stalking in the Fourth Degree (a Class B misdemeanor). A person is guilty of stalking in the fourth degree when he or she intentionally, and for no legitimate purpose, engages in a course of conduct directed at a specific person, and knows or reasonably should know that such conduct:

1. is likely to cause reasonable fear of material harm to the physical health, safety or property of such person, a member of such person's immediate family or a third party with whom such person is acquainted; or
2. causes material harm to the mental or emotional health of such person, where such conduct consists of following, telephoning or initiating communication or contact with such person, a member of such person's immediate family or a third party with whom such person is acquainted, and the actor was previously clearly informed to cease that conduct; or
3. is likely to cause such person to reasonably fear that his or her employment, business or career is threatened, where such conduct consists of appearing, telephoning or initiating communication or contact at such person's place of employment or business, and the actor was previously clearly informed to cease that conduct.

§ 120.15 Menacing in the Third Degree. A person is guilty of menacing in the third degree when, by physical menace, he or she intentionally places or attempts to place another person in fear of death, imminent serious physical injury or physical injury. Menacing in the third degree is a class B misdemeanor.

§ 485.05 Hate crimes. A person commits a hate crime when he or she commits a specified offense and either: (a) intentionally selects the person against whom the offense is committed or intended to be committed in whole or in substantial part because of a belief or perception regarding the race, color, national origin, ancestry, gender, religion, religious practice, age, disability or sexual orientation of a person, regardless of whether the belief or perception is correct; or (b) intentionally commits the act or acts constituting the offense in whole or in substantial part because of a belief or perception regarding the race, color, national origin, ancestry, gender, religion, religious practice, age, disability or sexual orientation of a person, regardless of whether the belief or perception is correct . . . or any attempt or conspiracy to commit any of the foregoing offenses.[3]

Encouraged by what we found in New York State laws, we checked a little further and discovered that the National Conference of State Legislatures Web site (http://www.ncsl.org/programs/lis/cip/stalk99.htm) lists numerous state level computer harassment or cyber stalking laws, which are listed in Table 5.1.

**Table 5.1**
**Inventory of State Computer Harassment and Cyber Stalking Laws**

| | |
|---|---|
| Alabama | Ala. Code § 13A-11-8 |
| Alaska | Alaska Stat. § 11.41.260, 11.41.270, § 11.61.120 |
| Arizona | Ariz. Rev. Stat. § 13-2921 |
| Arkansas | Ark. Code § 5-41-108, 5-27-306 |
| California | Cal. Civil Code § 1708.7, Cal. Penal Code §§ 422, 646.9, 653m |
| Colorado | Colo. Rev. Stat. § 18-9-111 |
| Connecticut | Conn. Gen. Stat. § 53a-182b, § 53a-183 |
| Delaware | Del. Code tit. 11 § 1311 |
| Florida | Fla. Stat. § 817.568, § 784.048 |
| Georgia | Georgia Code §§16-5-90, 34-1-7 |
| Hawaii | Hawaii Rev. Stat. § 711-1106 |
| Illinois | 720 Ill. Comp. Stat. § 5/12-7.1, 5/12-7.5, 135/1-2, 135/1-3, 135/2 |
| Indiana | Ind. Code § 35-45-2-2 |
| Iowa | Iowa Code § 708.7 |
| Kansas | Kan. Stat. § 21-3438 |

(*Continued*)

**Table 5.1**
**Inventory of State Computer Harassment and Cyber Stalking Laws** (*Continued*)

| | |
|---|---|
| Louisiana | La. Rev. Stat. § 14:40.2, La. Rev. Stat. § 14:40.3 |
| Maine | Me. Rev. Stat. tit. 17A § 210-A |
| Maryland | Md. Code tit. 3 § 3-805 |
| Massachusetts | Mass. Gen. Laws ch. 265 § 43, 43A |
| Michigan | Mich. Comp. Laws § 750.411h, 750.411i, 750.411s |
| Minnesota | Minn. Stat. § 609.749 |
| Mississippi | Miss. Code § 97-29-45, § 97-45-15 |
| Missouri | Mo. Rev. Stat. § 565.225 |
| Montana | Mont. Code § 45-8-213 |
| Nevada | Nev. Rev. Stat. § 200.575 |
| New Hampshire | N.H. Rev. Stat. § 644:4 |
| New York | New York Penal Law § 240.30 |
| North Carolina | N.C. Gen. Stat. § 14-196, 14-196.3 |
| North Dakota | N.D. Cent. Code § 12.1-17-07 |
| Ohio | Ohio Code § 2903.211, 2913.01(Y), 2917.21(A) |
| Oklahoma | Okla. Stat. tit. 21 § 850, 1172 |
| Oregon | Or. Rev. Stat. § 163.730, 166.065 |
| Pennsylvania | Pa. Cons. Stat. tit. 18 § 2709, § 2709.1 |
| Rhode Island | R.I. Gen. Laws § 11-52-4.2, § 11-52-4.3 |
| South Carolina | S.C. Code § 16-3-1700(A)(2), 16-3-1700(B) |
| South Dakota | S.D. Cod. Laws § 22-19A-1 |
| Tennessee | Tenn. Code § 39-17-308 |
| Texas | Tx. Penal Code 42.07 |
| Utah | Utah Code § 76-9-201 |
| Vermont | 13 V.S.A. § 1027, 1061, 1062, 1063 |
| Virginia | Va. Code § 18.2-60 18.2-152.7:1 |
| Washington | Wash. Rev. Code § 9.61.260, 9A.46.020, 9A.46.110, 10.14.020 |
| West Virginia | W. Va. Code § 61-3C-14a |
| Wisconsin | Wis. Stat. § 947.0125 |
| Wyoming | Wyo. Stat. § 6-2-506 |

In further considering the Megan Meier suicide case in Missouri, it is worth observing that prosecutors in that state declined to prosecute Lori Drew, who was eventually prosecuted and convicted in November, 2008 under federal laws governing unauthorized use of computer systems. At the time of the original state-level investigation there were reportedly deficiencies in Missouri law that precluded prosecution in state court. We do not dispute the state prosecutors' decision in that case. We do however note that the Megan Meier case should serve as wake-up call to the nation and individual states about just how insidious cyber bullying can be, and the need for governments everywhere to review the wording of their laws in order to prevent perpetrators of cyber criminality from escaping justice.

## POLICE AND COURT RESPONSE CAPABILITIES

"Where's a cyber cop when you need one?" Probably looking for violators of child pornography laws, computer hackers, or cyber terrorists intent on attacking national critical information infrastructure! This is not meant as a criticism, rather an acknowledgment that there is plenty and many forms of cyber crime to keep law enforcement officers who are assigned to very few high-tech crime units extremely busy. When it comes to cyber bullying, just as with classical bullying, the hard truth is that local, state, and federal governments do not have the resources to formally investigate every allegation of wrongdoing. Nor do prosecution agencies and juvenile courts have the capacity to process all cases of cyber bullying that could conceivably be reported for actual violations of *existing* state laws if these were to be reported and investigated to their logical conclusions.

There are exceptions of course, but singular cases even when prosecution occurs may not pertain to cyber bullying. Instead they may be regarded as related to bullying or perhaps online bullying, just depending on the explicitness of existing criminal laws and overriding community and political sentiment about cyber bullying. Remember the case we mentioned earlier in Chapter 2, in which a 17-year-old boy in Wisconsin was prosecuted for allegedly posting naked photos of his 16-year-old ex-girlfriend on his MySpace in order to get back at her? Warned prior to his arrest that he could face prosecution if he did not take the photos off the Web, he reportedly told an investigator, "Fuck that, I am keeping them up." He also reportedly told police investigators that he posted the photos, which were taken on a cell phone and given to him by the girl when they were still dating, and that he posted the photos "because he was venting." Alongside the photos were captions, one of which reportedly read, "Yo, U see how big her hole is! Its from me!"[4] The defiance and incivility exhibited in cyber bullying, has seemingly limitless bounds, and underscores a primary message of this book: that cyber bullying is fundamentally an ethical and complex problem—not primarily a technological problem—that affects educational, justice, and social institutions throughout society.

## CIVIL LAWS PERTAINING TO CYBER BULLYING

On July 24, 2008, MSNBC and Associated Press reporters revealed to the world that Mathew Firsht sued his former school classmate Grant Raphael for unauthorized posting of personal information to Facebook. The information had been posted for 16 days before Firsht's brother spotted it and it resulted in a complaint being made to Facebook and Facebook then promptly removed the material that reportedly included Firsht's sexual preferences, his political views, and that he owed money. Investigation revealed that all the information was posted in a way to make it appear as though Firsht had posted the content about himself, but it was traced to Raphael's personal computer. In his defense, Raphael claimed that an unknown third person must have accessed his computer while attending a party. However the United Kingdom court judge rejected this argument in ". . . awarding Firsht 15,000 pounds ($29,794) for libel and 2,000 pounds ($3,973) for breach of privacy. He received another 5,000 pounds ($9,931) for libel against his company, Applause Store Productions."

This UK civil case demonstrates the emerging reality that cyber bullying that involves online slander, libel, intentional embarrassment, harassment, intimation, and/or threats may bring about justifiable civil court action in lieu of and/or in addition to criminal prosecution. Note these forms of legal redress are not mutually exclusive: violations of crime laws may result in prosecution, or a lawsuit, both or neither; and violations of civil rights may result in a lawsuit and also in criminal prosecution (e.g., by a local, state-level or federal government agency) depending on circumstances. For example, a lawsuit can be brought against a cyber bully (or more likely his or her parents if the bully is not considered of legal adult age) if the incident meets the standards of an *intentional tort* (i.e., intended actions not intended to cause harm).[5] Commonly accepted legal elements of intentional torts that may apply in a given cyber bullying situation include: (1) *defamation* damaging a person's reputation,[6] (2) *invasion of privacy* that involves divulging private facts about a person considered offensive to a reasonable person,[7] (3) *intentional infliction of emotional distress*,[8] and (4) *negligence in providing reasonable levels of supervision* of a child that one has legal custody or guardianship of.

Decisions to sue are difficult and should not be taken lightly. Lawsuits are usually very time-consuming, can be expensive, distressing and result in countersuits. In general, to prevail or make relatively short work of a civil wrongdoing, a plaintiff must be able to demonstrate intentional, negligent, or reckless behavior on the part of persons responsible. This requires a sufficient amount of believable evidence that a tort occurred *and* caused harm and

## THE DESTRUCTION OF JOY, TRUST, AND HOPE

### "Hit Them Where It Hurts, in the Pocket Book!"

As related by a teenage boy:

My dad came from a generation of chicken farmers. They were a poor family, and the smell of chicken odor often clung to his clothes. Every morning while getting ready for school, he had the same scared, panicky, sometimes sick feeling in his stomach. It was as if he was going to the dentist to have his teeth drilled. Kids on the bus would greet my dad in the morning with the sound of "peyou," and then tell him how much he stunk and would hold their noses with their fingers. They would throw manure at him that could consist of cat, horse, cow, bird, rabbit, guinea pig, any type of manure they could find (they wore rubber gloves). They would knock dad down and would rub manure on his shirts, trousers, shoes, ears, head, and sometimes in his mouth. Everyone would stand around and laugh.

My grandfather told my dad to be a man and to grin and bear it. That's life and life is not easy. You might as well get used to it now and accept it. Besides, there's nothing you can do about it. Don't go complaining to anybody because they'll think that you're a crybaby and you'll really get it. Grow up and ignore it. My dad was only a 9-year-old at the time, but the bullying continued through high school. Dad never went to any school functions, because he knew that it was impossible to have a good time while being a target of vicious, verbal, emotional, and physical attacks. He only had a few friends and felt like the loneliest kid in the world. Dad once told me that when he was a kid, if he ever died, no one would have missed him. Dad hated school and did poorly. It was a constant struggle getting bullied day-in, day-out. No one ever defended him, not even the teachers who witnessed the abuse. He just barely graduated from high school.

Dad didn't want to carry on the family business, so he got a job as a laborer with a carpenter right after high school. He was a hard worker and was grateful for not getting bullied. It was a new, nice life for him. Then, Dad met my mom and it was love at first sight. They got married and had my two sisters and me. My parents were wonderful parents and we have a happy life. Dad has a successful construction business with 50 employees. I do well in school and I have lots of friends. I go to all the school functions and am involved in many sports. I like to play war and crime games on the computer with my friends. But my dad won't let me play games on the computer anymore because of what happened to me—I was bullied too.

My *friends* that I used to play with started threatening me and went too far. Whenever I would win playing computer games, they would say that they were going to beat me up and break my fingers. The threats were part of the game, and I didn't pay any attention to them. The e-mail threats started getting more frequent along with the instant messaging threats. I started getting migraines and stomachaches, but I didn't think anything of it. I'm the type of person that doesn't let anything bother me. My parents would ask me if I was all right, and I would say yes. After about six months, I couldn't take the pain anymore, so my mother took me to the doctor. After a physical examination, the doctor wanted to know if I had anything bothering me or upsetting me at home or at school. I told him no. Then my *friends* started threatening me in school. I told them that enough was enough and that I didn't like it anymore. There were even more threats.

My parents never knew about the threats until my father's computer froze up so he used mine. I was in the bathroom when I heard a big yell. "What the hell is this? Who is this? What the hell is going on?" Dad asked me if I knew who these kids were? "Yeah, they're my friends." "Those aren't friends," my father said. "Friends don't make terrible threats like that to you. Friends don't treat friends like that." I told dad that I didn't think that it was any big deal. They were my gaming friends and I had lots of fun with them.

The threats kept on coming while my dad viewed them. I never saw him that mad in my life. He went into a rage. "My life was ruined because of vicious bastards like these," he said. "I'll be damned if it's going to happen to my son. I'm going to protect my son and none of this bull-crap of being a man."

All of this didn't make any sense to me. I told dad not to get mad and that it was okay, because they were my friends and only kidding. "Friends don't threaten to bash in your head, to smash and break all your fingers, and to hurt you badly. How long has this been going on?" I told him a little over a year. Dad asked me if I was afraid to go to school sometimes. He made me look him in the eye and told me not to lie because he would know if I was lying. I told him yes—sometimes. "What about your migraines and your stomach aches?" I told him that I didn't know. "Do they do anything in school?" I told my dad that they called me names and made threats. Sometimes they pushed me down and did other things.

My father called the police immediately and *demanded* that they take a report. They did. The next day Dad took off work and went to the principal's office. He was yelling and demanded that the principal see him immediately. Dad said that he wanted the names of the kids that were threatening me. The principal said that he went look into it. Dad said that he didn't want it to be just looked into but to do something about it. My five *friends* were called into the office and told not to make threats to me anymore. Dad put my computer in his home office. I was really mad at him, because I like my privacy without my dad overseeing everything that I say to my friends and what my friends say to me. The threats kept coming. My dad filed more police reports and went to the school numerous times. He even talked to the kids' parents. The harassment and bullying continued.

My father was fed up. He felt that he tried everything in his power to stop it, so he went to his lawyer. Dad never told me the particulars, but I know he sued the school and the parents. Dad had kept a record of every incident . . . the time, place, date, e-mail, instant message, what was said and done in school and outside of school. He taped recorded every conversation over the phone that he had with the parents, police, school administration, everybody, and anybody. The school and the families of the five friends all settled out of court. My father had a gag order that went along with the settlement, so he can't tell me any details. One thing that he did tell me was that I was all set for college. I could get my master's degree and not have to come up with a dime. I was set and then some. I heard my parents talking that if it wasn't for battered women getting their justice in the court system that we probably wouldn't have stood a chance to stop the threats or win the case. My migraines and stomach problems have stopped.

suffering. As in the preceeding story, dates and times of incidents, identities of people involved, what they did, saw or communicated, and verifiable documentation of everything are essential forms of evidence. It is usually not enough to show improper actions of others. Plaintiffs must also demonstrate through testimonial and written or tangible evidence how they were harmed (e.g., photos of injury or property damage, medical records, computer files, or logs, etc.).

The minimum (and only) amount of proof required to win a civil case is known as *a preponderance of evidence*. This means that facts of wrongdoing and resulting harm are more likely to have occurred than not. The implication is that to win a lawsuit, a person does not need to "prove" every single fact, only that the overall case happened in the way they allege. During and after a case is resolved, it is common for "gag" orders to be issued by the court (when minors are involved), or as a condition of a settlement. A 16-year-old male from New Jersey when interviewed for this book said he could not talk about cyber bullying because his parents are suing the cyber bullies, the school, and the police department. In his words: "Some of my friends put a website up that I was a queer. My father is a minister and I am not a sinner. The lawyer has had other cases and won. My parents are suing for over $100,000 plus all expenses paid. I guess the parents have some kind of a personal liability policy or something like that. Kids better start laying off because there's a lot of parents suing, but I can't talk about the details."

Cyber bullying cases often raise questions regarding whether schools afforded learning and activity environments free from threats, intimidation, and generally offensive behavior. When evaluating whether schools may be liable and thus subject to being sued, courts consider the following four legal questions: Was a legal duty owed? Was there a dereliction or breach of this duty? Did demonstrable or actual injury result? Was there proximate cause?[9] Proximate cause means that the dereliction of duty was responsible for causing the injury. Breach of duty can be established in part by the nature of bullying activity involved in relation to levels of supervision, safety, and security afforded. Breach of duty can also be shown if the possibility of injury could or should have been reasonably foreseen.[10] Therefore, to successfully bring a negligence claim against a school district, school officials or school staff, a claimant must establish that an injury occurred and that adults responsible for student conduct should have foreseen that harm could result. Negligence cases can be strengthened if there are laws mandating the reporting of bullying to a principal or school board, and that these laws were not followed.

Legal responsibility of schools to ensure safety and security for students extends to their use of computers and the Internet while on school grounds. If students are allowed to bring IT devices into schools, legal duties may extend to their use of cell phones. As previously indicated, this is an emerging area of law, as is school liability in bullying situations that link campus behaviors to Internet communications between students after school hours and while off school grounds. This issue is likely to become more problematic as more and more youth engage in mobile social computing, slip into cyber bullying behavioral patterns, and parents file lawsuits alleging school misconduct.[11] However, if courts approach cyber bullying cases like they have addressed negligence claims for school violence, school officials may not have much to worry about.

Some courts have set a very high standard for negligence claims against schools, even in cases that resulted in injury from a weapon brought onto school grounds by students. Thus, while courts have often ruled against schools for disciplining for off-campus conduct, they have also ruled in favor of schools in cases alleging supervisory negligence of on-campus behaviors. However, since civil liability for schools is usually established through case law, standards vary from state to state according to the circumstances of cases decided.

A detailed analysis of the laws is beyond the scope of this book. It is up to the individuals and schools, with guidance from competent legal counsel, to know and understand relevant statutory and case laws of their state government along with those of the federal government. We therefore conclude by reaffirming that schools are legally bound to provide for the safety, security, and welfare of students. Schools must be reasonable, cognizant, and competent in their preventing and responding to bullying and cyber bullying. As we have described, case law now establishes that schools can be held liable for failing to take action when students are bullied at school in the absence of adequate provisions to prevent this. These legal precedents are consistent with societal expectations that the mission and vision of schools is to assist students in reaching their full potential. Case law rulings in civil cases also support our beliefs that schools are ethically and morally obligated to act in the best interests of students in campus-related cyber bullying situations. Courts will decide this matter in due time.

# Closing the Digital Divide for Parents

*Cyber what? That's kids stuff. My kids have temper tantrums if I dare go near their computers. Peace of mind means more to me—it's not worth upsetting the apple cart.*

—*Mother of three teens*

In this chapter we provide help for parents to close the digital divide that separates them from knowing what their kids are up to and experiencing online. This is really important because, as it turns out, many parents are oblivious to what is actually taking place by and among youth online. To begin with, lets again return to an aspect of Rochester Institute of Technology's "Survey of Internet and At-Risk Behaviors" study in which youth perceptions of parental supervision were compared with parent's self-reporting of supervising their kid's online activities. As Figure 6.1 illustrates, what youth believe does not square with what parents believe about supervision! For example, while only 7 percent of parents surveyed believe they provide no supervision of their children's online activities, 65 percent of 10–12th graders believe their parents provide no supervision whatsoever. On balance, the figure indicates a similar, though less significant difference in perceptions between youth and parents about supervision. What do you think about these data?

We begin this chapter with a short pep talk for parents—a little tough love for adults about the necessity of becoming actively knowledgeable about

**Figure 6.1**
Perception of Supervision

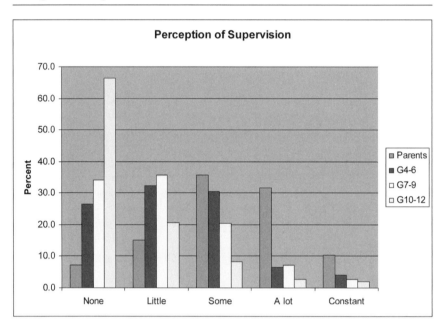

their children's online affairs, and the need to become appropriately engaged with them in online activities. Next we'll consider information about child and youth brain development, which will help parents to understand why normal kids sometimes act so foolhardy. Then we offer insights for parents about how to effectively supervise online activities of youth. The good news is that you don't have to be a technological genius to be very effective, and our guidance for proactive engagement if followed is likely to have some very positive results that may surprise you as well as the youth in your lives. When we get to the section on effective supervision and communication we'll teach you how to "be the parent"—to sound hip without being pretentious, over-bearing, or compromising of core family values. We will tie this into principles for ethical decision making and the need for ongoing education of youth and for parents amidst technologically evolving cyber abuse and bullying.

## You Didn't Get the Memo on Cyber Safety?

If you are a parent, and have not yet received "the memo," IT'S TIME TO EDUCATE YOURSELF ABOUT AND BECOME INVOLVED IN WHAT YOUR KIDS ARE DOING ONLINE! This includes making a list of the devices they use to go onto the Internet, when they go online, and from where they access the Net, how long they typically spend doing XY or Z, and specific places (e.g., Web sites they visit) along with whom they interact. In the process it is critical to express genuine interest and curiosity about who their online friends are. Parents should inquire about how those online relationships got started, how they are going, and what value online friends and associated content have for their children.

Parents also need to balance *their genuine need to be informed* with privacy needs of youth, in order to supervise and provide guidance regarding controversial Internet content. This needs to be accomplished with a firm conviction that Internet safety and responsible computing is not a one-time project, a short-term program, or technological fix. Instead, fostering Internet safety, information security, and cyber ethics is a lifestyle choice. The choice to be a responsible Internet user needs to be a personal choice in the context of stated, enforced, and reinforced core family values. This is analogous to using another powerful form of technology safely, legally, and responsibly—the family car. Whether driving or simply riding in a car, occupants need to take safety precautions and be responsible in order to avoid accidents. This attitude goes beyond analogy and extends to actually operating motor vehicles while calling or texting with cellular phones.

## THE DESTRUCTION OF JOY, TRUST, AND HOPE

### "When Negligent Use of Technologies Collide: The Tragic Death of Five Senior High School Students"

As known by the authors and from media reports:

In early July 2007, five female seniors having just graduated from Fairport (New York) Central High School were tragically killed when the car they occupied crossed the centerline of a two-lane country road to collide head-on with a truck and then burst into flames. The investigation into the cause of the crash, which made national news reports, revealed that the driver's cell phone was used immediately prior to the collision to send a text message to another teen in a separate following car. An entire community still mourns the deaths of those five beautiful young women, and somberly reflects on how texting while driving may have contributed to the tragedy. For our purposes, this is not a driver's education issue: The more fundamental challenge here has to do with fostering appropriate use of information technology devices beginning very early in life and reinforcing this throughout the lives of youth with genuine interest, positive role modeling, and supervision. Failure to do so as parents, in our schools, and communities risk colliding cyber behaviors with physical consequences and vice versa. Such are the realities of how we now live and rely on mobile technological devices.

The issue of mobile talking and texting as forms of social networking and computing presents numerous special challenges for youth and for parents long before teens begin driving cars. The challenges are far less straightforward than youth learning rules of the road and acquiring a driving license. Sadly, thousands of teens (along with adults) illegally operate cell phones and other IT devices while driving or operating cars or other "vehicles" on roadways. Noting that most states (38 as of this writing) have banned cell phone use while driving unless used with headsets, hardly a day passes when we don't observe people using a handheld device to talk or text while motoring, peddling, or scooting around. At this moment, while composing this chapter (with a laptop computer), a boy appearing to be a 9-year-old is illegally riding by on a motorized skateboard at about 5–8 mph on the author's residential street holding a cell phone to his ear, steering with the other hand, and wearing no helmet!

While many parents today know they are not as tech savvy as their children and cannot watch them 24-7, not knowing even a little about computers and other types of IT devices that kids commonly use can be disastrous. Limited knowledge, skills, and abilities about IT devices and information/computer systems can lead to uncertainty and fear, made even worse if youth end up becoming involved in cyber bullying as either victims or offenders. Fear to become better acquainted with digital youth culture and information technology that tweens and teens now routinely use, sometimes with sly and reckless abandon as in abusive cases, allows unhealthy attitudes, poor decision making, and irresponsible physical and cyber behaviors to creep into the lives of otherwise great kids. It may also result in parents remaining in the dark about negative aspects of digital youth culture, coarse messages and content sent or received, interacting online or in person with strangers considered as friends, and so forth. Once patterns of physical-to-online use and abuse become established, it is invariably harder than ever for parents to span the digital divide that naturally separates so many of them from the cyber world occupied by today's youth.

"Oh my gosh! That boy on the skateboard, here he comes back the other way this time with no hands and text messaging—amazing! No, I'm not making this up!!" Texting is becoming increasingly popular as a primary means of communication for youth above and beyond verbally talking. Using any regular hardwired phone is much less common than using personal cell phones. It would seem that social networking for young people is increasingly social computing and therefore mobile computing . . . Hence, mobile networking through which youth socialize with "friends" a concept that is simultaneously a noun and verb, as when kids "friend" (i.e., befriend) each other online. The implications for parenting are monumental, as parents and even their children can no longer expect to physically meet, interact or become intimate with friends. Unlike days of old, neighborhood friends can live or go to school anywhere in the world, and relationships can be based on third-party associations rather than geographic proximity. To repeat and emphasize a concept discussed earlier, cyber bullying therefore is limited only by the cyber neighborhoods that kids frequent in cyberspace. Again, the implications for parenting are huge.

## The Destruction of Joy, Trust, and Hope

**"A Case of Caring Parents beside Themselves over Threats of Sex and Possible Fraud"**

Concerned parents of 16-year-old boy:

A concerned father and husband recently contacted this author about a disturbing U.S. mail letter with no return address, an out-of-state postmark and hand addressed to his 16-year-old son. The man's wife also knew about the letter. Ordinarily they would never have pried, but this letter was very unusual and the parents were very protective and concerned for "Paul" who had been mildly developmentally challenged since birth. The parents discovered that the "snail mail" addressed to their son was a handwritten love letter, apparently written by a girl, who gave her name and other personal information about herself. The letter included sexually graphic information about what the girl wanted to do physically with Paul's private parts now that they had *already established* a great online relationship that had apparently began via Paul's Web site . . .

The parents confessed they did not know what their son's Web site was or what its contents consisted of, nor did they know anyone in the state of Kentucky from which the letter was sent. I explained their options were some combination of: (1) respect their son's privacy, do not confront Paul immediately because he did not appear to be in immediate danger, but do continue to monitor the situation; (2) Web search the names of the girl *and their son* to learn more about what might be going on in their social computing worlds; (3) then engage Paul about his Internet activities especially those involving online friendships; (4) when the time is right confront Paul about the letter and use it as a teaching instance about Internet safety and information security (e.g., possibilities that the girl could actually be an adult fraudster or pedophile, or someone else of a younger age); (5) depending on what is found out, involve the National Center for Missing and Exploited Children and/or law enforcement authorities; and (6) implement closer supervision or restrictions on IT-usage if Paul's safety and welfare cannot be assured through lesser invention strategies and his voluntary willingness to use the Net in sound ways.

In the end, the parents opted for a measured inquiry about the letter and Paul's online activities after acknowledging they opened it out of concern for his safety.

Confusion among parents surrounding the most likely dangers of their children using the Internet, including all forms of abusive and illegal behaviors, along with receiving unwanted sex-related content (e.g., pornography) and cyber attacks (e.g., viruses, spyware, phishing probes, etc.) can be worsened by advertisements that employ scare or guilt tactics. Television, radio, Net, and print ads that advocate purchasing Internet filtering and blocking software, identity theft prevention insurance, computer tune-up services, and so forth do serve a useful purpose, but not when they are pitched *as if these were substitutes for parents routinely engaging their kids about what they are actually doing online, who they are interacting with, and for what specific purposes.* Unlike "purchasing the problem away" with some partial fix, engaging youth will help expose ways in which youth, along with an entire household of IT users, may be exposed to various forms of cyber threats and offending, including but not limited to cyber bullying. Remember that many types of cyber crimes occur because someone was manipulated into giving up personal information combined with not properly and regularly securing computer/device operating systems and software applications. In short, all users need to be informed and regularly back-up, patch-up, and beware of potential cyber threats!

The inevitable truth is that few parents are fully aware of what their children are doing online. As with most of society, although we are getting better, parents as a group are information security minimalists. In other words, parents know little more and perhaps less than youth about how to protect themselves, their data, devices, and technology systems online. When it comes to cyber bullying as one important form of cyber offending threat that kids face, they are not sufficiently familiar with technology, net/leetspeak, and digital youth culture. Research substantiates that relative few parents actively monitor much less intelligently supervise online activities of youth. Others do not engage their youth out of respect for their privacy. Some parents trust what their kids tell them and/or believe their children will do the right thing based on years of solid parenting, intervention, and appropriate discipline. Other parents are truly busy, holding down at least one full-time job while trying to provide for, be supportive of, or engage in traditional sports, recreation, and cultural activities of their children. We understand, we respect that, and we empathize. After all, as previously discussed, parents have been setup by several societal factors to take the hit on this one!

Factors beyond the control of individual parents that have also contributed to cyber abuse, cyber crime, and cyber bullying by and among youth and young adults include: (1) negative aspects of digital youth culture having emerged largely unseen and not articulated by society; (2) media, legislative, and law enforcement emphasis on cybersex predators while ignoring worsening youth online sexual promiscuity (e.g., using cell phones to take and send naked pictures of each other as pseudo-child porn); (3) formal education systems embracing, endorsing, and espousing computer technology and benefits of the Internet while providing minimum Internet safety, information security, and cyber ethics instruction; (4) technology innovation and marketing forces that push development and sales of IT devices and technology solutions such as Internet filtering and blocking software that kids readily figure out how to defeat and share with each other online; and (5) lack of positive role modeling and supervision by responsible adults, not limited to parents, many of whom actually delude themselves into believing (more likely hoping) that all is right in cyberspace, "at least with my kids, who would never get mixed up in anything wrong." All of these factors have combined to create conditions ripe for many forms of cyber abuse and offending now engaged in by millions of youth. That in short, is the memo!

## Teenage Brain Research: Another Reason to Get Involved

When attempting to understand where teenagers are coming from in terms of their thinking and behavior, it is important to consider what is inside their heads: literally! Recent research on the brains of teenagers can help explain why they sometimes behave and misbehave the ways they do. Researchers used to believe that the brains of teenagers were much like those of adults. However, research now shows that the pre-frontal cortex of teens (the part of the brain that controls judgment, insight, and emotions) is not fully developed until human beings are in their early 20s![1] As a result, adolescents do not fully analyze and rationally think through situations as thoroughly as do adults. The neural structure for their being able to is simply not in place.

Slow human brain development relates to cyber bullying in significant ways. Harvard researcher Deborah Yurgelun-Todd has shown that teenagers are less able than adults to correctly identify emotions on each person's face from a series of pictures. For example, rather than identifying a picture with a face showing fear as fear, many teenagers saw something different, such as anger or shock.[2] Therefore, teenagers already unable to read facial expressions of peers in oral communications may find it even more difficult to accurately interpret what is happening when interacting online. Without visual cues, all people, but especially tweens and teens, are disadvantaged and prone to make mistakes. False assumptions, egocentric needs, and gut reactions dominate rational and circumspect decision making about what and how best to communicate. Impetuous and even risky communications are synonymous with what teenagers are as they mature into their bodies and brains!

The lack of maturity in the teenage brain combined with the ability to instantly communicate with the cyber world is a dangerous combination. Add teenage hormones into the mix along with a sense of anonymity when online, and the possibilities for impetuous risk taking escalate exponentially. Further, a lack of life experiences—the proverbial school of hard knocks—to help guide informed decision making while in the fast-paced online world of digital youth culture, sets up youth for crashes with emotions, egos, and self-esteem! The struggle to win as in online gaming, takes hold amidst conflicting feelings of fear, invulnerability, and (as previously discussed in chapter 2) disinhibition.

Insufficient biological development of a teenager's brain may contribute to cyber bullying, because teens routinely experience difficulty making decisions that involve consequences of their behaviors, and they frequently fail to take into consideration alternative explanations for and contexts in which messages are being sent or received. In short, they may not consider the harm they are causing or are able to cause, nor are they even able to adequately contemplate factors that lead them to interpret things in the way that they do. As victims, teenagers may allow cyber bullying to continue because of difficulty thinking through how to respond to aggressive situations they are caught up in. Confused about the meaning of true friendship, along with all the issues mentioned above, teenagers are among if not the most vulnerable people online. This is especially important to keep in kind as we now shift into the role of supervision and communication in dealing with the issue of cyber bullying.

## The Scoop on Supervision—Build Trust

Most advice given to parents about how to supervise youth online includes a series of tips such as "keep home computers in common or high-traffic areas," "buy Internet filtering/blocking software," and "monitor online activities and limit use of computers by youth." While this may be sound advice depending on a particular family situation, it is not enough! More important than computer location, technology purchases and time limits are needed lines of communication between parents and children. Just as cyber bullying is bullying with a technological twist, actively supervising online behaviors of youth entails routine supervising with some technological savvy and arm twisting! The key is to establish core family values about responsible Internet and device use, and maintain interpersonal communication with youth, for example, engage them in face-to-face and technological ways that command their attention and respect.

We as parents can put our children on the defensive when we demand to know what is happening in their lives. Consider an example of a parent dealing with a 4-year-old child. Upon discovering that a wad of gum has been placed behind expensive new furniture in the living room, an upset parent confronts her child and yells, "Did you put the gum behind this couch?" Silence. The question is yelled even louder . . . Silence again, followed by a whimpering, "No." While the child obviously *did* place the gum behind the couch, a lie was told out of fear of repercussions. Although simplistic, this example can be applied to a teenager who is being cyber bullied, but willing to endure in silence to avoid feared repercussion of having their computer/IT device taken away or time spent online restricted—their very lifeline to their friends and social network via cyberspace! Unfortunately, and perhaps due to unfamiliarity with the teen technological scene, parents may be too quick to blame victims of cyber bullying for putting themselves in a position to be bullied.

In 2006 an ABC News primetime special on cyber bullying featured several girls being interviewed. One of the girls shared some cruel messages that had been written about her online. The remarks were in response to her online journal about a recent vacation, and included messages calling her a slut and making other nasty insults. While sharing the information to the interviewer, the father walked into the room and learned about the online journal and insults for the first time. While showing obvious concern and stating that he did not know she was keeping an online journal, the daughter stated that he shouldn't be mad or freak out about the insults. Their dialog continued:

Father: "I don't like this at all."
Daughter: "Dad. You're better off not knowing. It is a harsh reality. It's high school."
Father: "It may be a harsh reality, but the fact is that you set yourself up for this essentially."
Daughter (while wiping away tears from her eyes): "See. I just got myself in trouble."

Blaming the victim is easy to do, especially when a child or teenager is involved. Parents after all, have an obligation to be in control, right? The example above demonstrates some of the important issues surrounding open communication and natural reactions to finding out about a cyber bullying situation. The father was unaware of her online activities and reacted quite emotionally when he found out. His goal was to immediately control the situation by inadvertently blaming the victim, his own daughter. Ironically, he was also motivated by concern and love for his daughter. However a more informed parent would have engaged their teenager by asking about the journal not with regard to its private contents, rather as one among various likely activities she might be engaged in online (e.g., social networking, Web browsing, electronic gaming, IM-ing, texting, etc.). Then out of concern, he could ask the teen to share why the diary was important to her and with respect, inquire about some of the content that lead to her being cyber bullied. In the process, the real and possibly fake identities of people involved as offenders, witnesses, and potentially other victims could be established. Lessons about how to protect oneself online could also be imparted. The daily patterns of online communications in relation to physical activities and interpersonal interactions could be discovered and assessed for their value-to-risk potential.

By engaging their child, tween, or teenager, a parent can determine what their kids are engaged in. The goal is to develop and maintain a relationship where kids feel they can openly communicate with parents about issues that are important to *them* (i.e., the youth). In other words, *this needs to be about kids,* not parents primarily, though in the end the needs and responsibilities of parents will be fulfilled to the extent that trusting relationships can be fostered. This well known parenting edict emphasizes the natural importance of youth to parents. The engaging approach also acknowledges the central role of youth in cyber bullying as victims (or as offenders or witnesses). Both are the result of being proactive and positively involved in the online lives of youth and through developing mutual trust and clear lines of authority and responsibility. Put another way, parents need to routinely reveal to their kids that they understand digital youth culture and are trying to respectfully learn what they and other youth do online. They should plainly acknowledge their understanding of current events, popular child and teen blogs, and controversial issues that kids chat about online, including sex, among many other things.

Parents must also convince youth they are there for them and respect their wishes and their privacy, provided that online activities do not involve violations of predetermined rules, abuse of anyone online, or violations of law. Without mutual trust, there is very little chance youth will look to their parents when they need help, or that parents will trust them to behave and report problems when they arise. Failure to establish trust or having trust once established breakdown will in turn mean that youth are more likely suffer

## THE DESTRUCTION OF JOY, TRUST, AND HOPE

### "The Effects of Not Communicating about Computing"

35-year-old mother of 13-year-old daughter:

Computers should be outlawed. I used to have a relationship with my daughter and she's turned into a beast. We have had trouble with computer, cell phones, Web sites, chat rooms, blogs, text messages, online postings and then it gets carried over to school. It always starts on the computer, always. My daughter got so upset at one of the blogs that was posted about her that she threw our brand new $2,000 computer out through our home window!

My husband and my work records, everything was on it. It was storming (raining that day) and the computer was out in the rain all day while my husband and I were at work. I am starting a petition to outlaw chat rooms, blogs, and everything that kids have access to online. We were stupid. We didn't backup any of our information. We never imagined this could happen. Please tell parents out there not to allow their kids on the computer. If they need information for homework, look it up for them.

in silence if they are being picked on (or ostracized) by bullies or "friends" rather than risk intervention from parents. Youth who cannot trust parents will also more likely fear that parents will intervene inappropriately in ways that will ultimately prove ineffective in the long-term.

## FOR PARENTS OF A CYBER BULLYING VICTIM

If a parent becomes aware that their child is a victim of cyber bullying, the initial response should be supportive, not accusatory. This is especially true if the child told their parent on their own. However, as in the example above, a natural tendency is to react impulsively and emotionally. With this in mind, parents should begin with their own threat assessment including a complete review of the situation by conducting an investigation consisting of in-person and online queries. Although not trained as professional investigators, parents are naturally good snoops when it comes to finding things out that involve and threaten their children! The key is to ask questions—LOTS OF QUESTIONS—of several people. This has to be done in a cautious and supportive manner so that youth feel free to share facts honestly, and so that trust crucial to maintaining solid relationships is not jeopardized. Always remember that when a child tells a parent about cyber bullying, they are among a minority of youth who do so; they are reaching out for help, and will immediately pull back if they perceive an overreaction or punishment coming their way.

When asking questions, *REALLY LISTEN* to the answers you are given. Use the information you have in this book to ask more probing questions, and to empathize with what youth are saying, experiencing, and feeling. Use basic nonthreatening interviewing methods: sit quietly without crossing arms or legs if possible, make eye contact, touch your child if appropriate, and avoid stern or judgmental words. The goals are to obtain as much information as possible, so that the best assistance can be given. Missing pieces of the puzzle will hinder an appropriate response by parents. Also, each situation is unique so a perfectly choreographed response does not exist. The next steps will be guided from what is discovered, and should take into consideration the age of the child victim, age and friendship status of offenders, and potential seriousness of the offense. In reality, a cyber bullying situation may involve a simple misunderstanding, a benign case of teasing, an embarrassing event, or something more serious like a threatening, abusive, humiliating, or ongoing situation. If potential danger exists, school and/or law enforcement authorities should be contacted immediately.

Depending on the type and methods used in the cyber bullying, the next step is to find, save, and preserve the physical and cyber evidence. Bullying as with other forms of crime nearly always creates and leaves behind evidence that should be preserved in the original state, and whenever possible left for trained professionals to locate, gather, and forensically process. This can be done in a number of ways depending on the nature of evidence involved and technology available. For example, if the bullying took place 'via e-mail, it will likely be saved by the computer program(s) used to create, send, and receive it. Copies of messages should always be printed out, copied, and saved into a word processing document, along with notes about when, where, how, and by whom this was done. Original message headers showing dates, times, senders, and receivers of messages should be included, for every "piece" of digital evidence.

Instant and text messages can be processed in much the same way so long as messages have been saved on device hard drives. Once messages are deleted, it takes a specially trained computer forensics examiner to recover the data and there are no guarantees this is possible. If the bullying happens through a Web site, taking a screen shot that includes the offensive messages or images is appropriate. From a personal computer, this can often be done by pressing the "print screen" button on the keyboard and then "pasting" the screenshot into another file such as a Word™ document. Practicing this simple process using data not involved as evidence is a good idea to develop skills and confidence, and depending on circumstances it may be appropriate to involve your victim-child if they are more familiar with the functioning of a particular device.

Recording of online chats through note taking inclusive of dates, times and screen names of people involved in cyber bullying can assist with potential tracing of e-mail, instant messages and texting. No matter how it is done, printing hard copies is always a good idea, provided it is done in such a way that does not alter or delete the contents of the original message. Also, viewing the Web history of a child's Internet browsing can aid parents in discovering gaps in cyber bullying case scenarios. The idea is to get a feel for what a child does and does not do online, with whom they interact, when, why and from which device(s). Again, depending on circumstances, this can be accomplished with assistance from the child victim as a way of discovering truth and building their confidence that you are on their side.

Another step, if appropriate based on the situation, is to make contact with the Internet Service Provider, Instant Message Service, social networking service, or cell phone provider. As the problem of cyber bullying has become of larger concern in society, these organizations are increasingly taking steps to assist with inquiries and complaints. For example, MySpace has a "report abuse" link that enables users or parents to report an issue that may constitute abuse. Upon clicking on the link, the user is asked to provide their name and e-mail address, choose a type of issue from a list, and describe the issue with as much detail as possible. Not surprisingly, cyber bullying is at the top of the list.

MySpace also has advice sections that assist with response to harassment, blocking annoying users, and deleting offensive comments and false Web sites often used in phishing schemes. Often, complaints will lead to removal of the content. Another popular social networking site, Facebook, pledges to quickly remove any harassing or offensive content. However, while some so-cial networking sites are very cooperative, they are not universally regulated, and may never be given controversial debates over free speech and the inher-ent freedom of expression nature of the Net. Remember, a hallmark of digital youth culture is creative freedom online, which is fundamentally appealing to kids searching for their places and spaces in cyberspace. Therefore it is pri-marily up to parents to police the online activities of their children. Further, parents need to recognize that with millions and millions of users it is very difficult for Internet companies such as Google, America Online, MSN and Yahoo to police all of the Web sites accessible through their search engines. They rely on providing parental controls and search filters that parents are encouraged to check out and use, along with reporting abusive online ex-periences and offensive content that violate terms of service agreements or policies.

When cyber bullying takes place via a cell phone, parents should contact the cell phone provider for assistance in identifying the phone number from which the calls or text messages were made. Future contacts from that cell phone can be blocked. Although it may be difficult to legally prove who actu-ally sent a text message, one primary goal is to stop cyber bullying messages from recurring. Although contacting the ISP or cell provider may not be the most appropriate option based on the circumstances, it is important to know that it can be a valid option: make your voice heard.

The video hosting Web site YouTube has also not been immune from cases of cyber bullying and has also provided means of reporting abusive or offensive videos. For example, on March 30, 2008 a Florida teenage girl was allegedly repeatedly beaten by six fellow teenage girls, ages 14–17, who taped the assault and posted it on YouTube.[3] Two teenage boys waited out-side the house where it occurred as lookouts. Afterward a few of the assail-ants allegedly said they beat the girl up because she was trash-talking them online. A police official described the incident as showing a pack mentality and that they did not care how bad they hurt the victim. Although YouTube does not prescreen videos, it does remove violent or offensive videos when flagged. According to guidelines from YouTube.com, "If your video shows someone getting hurt or attacked, don't post it."

In another instance, YouTube removed a video of a violent fight that was captured on camera. Some individuals involved in the attack were later ar-rested and charged with assault. Although this did not appear to be a case of cyber bullying, it does provide an example of teens taping criminal acts, and then getting caught due to posting the evidence online for all to see. In digi-tal youth cultural speak, this is a classic example of candidates for the "Darwin Award" as in Charles Darwin's famous theory about evolution, survival of the fittest, and how the dumbest among species are doomed to fail! (In leet-speak, this concept, which is a huge insult among savvy online users, would be written as "Epic Fail"—check out http://www.darwinawards.com/ that portrays numerous criminals who, in their stupidity, left evidence of their crimes online or at crime scenes.

If suspected cyber bullying occurred at school or occurred through the school network, or otherwise using school technology, then the school should be immediately contacted. When incidents happen on campus and during school hours, the school has a responsibility to intervene. If the cyber bullying is occurring away from campus, where it most often does occur, then a decision must be made whether the school should be notified. Many school officials appreciate being notified as a courtesy even if they have no legal basis or responsibility to intervene. In their minds, even if bullying is not yet school related, it could become so and they would rather prevent this if they can rather than deal with the consequences later. Besides, school officials have lots of experience with students bullying each other and may be able to offer assistance or provide advice. Sometimes notifying school officials can lead to careful monitoring of classmates or teammates, particularly during or after school activities. Officials are usually highly attuned to potential safety or security problems that stem from bullying, and may elect to notify police.

Age of the students involved can also influence decisions as to whether or not to contact school or law enforcement authorities. If cyber bullying is occurring at the elementary or middle level, it may be appropriate for parents to contact school officials despite the wishes of their victim child. However, older teens may not want you to contact the school because they fear being labeled "a rat" and ostracized or bullied even worse. Therefore, parents should resist impulsively contacting the school without communicating with their child about their wishes, and how they view you assisting them. Overall, regardless of whether school officials can or cannot impose formal discipline, schools have resources that parents are ultimately helping to pay for and are entitled to, as are their children.

Some districts have designated safety, security, or lead bullying prevention officers who work closely with local law enforcement agencies, which may also have designated school police officer, D.A.R.E. (Drug Abuse Resistance Education) or GREAT (gang resistance education and training) officers positioned to help or intervene if warranted. The value of parents partnering with school officials was nicely summarized by a principal who said, "We (schools) need an awareness of its (cyber bullying) frequency. We can monitor in school as much as possible, but parents play a vital role and without that partnership with parents and the community we cannot effectively address this issue."[4]

Contacting parents of a cyber bully may also be an option if a child is victimized. Again, parents should talk with their child first to get a better understanding of the seriousness of the particular situation. Although it may be instinctive, parents should not impulsively rush to confront the parents of a cyber bully without careful thought. Some parents may be receptive and will do what they can to understand what happened and take steps to stop the cyber bullying. Other parents may react defensively and blame the victim for what is happening, blame the parents of the victim, or both. Remember, parents often do not know what is happening with their kids online, and therefore may be equally surprised to find out that their child actually started cyber bullying—RIT's research shows that all age levels of children who are bullies are likely to be victims of bullying, and vice versa.

To avoid potential confrontation or difficulties with face-to-face communication, the parents of a true victim can present allegations in writing, including copies of any saved evidence, and send this information to the parents of bullies in a way that asks for their assistance in stopping the cyber bullying. As indicated previously, school officials may also be of assistance for communicating with parents if bullying is connected even indirectly to school activities. And, depending on the response provided by a parent whose child has been shown to be a bully, law enforcement can also be contacted merely as a means to officially document the problem, even if no investigation is warranted or desired. If a situation escalates, this police documentation of the allegations along with evidence gathered will be invaluable to prosecution and/or in a civil lawsuit.

## FOR THE PARENTS OF THE CYBER BULLY

Every bullying situation has at least two sides to the proverbial story. Sometimes bullies when confronted will lie or exaggerate to explain their actions or simply deny any harassment, threats, or that physical touching took place. "I never touched him!" and "That's a load of crap, she started it!" are common things bullies say when accused. Just the same, they may be telling the truth, or at least to some extent. So what advice can be offered to parents of the cyber bully? While some parents may indeed be guilty of inadequate supervision, or may have otherwise influenced or contributed to inappropriate behavior, becoming aware that their child has been cyber bullying is often completely unexpected or even shocking. This is especially true in first-time situations. And since there is no one profile of a cyber bully, nor is there one cause of cyber bullying, parents presented with evidence their child is responsible or involved in bullying may naturally be confused, doubtful, protective, and defensive.

Keeping this in mind, if a parent becomes aware of the possibility that their child has bullied someone online or otherwise, it is important to not overreact and become defensive. After all, most children experience some level of bullying by other kids as they grow up so the odds that any parent's children are not involved in some way may be slim. Not every allegation is true; rarely are allegations completely false. Therefore, if the allegations are coming from a school official or another parent, parents of accused bullies should listen to the allegations and ask to review any evidence before responding with anything other than *reasonable concern for all children who may be involved.* Certainly evidence must be carefully considered before parents of accused bullies commit to a course of action. Consider how we have already discussed how easy it can be to set someone up online, and to engineer content that falsely implicates someone in wrongdoing.

If an admission of cyber bullying is coming from a child, it is again necessary to dig deeper to understand the situation and its root causes. If allegations are found to be true, then the cyber bully must be held accountable for their actions through appropriate disciplinary measures. They must also be informed of potential involvement of police or lawsuits, while at the same time being educated as to how their actions have hurt or otherwise impacted others at school, in the community, and even online friends in cyberspace. In so doing, responsible parents must also endeavor to build trust with their children. It was one thing to be disappointed in one's child, and quite another thing to abandon them because they erred in judgment, which all kids are prone to do.

The seriousness of harm caused, and whether school officials or law enforcement are compelled to become involved, are useful guides to meting out appropriate levels of punishment and future supervision. These should be in accordance with established family values, societal ethics, and laws governing corporal punishment and child abuse. The worst thing a parent can do is make a bad situation worse by overreacting, not taking appropriate action, or betraying the trust of a child by abandoning their parental responsibilities. Obviously consideration of denying or restricting future use of computers and other IT devices, along with instruction in appropriate use of the Internet, are vital concerns that must be incorporated into any action taken. Here parents must make perfectly clear what the abusive child can and cannot do online, and how family units can work together to prevent future bullying.

## PREVENTION THROUGH ESTABLISHING AND ENFORCING RULES

Research by the Pew Internet and American Life Project in 2005 indicated that just more than half (54%) of American families had parental control software on their computers, which translated to about 12 million households.[5] This was compared to about 7 million households using parental control software in the year 2000. In addition, the survey also found that 62 percent of parents were worried that their child would read inappropriate content online. Further, 64 percent of parent survey respondents said that they have rules governing time spent by their child online. The survey also found common ground in terms of responses by parents and teens—the majority of both parents (81%) and teens (79%) agreed that teens are not careful enough about revealing personal information, and also that teens are doing things online that they do not want their parents to know about. On a more positive note, the results did show that parents are increasingly using filters to limit access to inappropriate or harmful content, and also showed that parents are trying different ways to monitor the online activities of their kids.

A similar study by the Pew Internet and American Life Project in 2006 also found that many parents (65%) reported being involved in the online activities by checking to see what Web sites were visited.[6] The point is made that parents are not completely out of the loop, and as ignorant about teen technology use as many have come to believe. For example, the study also showed that nearly three-fourths of parents could correctly determine whether their teenager has created a social networking site. However, this must be interpreted with caution as many teens have more than one social networking account, meaning that the parents may not be aware of all social networking sites that their teen may be using. Also, more than two out of three parents (68%) reported that they have rules about which sites their teen could visit, as well as rules about the type of information that their teen could share online with others.

A more recent study, conducted by Harris Interactive in late 2007 for Symantec's *Norton Online Living Report* surveyed more than 4,500 adults and 2,700 8- to 17-year-olds in several countries, including the United States, United Kingdom, Australia, Germany, France, Brazil, China, and Japan. Results of the study revealed that many parents are unaware of their children's online activities and the security threats that surround those activities. Specifically:[7]

- Parents underestimate how often their children experience requests for personal information, being approached online by a stranger and experiencing cyber bullying.
- While 25 percent of U.S. children reported being requested for personal information, fewer than 20 percent of parents think this is happening to their children.
- In the United States, 13 percent of children reported "cyber pranks," while only 2 percent of parents surveyed believe their children are being cyber bullied.
- About 20 percent of U.S. children surveyed, reported they do things online that their parents would not approve of.
- United States children also reported spending 10 times as much time online than their parents reported they do. While parents believe their children are online about 2 hours per month, youth surveyed reported spending an average of 20 hours per month online.

"This 'digital disconnect' between parents and their children can be attributed to a lack of communication, the report says. The survey reveals that only half of parents say they've spoken to their children about practicing safe online habits. This is upsetting, the report says, considering that 81 percent of U.S. children say they are comfortable talking to their parents about their online experiences. What's more, this digital disconnect is not just happening in the United States—it's happening in most major countries around the world."

According to Marian Merritt, Internet safety advocate for Symantec, "This report clearly demonstrated a global digital divide. We've always taught our children to not talk to strangers in the offline world, and now we must teach them how to safely exist in an online world filled with strangers."[8]

Every responsible organization in the United States that relies on computer technology now has an acceptable use policy (AUP) in place. This is true of government, private, and nonprofit organizations across employment sectors. When it comes to online safety and security, as well as ethical use of computers and data, sectors such as the health care administration and financial services are regulated by the federal government to guard against hacking, identity theft, and abuse of information systems by employees. It all comes down to protecting data, devices, and networks that everyone depends on for their personal and employment security and privacy needs. Parents who manage households can learn a few lessons from managers of such organizations. After all, computing environments in organizations and households have people using similar devices to access the same Internet and share sensitive information.

Just as employing organizations, including school districts, develop and train staff in AUP requirements, parents need to develop rules for using computers, cell phones, and other types of IT devices for their children. Developing rules will help all users of these devices within households to individually and collectively stay safe online, and help to prevent family members from becoming victims of cyber bullying or other forms of online abuse and cyber crime. Sound rules for responsible computing will also help youth to recognize many types of online threats and prevent them from slipping into abusive or offending behaviors.

## EDUCATE, BETTER EDUCATE, AND RE-EDUCATE (YOURSELF)!

To maximize parenting effectiveness in cyberspace parents must commit to self-education about digital youth culture, social computing, ways in which social computing is harmful, and cyber bullying as one important form of online abuse and possible crime. Reading this book is an excellent start! Parents should not wait until their child is a victim or perpetrator of cyber bullying to start increasing their awareness about this vast social problem. Make it a point to learn from your kids who may be very happy to share their technological prowess! Become an expert in their online language, and continue to explore and research in order to develop a parental toolbox of information that may help guide the decision making of both parent and child.

There are many useful tips and suggestions now offered to parents for safe and appropriate use by children of computers and other types of IT devices. Nonprofit organizations, such as iSAFE, Inc., the National Center for Missing and Exploited Children (NCMEC), and WiredSafety.org are among numerous organizations that list tips for youth, parents, and educators in how to remain safe, secure, and ethical when online. The Family Online Safety Institute (fosi.org) is an International non-profit organization dedicated to promoting online education for many stakeholders ranging from government leaders to parents. Also, the mission of ikeepsafe.org is to give empowering online safety information to parents, educators, and policymakers. Some information provided by these organizations is specific to preventing cyber bullying. The signature NetSmartz program of NCMEC has online games for children to learn about cyber bullying. iSAFE.org has role-playing exercises for teens that cover various social computing scenarios.

WiredSafety.org has specific suggestions and guidance for all ages to prevent cyber bullying, as does cyberbullying.us. In addition, OnGuard Online represents a consortium of leading federal government agencies that provides numerous cyber crime prevention tips for home and business users, many of which are easily understood by middle and high school aged youth. We'll be talking about these resources and other online resources more later, all of which can be easily found online with a simple Web browser search. For now parents need to understand that even long lists of good suggestions will not provide complete protection for their family, nor alone will any combination of technological fixes such as wireless routers with built-in firewalls or Internet content filtering/blocking software.

## THE IMPORTANCE OF INFORMATION SECURITY AND FAMILY ACCEPTABLE USE POLICIES

Although we are consistently cautioning parents not to rely on technological solutions to prevent cyber bullying, in the end cyber bullying is a technology-enabled problem that requires some understanding of how data needs to be managed for safety and security purposes. The reason for this is threefold, and each has to do with cyber bullying.

First, information security, which is fundamental to safe computing, is like a chain: it's only as strong as its weakest human link. If a user of a device leaks their password, fails to update their system with security patches, or allows themselves to be manipulated, voluntarily give up personal information, *or is perceived to be vulnerable to other users,* they along with their network devices and data residing on their devices may become vulnerable to attack. Remember, bullies single out and target victims because they appear vulnerable, and because they may in fact be vulnerable in one or more ways, including social or technological ways. Youth who are computer savvy, in both the technological and social computing sense, are far less likely to fall for online bullying gimmicks such as those identified in prominent cases featured in Chapter 1.

Second as implied above, computers, other IT devices, and Internet safety primarily depends on human judgment along with technological prevention steps. If a user visits and interacts through unsecure Web sites (i.e., those for which the little yellow padlock symbol does not appear), or does so while using default passwords setup by device manufacturers, or without running antimalware software (to guard against viruses and spyware, etc.), or posts personal attack-style, embarrassing, or clumsy messages to social computing Web sites, they are just asking to be attacked by a computer criminal or online bully. Remember, many forms of computer abuse and cyber crime result from personal information being illicitly acquired about people and then used against them in some online scheme. Unfortunately, negative aspects of digital youth culture and the fickleness of friendships in primary and middle school means that people who are online friends today may prove to be preying strangers or enemies (e.g., cyber bullies) tomorrow! These are the realities and dynamics of fast-paced interactions and fundamental concepts of cyber bullying discussed earlier in the book.

Third, remember that computing and telecommunications technology is continually improving. This makes it inevitable that new ways to manipulate networks, devices, and data for illicit purposes will also get better and thus more problematic. This is the never ending cyber game of cat and mouse that we discussed in Chapter 3 in the theoretical context of "Technology-Enabled Crime, Policing and Security." Recall that the large point of the theory is that technology continually empowers people to commit abuse and crime in new and more sophisticated ways. The implication is that technology-enabled safety, security, and ethics is a lifestyle choice, just as deciding to be a defensive driver is. Accidents may still happen, but they are less likely and when they do likely to be less damaging if victims were driving defensively to begin with. This is something that all IT device users must embrace and practice daily while navigating cyberspace, as a matter of routine. Children must be taught this concept from the time they first begin using computers. Parents must model from *Day One* what responsible computing and telecommunications means.

Preventing cyber bullying also requires parents to learn as many safety tips as possible, from online resources such as those mentioned in the previous section. Doing so will enable parents to make adjustments that best fit a particular family, school, and bullying situation. Establishing rules and enforcing these are crucial. Researchers Sameer Hinduja and Justin W. Patchin have devised what they call a *Family Internet Use Contract* that specifies expectations for children and parents. It identifies basic responsibilities to help raise awareness about preventing cyber crime and respecting privacy, and it provides a place for youth and their parents to sign in agreement to what amounts to an acceptable use policy (AUP). It is similar to AUPs increasingly used by school systems, which sometimes require students and parents to sign. In effect, parents should consider devising an *AUP for Preventing Cyber Bullying,* though a one-pager or short document, even when signed by parents and youth, is hardly a substitute for active parenting to model and supervise responsible computing.

An AUP of sorts may provide an initial basis for further understanding and trust building over time. Such a document should specify in clear terms what families can and cannot do online, or while using cell phones and so forth. Family AUPs should also describe what family members can expect from one another for digital safety, security, and ethics including, but not limited to, cyber bullying and privacy issues. Expectations of appropriate behavior while using technology need to balance specificity with general concerns. After all, no list of rules or expectations can cover every conceivable cyber bullying situation, but certain things as indicated in this book should stand out in plain terms as examples of "shall and shall nots." Along with this, consequences for breaking rules should also be clear and consistently enforced. This does not mean parents should watch over the shoulder of their kids online activities. Rather, they should employ reasonable monitoring methods and when violations of the family AUP occur similar penalties should be imposed for similar violations.

Rules will vary depending on variables such as age level, history of problems, and maturity level of youth involved. Parents need to make the rules, preferably in consultation with their kids, but this too depends on their ages, history of problems, and maturity level. This book will help parents to understand core issues at stake and decide upon appropriate precautions in the form of rules. At the end of the day, it is the responsibility of parents to set the rules, enforce the rules, and to lead by example. Any violation of rules (or cyber laws) by parents will ultimately undermine their own legitimacy. Parents who are mean on the phone or in their e-mail messages can hardly expect their children to act differently. Illegal pirating of music, movies, or software by parents also sets a bad example. The same holds true for all areas of cyber abuse and offending.

Young individuals must learn that they do not own the Internet, nor for that matter the concept of social computing! There *are* legal and social boundaries even in cyberspace, which seemingly has no natural boundaries. Hence, *the rules* should set Internet time use limits and Web site content restrictions, if appropriate. Parents should also learn how to check Web traffic logs for computers setup to connect to the Internet through a router or wireless access point (which is always a good security precaution). If this is the case, parents should enable logging on the device control settings when installing the unit. Afterward they can periodically check all incoming and outbound Internet traffic via all devices connected to the home network.

Parents can also prohibit tampering with Internet browser histories of devices. However, savvy youth intent on deceiving parents can easily develop technology *work arounds* such as installing multiple instances or different browser software and hiding these on a hard drive. The use of filtering or tracking software can also assist in blocking access to undesirable Web sites, or in tracing what sites have been visited. Although simple history checks can be done by viewing history through the Internet browser, more comprehensive software programs exist that allow for greater control of the computer use of a child. For example, programs allow for restricting times including when the child can or cannot use the computer for purposes such as entertainment, to browse the Internet, or play games.

Programs also exist that allow parents to control online use, and thus can reduce exposure to inappropriate or harmful material. More specifically, this can be done by blocking inappropriate URLs, Web sites, or keywords. Conducting an online search on parental control and Internet filtering software can give parents information about software that will best match a particular need. However, some of these parental control settings may be so restrictive that youth may not be able to function online in ways appropriate for their age, social interactions, or required school work. As indicated elsewhere, parents need to be mindful of the technological abilities of our children today, and the very real possibility that they can beat or get around the program you are using, or simply go to a friend's house where there are no rules for technology use! Mobile computing has changed everything. Even taking away a child's cell phone will not necessarily prevent them *at any age* from acquiring another one for less than $10 at a discount store and establishing a short-term pre-paid cellular account to use in secret!

As mobile Web browsing via cell phone becomes more and more common, parents will need to better understand what they can do to protect their kids from online abuse of other kids using such methods, as well as prevent such abusive tactics by their own disobedient children. When thinking about monitoring, effective communication with tweens and teenagers is vital to continually build and preserve trust. When trust is not fully in place, parents may consider limiting the types of cell phones they allow youth to have (e.g., devices that are not capable of Web browsing, texting or e-mail). Still, for Web-equipped phones, there are some options that exist for parents to limit what their child can do with the phone. For example, Verizon Wireless recently added some new controls for parents to filter content based on a rating system that considers the age of the user. On the most restrictive setting, access to e-mail, instant messaging, chat groups, and social networking sites is completely blocked. This setting may be useful for a younger child who has a phone. A drawback is that the parental control settings do not work on all phones, especially older cell or smart phones.

Other companies such as T-Mobile USA, Sprint Nextel have Web browsing filters that can block inappropriate sites. If blocking content isn't enough, another software application offered by eAgency called RADAR, monitors incoming and outgoing calls, e-mails, text messages, and other content such as photos. With this software, parents can receive an e-mail or text message alert when their child uses the phone in any manner, they can receive a copy of the content exchanged, or they can log on to a Web site to check Internet activity. The software is currently limited to use on particular devices (e.g., the BlackBerry Pearl phone). In the future, as the technology improves, parents will have increased options for blocking and/or monitoring the Web activities of their children. Whatever technology-supported supervision methods are used, these should be supplemented with open conversations about what the parents are doing and why.

## The Destruction of Joy, Trust, and Hope

**"Effective Communication and Engagement between a Divorced Father and His 12-Year-Old Son"**

Divorced father making an effort to learn about IT:

"My wife and divorced three years ago, and I get to see my son two weekends a month and sometimes during the week. He's really into the digital stuff. He's got a cell phone and iPod that he listens to tunes on, and he always seems to texting (the father motions with his thumbs as if using a BlackBerry). I'm not into technology, other than my cell phone, which I use all the time for working out in the field. Sometimes my boy comes along with me to job sites when I assess and bid on work to be done by the company. Whenever I can, I try to relate to him on his terms, which usually has something to do with technology. Recently I asked him about the types of songs he listens to . . . Rap mostly, I hate it. The words are foul. I introduced him to jazz and even took him to a jazz concert where the band did some jamming. He liked that, and now we listen to jazz (and some rap) using his iPod, which I connect to the speaker system in my company truck.

We also started texting a little, and I told him that if I ever catch him using foul language in his messages, or downloading porn, that will be the end of that! I set the rules man, and I lay down the law. But kids are kids and bound to screw up at some point. I found out from one of his friends that he did something online that he wasn't suppose to. I didn't tell him how I knew, and I didn't go into specifics because I did not want him to think I was going to his friends to spy. But he got the message and now walks a straight line. I keep on eye him though, best I can. These days, you have to."

## Effective Supervision and Communication

While the suggestion of placing computers in a common area of the home should be part of the established rules, portable electronic devices, and mobile computing has made this long-emphasized rule a worthwhile but inadequate one that depends on the level of trust afforded to and demonstrated by youth. Children may be experiencing cyber bullying as offenders, witnesses, or victims from within a family room while a parent sits nearby. Effective supervision requires active monitoring, communication, and engagement with children in their online activities, within reason. For example, learning to play online games as foes against or team members with one's children is an excellent strategy that some parents are doing. Many parents find they enjoy online gaming themselves and that gaming creates new opportunities to bond with their children at all ages. Other ways to positively and proactively communicate through computing activities, rather than talking to kids provides entirely new ways to role model and practice what we preach as parents. Sure, using filters and blocking software can certainly help, but as indicated above and akin to the "computer in a public room strategy" it also is not a satisfactory stand-alone solution.

Active communication through engagement with kids on their social computer terms implies the need to be increasingly sensitive to youth privacy needs and rights as they age. Adequate supervision versus their need and right to privacy may at times pose particularly challenging situations and decisions for parents. Trust built over months and years of successful computing experiences can ease difficulties in this area. However, just as with noncyber activities, youth who violate rules and trust will need sufficient "cyber out time" to reflect on and change inappropriate behaviors, with extra careful monitoring, guidance, and support from parents. The same principle holds true for victims of cyber bullying, who with parental involvement may need their time, activities, and interactions online restructured for well-being rather than disciplinary reasons.

When parents are actively involved with all aspects of their child's life, it is much easier to make *informed decisions* about supervision based on a totality of circumstances: age, level of trust, maturity, technological savvy, dependence on computing rather than in-person encounters for social networking, and so on. A word of caution: when engaging youth on their terms be careful not to come on too strong or as the proverbial "nosey parent" or as an online snoop as these approaches can drive kids into technological hiding! Instead, adopt and practice the following: (1) Educate yourself about online activities routinely engaged in by youth so you don't fall (further) behind the technological times, (2) determine what your children do online, (3) establish computing rules inclusive of in-home and mobile activities, (4) find mutually acceptable ways to engage youth as a way to monitor while role modeling, and (5) trust but verify out of love and respect. That's it, in a nutshell!

If however rules for computing are overly strict and unreasonably punitive, youth may not only hide their online and physical activities from you, they may also defy you by acting out with stern independence. Being overly rigid can also lead to an unintended consequence of closing off communications and making it difficult to reestablish or build upon trusting relationships. Remember, kids may endure repeated victimization and cyber bullying if they fear that their access to the Net or use of IT devices will be taken away or restricted. Also, keep in mind the trends in technology, and that more and more children will have access to the Internet via cell phones and PDAs as this is now expected by peers and everyone else in our increasingly connected world.

Lastly, parents cannot rely on schools alone to protect kids online from inappropriate content, including that which involves cyber bullying, or trying to block youth from every inappropriate site in order to prevent exposure to cyber bullying is simply not enough. Parents need to take an active role in teaching acceptable and ethical behavior while online.

## ETHICS AND EDUCATION THROUGH POSITIVE ROLE MODELING

So how do you teach acceptable behavior and ethical behavior in general and online? A detailed answer to this question is beyond the scope of this book, but research demonstrates that students learn how to behave responsibly when instruction is "salted" across formal curriculum instruction, exemplified with real life and pertinent examples, and reinforced by family values and active parenting. Remember that the teen brain is still developing, so have those conversations with them about the moral issues associated with cyber bullying, with hate speech, with exposure to violence or other controversial content, about how to react when they see this type of content, and this all needs to be undertaken with care. Most theories on the development of moral behavior presume that very young children are substantially influenced if not controlled by the actions of others. This includes primary caregivers such as parents, schools, and also churches. Societal, community, organizational, and family values set the tone and behavioral norms for children, tweens, and teens. This can happen through direct teaching and instruction, appropriate supervision, correction, rewards, and punishment.[9] All of these function interactively and over time as part of culture building.

As children develop, two of the most important aspects of establishing moral behavior include what are known as *internalization* and *modeling*. As children develop they begin internalizing the moral rules and values of authority figures such as parents and teachers who have guided them. Over time they imitate respected adults, peers, and other people in their lives who they hold in esteem.[10] This is also known by some researchers as scripting.[11] Upon misbehaving, if children are given clear and understandable reasons, often emphasizing the impact of their actions on others, they are more likely to internalize and imitate societal expectations for ethical, moral, and law-abiding behaviors. This holds true when faced with the ultimate test, which is continuing to align behaviors with morals *even when not being watched*. This is significant when considering behaviors while using IT devices, where increasingly it is the case that no one is watching, a condition that grows as youth age and come to expect and hopefully deserve less supervision and more privacy.

Some ways to help children internalize appropriate behavior when using technology includes teaching kids how their actions can be even more emotionally harmful when done online. Absent the visual cues or body language, the meaning and tone of online communication can be hard to convey and to interpret. Serious teaching and discussion should occur on the topic of disinhibition (see Chapter 2), and that although they may be typing words into a keyboard in front of a screen, the receiver of the message is a real person with real feelings. Feelings by message receivers are heightened during teen years, when socialization and fitting in are paramount, and when sensitivity about how one is perceived by others is heightened. However, for the sender, a decreased sense of self-awareness combined with establishing independence means decreased concern for how they are perceived or judged by others. A good general suggestion is to evaluate: "Would you say face-to-face to others what you are about to type or post online? If this answer is no, teach kids not to! Our message to kids should be to "think, and think again, before you send." Kids must be taught to use their own filters based on expected standards and established rules to effectively self-monitor and police their behaviors. In short, they need to consider how the message could be perceived by others.

Another way to possibly help in the internalization process regarding cyber bullying is to seize a teachable moment and use the technology to do so. Conduct a search of cyber bullying videos online, or visit YouTube to perform of search of cyber bullying videos. Look for a video that may have an emotional impact on youth and help your own kids to learn how cyber bullying has impacted real people. Although some cases are extreme and have lead to suicides or other forms of violence, other cases have caused emotional scarring on a number of different levels, as well as problems for family members, friends, and other people in schools or communities. Although videos on cyber bullying can portray how damaging cyber bullying can be, it is up to parents and individual users to decide what is acceptable and appropriate based on established principles of conduct, rules, and laws.

Returning to influence and modeling, these concepts when not established to promote responsible computing can to the contrary result in inspiring and reinforcing irresponsible and aggressive behaviors that can extend in the cyber world. Recent research has shown that moral approval of bullying, a perceived school climate tolerating bullying, and peer support for aggressive behaviors are all predictors for someone becoming a bully.[12] As has been indicated, family violence, deficient school environments, poor problem solving, and associating with violent groups (of other kids) have been shown to influence bullying. As also discussed earlier, negative modeling occurs through mass media such as television, radio, movies/videos, electronic gaming, and various other forms of social computing. Perhaps these media influence some youth to act aggressively toward other youth, and some researchers believe the connection is undeniable.[13] For all these reasons, parents must first teach their kids that bullying and cyber bullying are wrong! Next, parents must be mindful of the influences that both schools and peers can have on bullying and cyber bullying attitudes. Finally, parents need to remember that peers are very influential while online friending is the new reality of social computing in which mean messaging can become viral and spread through rapid-fire texting.

Unfortunately, some parents fail to educate themselves and proactively engage in influencing and role modeling appropriate behaviors for their children. They fail to do so for various reasons, including rationalizing bullying, making excuses for their children, disbelieving *their* children could be involved, and even fear induced by a bullying spouse who creates negative role modeling for children. One mother from Baton Rouge, Louisiana for example, commented about her 13-year-old son being a cyber bully: "Yes, I know about cyber bullying. Cops have been at the house different times. I just tell the police he is only having fun and doesn't mean to hurt anyone. I know however, my kid was born a bully. It's either them or us that gets bullied . . . He has a mean streak in him just like his father. If he doesn't bully and take out his anger on other kids then we get it here at home. What's the big deal, anyway? It's only words on the chat rooms and blogs—better my kid express himself and take out his anger that way than to make matters worse around the house." Despite such difficulties, parents must take a stand, or else who will?

## BE ON THE LOOKOUT FOR WARNING SIGNS

Another prevention or early intervention strategy is to be mindful of potential indicators on victimization. If a parent is involved in the life of the child, then they should be observant for possible warning signs caused by cyber bullying. Unlike certain forms of physical bullying in which injuries may be visible, victims of cyber bullying may present warning signs in more subtle ways consistent with victims of nonphysical traditional bullying. For example, they may exhibit emotional distress such as anger, show fear, or feel or become depressed. Many youth are careful not too show the emotions around parents. After all, tolerating the rough and tumble aspects of digital youth culture is expected of online participants. Their distress may be displayed immediately after using a computer or another IT device, but not necessarily. Parents should be alert for suspicious activity by their child upon seeing the parent, such as quickly attempting to close out of programs or discontinue a particular online activity. Quickly closing a computer screen or flipping a cell phone cover shut is not a good sign: youth who do so are often doing or experiencing something inappropriate.

Other possible indicators could be the avoidance of friends or former friends, or an increasing or sudden reluctance to use technology such as the computer. Further warning signs could be school related such as fear of going to school or decreased academic performance. A victim of cyber bullying may also be disciplined more often by the school for other reasons including weapon carrying, or become involved in traditional bullying because of what they are experiencing online. Other changes in behavior, including negative comments about online activities, or communicating about revenge, violence, or suicide must be *genuinely listened to* and considered serious warning signs. Overall, it is important for parents to know their child, and to attempt first to understand why it is that their child is behaving in certain ways. Discerning between a real online problem versus those attributable to growing pains of the physical and emotional variety is essential. Each of the potential warnings signs could indicate cyber bullying victimization, but could also be signs of some other forms of trouble. Either way, parents are usually best positioned to recognize warning signs and intervene in appropriate ways.

## THE DESTRUCTION OF JOY, TRUST, AND HOPE

### "My Baby Is Gone! The Disturbing Story of Another Victim of Suicide"

Reported by mother in despair:

After my daughter committed suicide, my so-called friends, acquaintances, co-workers and neighbors sent me their condolences along with stupid statements that "many teenagers are committing suicide from depression these days." They would say in a matter of fact tone that my daughter "must have been depressed" and then follow with the question: "How long had she been depressed?" My daughter never suffered from depression until she began to hang around certain girls who I never liked nor trusted. My daughter brought over a new friend from school. She reminded me of someone, but I couldn't put my finger on it.

One day I was at a parent-teacher conference for my daughter. I looked across the room and I saw a woman, who years earlier I had known as a girl and passionately hated in high school. This woman and I were rivals throughout our school years. She especially hated me when the guy that she was in love with broke up with her and started dating me. I didn't go out with him because I liked him; I went out with him because I hated her. Later when I found out that my daughter and her daughter were best friends, I could have died!

I didn't want to go into detail, but I told my daughter to be very careful, because her best friend's mother had always been a big manipulator. She could convince her worse enemies that they were her best friends. But my daughter wouldn't listen. After my daughter entered 9th grade I began to notice something disturbing. Whenever my daughter made a new friend, my ex-rival's daughter would somehow lure him or her away. Eventually the new friend would have nothing to do with my daughter.

My daughter started going with this really nice, respected guy. I really liked him. It was probably the first friend she had that I really liked. Her so-called best friend tried to lure him away from my daughter, but this time it wasn't working. The more my daughter's boyfriend resisted, the more my ex-rival's daughter persisted. This was the first time that she wasn't winning, and she didn't like it . . . About two years later, my daughter's boyfriend gave her a pre-engagement ring. The agreement was they would both go to college and after college they would get formally engaged and then married.

After this became known *my ex-rival* put up a Web site stating that my daughter was going to break up with her boyfriend and that she was sorry, but that's life. She stated that their lovemaking was unbelievable and he loved that fact that she is bisexual. Some other guys went into the chat room and were saying what a sap her boyfriend was . . . They asked, "How could he be so stupid?"

His mother was shown the site by my ex-rival. She said that she was only showing her because she thought a lot of her son. The mother called my daughter and told her that if her son had anything to do with her again, he would be disowned and they would not pay for his college. My daughter asked her what the problem was and she just replied "as if you didn't know." My daughter got an e-mail from her boyfriend saying that they were finished, and by the time that he got done with her, she wouldn't have a guy within 10 feet of her. She would never have a boyfriend, much less a husband and kids, which she always wanted.

Toward the end of my daughter's life, people were saying to her online, "Why don't you just end it all? I bet you don't have the guts." "Do society a favor!" My daughter's last words were "I'll show you! I do have the guts!" The autopsy showed that my daughter took her life with a bottle of pills.

I have been to the school, the police and to lawyers, and they all ask me, "Where's the proof?" I have the proof. The proof is I saw my daughter's spirit slowly get eaten up alive. Every time she went to the chat room it was like a sword going through her chest. She started getting migraines and night terrors. This never happened before the Web site started.

One night, about six months after my baby died, in a drunken stupor, my ex-rival admitted to a few people that she finally got even with me. "It might have taken a lot of years, but I did it. I got the ultimate revenge." One of my friends told me about my rival's confession and there were several witnesses. I immediately went to the police. They said that they wanted to talk to the witnesses. I called everyone what was present who heard the confession, and they all changed their story. "Well, we were drinking too, and maybe we heard it wrong or she was only joking." One of my friends said, "Listen, nobody wants to get involved. Your daughter is dead, and there's no bringing her back. Let it go. After all, if she did it to your kid, what's preventing her from doing it to ours? Our kids already get more than enough bullying, online and off-line."

I'm not letting this go. That low-life took my baby's life. She didn't commit suicide, they drove her to her death. She was never, never, never—and I mean never—depressed until my ex-rival started putting all the crap on the Internet—imposing my daughter's face on a nude centerfold and pretending that it was a guy that she had been to bed with and had two-somes and three-somes with. So, I'm on my own. I guarantee that my daughter didn't die in vain. I may end up behind bars, but I don't care. Someone is going to pay for this. I will make sure of that.

# Emerging Best Practices for Schools

*Parents who are concerned have a tendency to block their children from using the computers, rather than teaching them how to do so correctly and then supervising more consistently. They expect that to happen in school alone.*

—*A school principal*

In Chapter 6 we reviewed legal issues and laws bearing on cyber bullying. A major implication from that discussion is the reality that cyber bullying does not neatly come under the responsibility or jurisdiction of one element of society such as schools, law enforcement, or parents. Addressing cyber bullying must be a shared responsibility with each stakeholder including parents, adolescents, schools, police, and the overall community having some degree of ownership. However, given the amount of time youth spend in schools and the reality that much bullying begins within or spills over into school environments regardless of being traditional physical and/or cyber in nature, schools have a special, increasing role and responsibility to be on the lookout for bullying and to intervene when necessary. Further, school officials as educational leaders within communities should assume responsibility for raising parental awareness about the nature and extent of cyber bullying their school districts face, and thereby convey a sense of urgency to close the digital divide between adults and youth. Unfortunately, sound and best practices for addressing cyber bullying through education about information security, Internet safety, and cyber ethics have yet to be widely established. For this reason we advocate that school officials do as much as possible to protect students based on what we do know, and continue to learn. Rather than offering a specific, one-size-fits-all guide to what can or should be done to address cyber bullying, this chapter provides a framework for cyber bullying intervention, prevention, and education. An ongoing dialogue and discussion about what can work for different schools in different communities must take place.

## ADULT RESPONSES TO BULLYING

An issue pertaining to bullying and cyber bullying involves the response by people who observe or become aware of it. As stated earlier, youth bystanders who observe bullying often do not take action to stop bullying. Given the reluctance of many children to intervene in bullying, teachers and administrators play a critical role in prevention and intervention. However, adults often overestimate their ability to identify and intervene in bullying situations. Research findings, supported by additional observational studies, suggest that teachers may be unaware of the bullying that occurs around them.[1] Also of note is that children may question the commitment of teachers and administrators in stopping bullying. For example, another study involving 196 9th grade students showed that only 35 percent believed their teachers were interested in stopping bullying, as opposed to only 25 percent who believed administrators were interested in stopping bullying.[2]

Perhaps these student beliefs also relate to student reticence to report cyber bullying for fear of losing friends, being labeled a snitch, or having their computer and cell phone privileges taken away. Recall the Fight Crime study (Chapter 4) that showed that only 9 percent of 12- to 17-year-olds who had been cyber bullied told a teacher about it![3] How can teachers and other school staff members be held responsible for bullying that is not reported to them? Further, when considering covert aspects of online bullying, levels of awareness and confidence among teachers and administrators in dealing with cyber bullying are undoubtedly even lower. Indeed, other researchers have found that few teachers and administrators are aware that students are harassed through electronic communications.[4] This makes a lot of sense as cyber bullying is unseen unless school officials go looking for it on the Internet. Lacking adult education, staff development, and training about cyber bullying perpetuates unseen aspects of the problem—off campus, after school hours, out of sight, out of mind! These and other factors combine to undermine confidence of youth in the abilities of schools to support them when they are bullied, and undermine the ability of genuinely caring teachers and school officials to take individual and collective action on a building or districtwide basis, according to the nature and extent of actual, potential, or perceived bullying problems.

## TEACHER ATTITUDES TOWARD BULLYING

Teacher and administrator attitudes about cyber bullying are rarely researched. Our review of literature indicates that whole-school approaches for preventing bullying can be more effective than ad hoc practices of individual teachers or administrators. Getting educators invested in the effort is key. One study was conducted that explored how teachers' attitudes shape school climate, and can therefore influence bullying.[5] The researchers surveyed 797 teachers and paraprofessionals from 18 Wisconsin primary and secondary schools. Results indicated that 57 percent of respondents felt that students would not intervene if they saw another student being bullied. On the other hand, 93 percent reported that adults would stop verbal bullying if they witnessed it, with 65 percent reporting that the staff has received training on how to intervene.

Bullying pioneer researcher Dan Olweus noted in his research the importance of the attitudes and behaviors of school personnel in preventing and controlling bullying.[6] He also emphasized that comprehensive intervention programs should establish acceptable behaviors for students, allow for relationship development between teachers and students, and increase cultural sensitivity and diversity acceptance by faculty. The research suggests that in order for school personnel to be successful in combating bullying, a culture of respect must be fostered.[7] Other researchers discussed the importance of leadership of the school principal in supporting the reduction of bullying behavior.[8] Further, they emphasized that principals must (1) understand the seriousness of bullying, (2) provide clear definitions and direction to faculty and staff, and (3) enforce building and district policies that outline acceptable conduct. However, teachers do not always feel the support of administration, which can lead to a sense of hopelessness, as indicated from interviews with two teachers (7th and 8th grade) from upstate New York: "We both are considering thinking of career changes. We have received threats when trying to stop cyber bullies, and it has not been taken seriously by administration. We have tried to apply justice, and the cyber bullies turn around and threaten us as teachers."

Despite the importance of their role in establishing climate and addressing violence, research prior to our book had not sought the view and experience perceptions of building-level school administrators about online bullying. However, a recent doctoral dissertation research survey was administered to 107 school building administrators (principals and assistant principals) who oversee all grade levels in a large metropolitan county located in western New York State.[9] The mean number of students from each of the schools of building administrators surveyed was 828 students. Results of the survey indicated several important findings:

- Of the administrators, 74 percent reported that cyber bullying among their students occurred more often outside of school, but is still an issue in our school. This supports the notion that although cyber bullying does take place outside of school, administrators believe that it is an issue that the school has a role in addressing.

- Of the administrators, 57 percent reported that cyber bullying among their students is increasing, and 58 percent reported that the reporting by student victims of cyber bullying is increasing. Therefore, the majority of the school building leaders reported that the schools are increasingly hearing about incidents of cyber bullying by student victims.
- More than half (54%) of the administrators reported that the reporting by student bystanders is *not* increasing in their building. This can be problematic given the importance of empowering bystanders to take action to assist in instances of cyber bullying victimization.[10]

## THEORETICAL FRAMEWORK: EFFECTIVENESS OF PREVENTION PROGRAMS

There is general agreement that comprehensive social-ecological (i.e., whole school) approaches are necessary to reduce all forms of aggression in schools.[11] This necessarily involves a coordinated effort at a number of levels including: (1) individual, (2) classroom, (3) school, and (4) community.[12] A systematic review of school-based interventions to prevent bullying reveals that interventions that involve multiple disciplines were more effective in reducing bullying.[13] Fully 70 percent of studies evaluated found that whole-school approaches were more effective in decreasing bullying. Increased social work support and mentoring for *at-risk* students were also effective in reducing bullying. However, prevention programs that focus exclusively on bullies and victims can be ineffective, as they fail to take into account the role that bystanders play in the bullying dynamic.[14] Similarly, traditional bullying prevention programs may be ineffective for cyber bullying, given its sometimes anonymous nature, and that it often occurs off school grounds.[15] Although more research is needed to verify this, it still remains important to understand the role that schools can have in prevention and intervention of cyber bullying.

### PREVALENCE OF CYBER BULLYING IN SCHOOLS

Preliminary research seems to indicate that cyber bullying most often takes place outside of school, either at home or at a friend's house. But does this mean that the school has a lessoned responsibility for dealing with the issue? As we have stated, parents often look to schools to assist with problems related to cyber bullying, but schools have very limited authority to discipline students for off-campus conduct. Parents of victims would seemingly support the rights of schools to discipline for off-campus cyber bullying, while parents of perpetrators have sued schools for doing the same. On a similar note, parents are increasingly suing schools for not adequately protecting their children. Given the connections between cyber bullying and traditional school bullying, it is evident that cyber bullying can be closely related to the school. The survey results of school administrators support this given that three out of four administrators reported that cyber bullying is an issue in school, despite taking place more often off school grounds.

In the same survey, one principal commented: "Cyber bullying outside of the building greatly affects the inside of our building. School has made efforts to eliminate websites that may contribute to cyber bullying. However, it is difficult to control cell phones in the building. Students may be able to send messages when adults are not around or in class. We need to address this problem because it is going to increase. Too many students are communicating by phone and computer."[16]

Cyber bullying that occurs off campus often involves students that attend the school, and some evidence suggests that off-campus cyber bullying can spillover into the school. We also believe in-person or online bullying can begin in school and continue after school hours and off school grounds. Students often come to school very agitated and upset about cyber bullying that happened the night before, which can become a different problem when it leads to a face-to-face confrontation. This helps to explain research that shows that cyber bullies are often traditional school bullies, and cyber bullying victims are often traditional bullying victims, and sometimes even traditional school bullies themselves. In addition, about one in three victims of bullying report that its effects bother them at school regardless of when and where it happens.[17]

Thus, cyber bullying victimization is often related to school behavior problems such as skipping school or classes or carrying a weapon. Schools have a key role in addressing the issue of cyber bullying: Schools must educate to inform, create policies to establish limits, organize to prevent, monitor to intervene, and take swift and prompt actions against violators. After all, schools exist to promote academic learning, and to promote social, emotional, and ethical education. Schools also have a responsibility to produce students who will become respectful, engaged, responsible members of society. Therefore, schools should be tackling the issue of cyber bullying from frameworks that focus on prevention, intervention, and education. But they cannot and should not do this alone.

## PREVENTION STRATEGIES FOR SCHOOLS

Although not all schools are mandated to develop policies that specifically address cyber bullying, schools are increasingly doing so. Policies can be updated to include cyber bullying in an existing school bullying policy, or in a technology policy such as an acceptable use policy (AUP). Cyber bullying can also be specifically included in a school district's Code of Conduct, or included as a Board Policy. The New York State School Board Association provides guidelines for developing a policy framework that includes answering the following questions:

1. What is the current environment in your district's schools with regard to issues of bullying, cyber bullying, and harassment?
2. What are your policy needs and expectations?
3. How does this topic tie into your district's mission and goals?
4. What policies do you currently have that address these topics?
5. What is the focus of your current policies?
6. What policies do you need to develop and/or review?
7. What additional information do you need before developing policies on this topic?
8. How should this policy be communicated?
9. How does the Board and administration ensure that this policy remains current and effective?

The New York State School Board Association provides a sample policy on harassment and bullying that includes a reference to electronic communication. The policy should clearly state how students are expected to behave with regard to cyber bullying, and may include a statement that students have the right to report all types of bullying without fear of reprisal. In Minnesota, a law signed in 2007 required school boards to adopt a written policy prohibiting bullying and also cyber bullying. As a result, one district developed a policy that states: "The misuse of technology including, but not limited to teasing, intimidating, defaming, threatening, or terrorizing . . . by sending or posting e-mail messages, instant messages, text messages, digital pictures or images, or Web site postings, including blogs, also may constitute an act of bullying regardless of whether such acts are committed on or off school district property and/or with or without the use of school district resources." Consequences for violating the policy can range from a warning to suspension or expulsion.

Another school district in New York proposed some additions to its code of conduct that states: "Students may be subject to disciplinary action, up to and including suspension from school, when they engage in cyber bullying. Examples of cyber bullying include, but are not limited to: Bullying and/or harassment of a person or persons through electronic/digital means/devices such as cell phones, text messaging, online forums, online blogs or web logs, websites, and/or other online, digital, or electronic social networking means, such that the bullying or harassment to one or more others negatively impacts or endangers the personal behaviors, practices, outlooks, emotional wellbeing, in-school performance of activities, etc. of those persons and/or others within, on, or proximate to school premises."

According to one principal interviewed for the book, "Since our school district adopted a code of conduct last summer with a strict policy against students having electronic devices visible during the school day, the number of incidents has significantly declined. The first incident, there is parent communication regarding the rule, a contract is signed, the parent picks up the phone and the student has a detention. After the first warning, the consequences include in-school suspension or Saturday detentions. The third offense could result in out-of-school suspension and even a hearing."[18] However, in the larger survey of school administrators, while 76 percent of building administrators reported that their school had a board policy against bullying, only 36 percent reported that the policy included cyber bullying and about 45 percent were unsure if a board policy included cyber bullying. What does that say about the importance given to cyber bullying, and about knowing specifically what behaviors are addressed in school behavior policies once formulated?

We assert that it is important to have a policy that addresses bullying and that includes specific aspects of online bullying. Such policies should be developed in collaboration with parent, teacher, and student organizations. They should also be designed and periodically reviewed to comply with existing state and federal case law rulings applicable to bullying and cyber bullying situations.

## POLICIES BANNING TECHNOLOGY

Believe it or not, cell phones now carried by a majority of youth are not the first electronic device to give schools problems. Does anyone remember pagers? In the late 1990s, pagers were considered a major nuisance in many school districts and required school officials to figure out what to do about it. Today, many schools are implementing policies that outright ban the possession of technology such as PDAs and cell phones. In Milwaukee, Wisconsin, the school system banned cell phones in January 2007 after students used them to ask for reinforcements to a large fight. Further, individual school districts in New York State have also banned cell phones on school grounds. The issue of banning cell phones has been hotly debated and centers on the question of whether they are a nuisance or a valuable safety net. School staff may view cell phones as a significant distraction, a means to cheat via text messaging, or a tool for cyber bullying. However, parents often take comfort knowing they can communicate with their child in the event of an emergency.

Cell phones have been alleged to cause disruptions in emergency response situations due to large numbers of calls made to parents, who end up rushing to a scene and causing more problems. Considering the number of students who own cell phones, the outright banning of possessing them appears extreme and unenforceable. A more reasonable course of action would be setting restrictions on when and where cell phones can be used during school hours on school grounds. On computers, schools have also banned access to certain social networking sites but new questions are raised with increasing wireless access, and through the increase in "do-it-all" cell phones that can connect to the Web. Overall, schools will continue to wrestle with whether to ban the technology or to encourage its use. The technology can serve many useful educational, social, and safety-related purposes, so the answer probably lies in the middle with the placement of reasonable controls for appropriate use. As one school principal explains:

Banning cell phones and other devices is an easy "band-aid" approach, but I feel that schools should find ways to embrace technology responsibly. By bringing students together, and allowing them to use the devices they use outside of school, we will empower them to use these devices more responsibly. Schools can then have students using their devices in academic ways and they may be less likely to use the devices for cyber bullying . . .[19]

Text messaging via cell phone also appears to be causing disruptions on a larger scale as some schools have experienced widespread absenteeism due to text messages being sent by students to warn each other. According to a *USA Today* story, over two-thirds of students in two Maury County, Tennessee high schools missed school on April 21, 2008 after word of threats circulated via text messages after the funeral of two murdered youths.[20] Also, about one-third of students at George Rogers Clark High School in Winchester, Kentucky left school early in April 2008 after allegations were spread via text messages that a student would be bringing a gun to school. Further, almost a quarter of students at Tokay High School in Lodi, California did not attend school in April 2008 after text messages were sent that involved warnings of a gang shooting. At New Smyrna Beach High School in Florida, about two-thirds of students were absent after a threatening message that was found on a bathroom wall was circulated by students to each other via text messages. Given the large numbers of students with cell phones and exponential rumor-spreading capabilities, schools will likely continue to have to deal with instantaneous communication that could in fact be false and cause unnecessary panic. In the case of the Florida High School, the threatening message written on the bathroom wall turned out to be an empty threat made by a bored student.

## ACCEPTABLE USE POLICIES

Schools must have a comprehensive acceptable use policy (AUP) that students and parents must read and sign prior to students using technology at school. The policy should provide clear guidelines for appropriate use of technology, and hold those who violate the provisions of the policy accountable. However, the policy cannot be administered in isolation; rather it should be part of cyber safety and ethics instruction that will be reviewed shortly. Although the current mission of schools focuses on academic performance and results, this type of instruction—along with violence prevention in general—must be included on the to-do list of all schools. Acceptable use policies should also incorporate notification to parents about what is expected of students when it comes to using school computer resources as well as personally owned IT devices on school grounds, while engaged in school requirements regardless of physical location (e.g., doing homework assignments from a home computer), and at school-sponsored events (e.g., off-campus athletic events or student club activities that involve social networking via school or personally owned IT systems and devices). Many good examples of acceptable use policies are easily researched online through Web sites such as Cybercrime.gov, and through professional organizations such as iSAFE (www.isafe.org). Also, the Virginia Department of Education provides examples of Acceptable Use Policies for educational institutions, and includes specific guidelines and recommendations about what the policies should contain. This information can be accessed at http://www.doe.virginia.gov/go/VDOE/Technology/AUP/home.sthml.

## INCORPORATING CYBER BULLYING INTO EXISTING BULLYING PREVENTION EFFORTS

As previously stated, comprehensive social-ecological, or whole school, approaches appear to be effective in reducing bullying aggression in schools. It makes sense to include cyber bullying in these systemic efforts while recognizing the differences that exist between cyber bullying and traditional bullying. The Health Resources and Services Administration (HRSA) listed 10 "Best Practices" in bullying prevention and intervention:[21]

1. Focus on the school environment
2. Assess bullying at your school
3. Garner staff and parent support for bullying prevention
4. Form a group to coordinate the school's bullying prevention activities
5. Train school staff in bullying prevention
6. Establish and enforce school rules and policies related to bullying
7. Increase adult supervision in places where bullying occurs
8. Focus some class time on bullying prevention
9. Intervene consistently and appropriately in bullying situations
10. Continue these efforts over time

If schools are implementing these practices, then cyber bullying can be incorporated into the existing efforts. In schools, one of the most important of the best practices is the garnering of staff support, which should begin with the recognition that cyber bullying has become a considerable problem. Although there has been an increased awareness that cyber bullying is a problem, the awareness does not reflect a deeper understanding of the issue that is grounded in research. Therefore, cyber bullying should be considered an organizational development issue with a main goal of closing the awareness gap that exists among adults and students. An important first step in order to close the gap is to conduct an assessment of cyber bullying among students at a school. The assessment should also include questions about specific cyber offending behaviors, how and where it happens, and whether adults were told or otherwise made aware of the problem.

Educators and parents are increasingly dealing with the complex issue of cyber bullying. However, they have difficulty intervening due to the lack of knowledge of what cyber bullying is, and what can be done to address it. This can be remedied, at least in part, by training, training, and more training. In a recent survey of school administrators, 52 percent of school building administrators reported agreeing that they have the required skills and knowledge to intervene in cases of cyber bullying. Of the administrators, 10 percent reported strongly agreeing that they have the required skills and knowledge to intervene in cases of cyber bullying. However, only 40 percent of the school building administrators reported that they received training. When asked to rank a number of preventative measures to address cyber bullying, school administrators ranked training as the top four measures! They were ranked in the following order:

1. Training for school staff
2. Training for administrators
3. Training for students
4. Training for parents

However, when asked about whether training was occurring in their school building, just 21 percent of the administrators indicated that awareness training on cyber bullying has been conducted for administrators. Similarly, 30 percent reported that cyber bullying awareness training was conducted in their building for faculty and staff, 24 percent for parents, 25 percent for students, and just 7 percent for school board members.[22]

Adults are often unaware of how and what students are communicating while online. In addition, adults are less familiar than students with how the technology works and the language that is used. This is made worse by the lack of policies and procedures in school districts related to the intervention and prevention of cyber bullying. Therefore, the organizational development strategy could be a public relations plan with the primary focus on improving the level of awareness of the problem, which includes a training component for all staff. Another desired result is to obtain staff buy-in by creating a sense of ownership of the problem. Once the staff takes ownership, they will be more motivated to be a part of the comprehensive prevention effort. The plan will also encourage and promote a higher level of understanding based on cumulative knowledge and research. The overall objective is to change the social climate of the school to one that promotes respect and responsibility.

## SAMPLE ACTION STEPS FOR A CYBER BULLYING PUBLIC RELATIONS CAMPAIGN

Armistead and Jackson describe public relations as "building relationships that change attitudes to bring about desired behaviors." Further, Jernstedt notes that in public relations, it is necessary to tap into the emotion, encourage understanding, and create a sense of advocacy.[23] The public relations plan should apply these concepts to change school staff attitudes about cyber bullying. The plan should be guided under the leadership of the district bullying prevention committee, and can be accomplished by using four action steps. The first action step is to raise the level of awareness of cyber bullying. This can be accomplished through a mass communication effort including e-mails to all staff, an informative article in the district newsletter, and through summaries and links on the district Web site.

A program action message should contain the goals and desired results of the plan, and should reflect the values and mission of the district. The effort should also tie into the district bullying prevention efforts if they are already underway in the school. The second action step should be to develop interest and ownership of the problem of cyber bullying. This can be accomplished by demonstrating the importance and relevance of cyber bullying to all staff members. The message will highlight the need to take action to address the negative impact that cyber bullying has on students. Mass communication can again be used to deliver the message, and can be supplemented by a detailed brochure and student-designed posters emphasizing the cyber bullying component of the bullying prevention initiative.

The third action step should be to launch the cyber bullying campaign with a "kick-off" event for staff at the beginning of the school year. The event can include a keynote speaker with expertise in the field of cyber bullying that will assist in raising awareness and developing interest. Staff should be educated on the definition of cyber bullying and the district bullying policies that explain duties, responsibilities, and expectations related to prevention and intervention. The fourth action step should be a follow-up training session for all staff on how to intervene consistently when cyber bullying is observed or suspected. Since the topic of cyber bullying has not been well researched, leadership by the bullying prevention committee must be exercised to stay abreast of current research and best practice. Staff will then be provided with up-to-date intervention strategies that are evidence based.

Overall, the process for engaging the target audience will be geared toward achieving the objective of obtaining staff buy-in for the overall plan. The level of staff engagement will increase as each action step is systematically rolled out during the school year. The process will focus on two crucial aspects of cyber bullying that have been academically researched, namely prevalence and impact. Staff will be motivated to take action with the enhanced understanding that cyber bullying is increasing among our youth, and may cause psychological, social, academic, and physical problems.[24] The staff will also be engaged as they discover the connection of this effort to the mission, vision, belief statement, and wellness policy of the organization.

By understanding that the plan is a leadership priority, staff will be further motivated to keep our students free from harm so that they may reach their fullest potential. Probably the most significant component of the overall intervention effort is the need for a leader, or champion, to step forward and drive the efforts. This could be the superintendent, principal, mental health worker, school safety and security representative, or teacher. Regardless of how the issue gets to the table, it needs to stay on the table. For this to happen, the top leadership must support and approve of the initiative and empower those in charge of the effort to make decisions and implement action steps. Without a leader or champion, bullying prevention efforts in schools are sporadic, unsustainable, or nonexistent. This is significant given the best practice that states that bullying prevention efforts should be sustained through time.

## SUPERVISING STUDENT USE OF INFORMATION TECHNOLOGY DEVICES IN SCHOOLS

One of the best practices in bullying prevention is to increase adult supervision in places where bullying occurs. Therefore, to prevent incidents of cyber bullying that occur at school, schools need to maximize efforts to supervise and monitor technology use by students. For computer labs and any classrooms that use computers, AUPs and any related policies should be signed and shared so that students are clear of what the rules are, and what the consequences are for violating them. The training component discussed previously must include information for all school staff on how to recognize cyber bullying when they see it, and how to respond if they become aware of it. At the very least, staff should be aware of and enforce school policies dealing with technology use. For example, with the increasing possession and use of PDAs and cell phones by students, school staff must be observant for students sending text messages or otherwise using technology during prohibited times. Also, schools should use filtering and tracking software, but with full knowledge that students often have the skills to get around this.

Supervision in big school buildings and complexes with hundreds and even thousands of students coming and going is not easy. Administrators surveyed for this book indicated that computer device usage possessed and used by students on campus complicates their ability to provide effective supervision, but this view was not universally held. Possession and use of smaller IT devices like PDAs, cell phones and iPhones were generally viewed as being potentially more problematic because they are smaller, more easily concealable, and quicker to use. In regard to computer use, one principal commented that: "we are as diligent as we can be," while another stated: "Our district is not prepared or ready to handle this. They place filtering systems that are easily bypassed with proxy servers and the filtering system that doesn't recognize foreign languages which is how students get through them."

Determined students can always find a way to defeat Internet blocking and filtering systems, and there is plenty of aid available online from other youth and young adults if necessary. Actually watching individuals use devices, asking trusted students what people are doing and talking about, keeping your ear to the ground so to speak, and potentially monitoring network user activity logs are all methods of aiding supervision. As put by another principal: "We do as good of job as can be expected for a school. However, I don't believe it possible to police all tech use to avoid cyber bullying. I see more issues arise out of misuse of cell phones than I do the misuse of computers."

## SOCIAL, EMOTIONAL, AND ETHICAL LEARNING IN SCHOOLS

From a more global perspective, there is some amount of debate taking place over the primary goals surrounding education. For several years federal and state education policies that guide school practices have been focused on test scores, especially in the areas of reading and math. While the goals of improving scores are worthwhile and important, they should not be at the expense of character education. Unfortunately, despite the desire by many parents and teachers to have schools support their children in becoming responsible community members, this is not happening in most public school systems today.[25] How can we reestablish a balance between knowledge and skill building on the one hand, to go along with character building of young men and women on the other? Why shouldn't our most precious resource, children and perhaps our most expensive tax burden at the local, state, and federal level combined, be devoted to developing tolerance, respect, and behavioral accountability in a nation that espouses ethnic diversity?

We assert that when it comes to countering the harmful aspects of digital youth culture schools have an important role to help ensure proper development of social, emotional, and ethical decision-making skills of youth. Schools cannot rely on technology and push the wonders of IT and Net-based learning without also teaching kids how to be safe, secure, and act responsibly when online. Failure to also push for this need in our society that is increasingly dependent on information systems represents a major educational policy flaw. Children also need to learn to listen to themselves and each other when online and off-line, be reflective, flexible problem solvers, and be able to communicate and collaborate in ways that do not give offense. The related essential dispositions include being able to respond to others in appropriate ways, to appreciate and have an inclination toward involvement with social justice, and to serve others and participate in good will.[26]

Recent studies have shown that there are two main areas that promote academic success and healthy development of students. One is promoting the social-emotional competencies and ethical dispositions from Kindergarten through 12th grade; the other is creating safe, caring, responsive, and participatory schools and homes.[27] On an intuitive level, this amounts to educating youth in ways and environments that do not tolerate bullying. Granted, it is not easy nor should such lofty goals be simply introduced into curricula, staff development and class instruction methods or mandates. Yet, to the extent schools must support well rounded community-oriented success of youth, how else except through instilling positive education, adult role modeling, reward systems and active discipline along with coaching, counseling, and mentoring for youth who need extra time and attention?

Teachers themselves through staff development processes need to learn more about social-emotional learning needs and capabilities of youth in developmentally appropriate ways, and then incorporate principles for this into their classroom content and teaching styles. The current national policies regarding education that focus solely on performance can leave other initiatives such as bullying prevention off the radar screen. According to a middle school teacher from Syracuse, New York: "cyber bullying often starts on the computer and overflows into the classroom. However, currently, there is no way to stop it. Kids deny it, or they keep it hidden from adults. Since our focus is on the No Child Left Behind Act, our hands our tied and we have to turn the other cheek."

Why cannot a math story problem be developed in a way that promotes anti-bullying and responds to challenges youth in 7th grade commonly experience when engaged in social networking online? Similarly, why cannot development of English reading, writing and speaking include lessons about Internet safety (from being cyber bullied), protecting oneself and their data, and ethical decision making? Why is it that the most waking hours in the school days of our children cannot be devoted to instilling and reinforcing these other primary needs they will have as adults: to be socially as well as technologically adept, discerning and circumspect? Why not flavor classrooms with instruction and assignments in these subject areas that allow and require them to use their favorite IT devices in constructive rather than destructive unsupervised ways so much of the time?

Americans parents and taxpayers of education would not be opposed to this, if they truly believe as the evidence indicates "that the primary purpose of public schooling is to prepare children to become effective and responsible citizens."[28] Still we must contend with the understandable view of a school principal who said: "Our top mission as school leaders should be student learning, not bullying prevention. All things that are not about curriculum, instruction, and assessment should receive secondary attention. In promoting such initiatives, do not forget the "opportunity costs" of what happens when staff energies are doing this instead of the core mission of schools, which is to educate young people to use their minds well. It isn't that this isn't important; it's that schools should not have primary responsibility for it. We will deal with bullies as they emerge; we will build an environment of respectful appreciation for differences, tolerance and empathy, as part of our mission. Cyber bullying prevention is way down my list, along with obesity prevention and drug abuse prevention—all worthy causes, and all secondary to the central mission." Given what you have read so far in this book, do you buy this? Can society really afford not to help youth better protect themselves online, and we don't mean from sexual predators only, especially given that the majority of online sexual offenders are youth themselves hitting on each other as they explore their sexuality in unprecedented promiscuous ways!

A fundamental question therefore is: if schools, families, churches, and communities cannot find the time to teach kids how to be good people, who will? The task does not fall on one or the other, but should be a shared responsibility. Ask yourself whether you think the levels of respect shown by today's youth and society in general have decreased over the last 20 to 30 years. What do you think educators think about this question? Perhaps the most significant question is whether we want to judge our school graduates simply based on what they *know* and are able *to do* principally to earn a living, or also on who they *are and their potential to be successful online and off-line in a world that increasingly does not differentiate these?* Let's face it. Preventing bullying whether off-line or online is a societal responsibility, just as are other sorts of abuse and crime prevention. We can't dump responsibility for this on schools, parents, churches, and other nonprofits alone. Businesses and government also need to step up and become involved. No one person, group or institution gets a pass on this. The consequences are too dire.

## CYBER BULLYING RESPONSE AND INVESTIGATION STRATEGIES

Along with the strategies for prevention and education, schools must also develop a strategic plan to respond to and investigate instances of cyber bullying. Teachers and administrators are often unsure of how and when to respond to reports of cyber bullying given the confusing legal interpretations, free speech issues, location of the offense, and simply being unaware that cyber abuse and crimes can (and probably are) occurring right from within school buses, grounds, hallways, classrooms, libraries, and so on. If students are not reporting online offenses like bullying to school officials or parents, then it often goes unnoticed and flies below the school radar. However, schools must take steps to be prepared to handle a report of cyber bullying by a student, or even a staff member who has been victimized. As has been stated, schools can take appropriate disciplinary measures against individuals found to have violated school rules on school grounds. However, the issue becomes cloudy if the allegations of electronic abuse originated off school grounds. This is why school procedures should be developed to provide for an effective and consistent response to cases of cyber bullying that go back and forth between physical places and cyber spaces, and may involve any number of individuals who participate online and off-line, in symmetric (real time) or asymmetric (delayed messaging, post and wait) ways. The latter typically play out over several days, weeks, or months and will almost surely become emotionally disruptive to victims while they attend school. Again, remember that as our world merges cyber and physical processes, physical locations are becoming less important to key issues of problems we encounter.

If a school official suspects or receives notice of bullying online, the first step is to *do something*. Part of the educational and professional development of school staff has to be to know when and how to intervene. A new saying being applied in the New York School Safety Program is "If you see something, say something." This can be modified to say, "If you become aware of something, do something." The crucial first step is finding out as much information as possible to determine the next steps. These will likely involve notifying an administrator such as the principal or assistant principal about what you have been told and discovered in your initial encounter with people or data that came to your attention. Taking immediate though measured action every time bullying arises in any form, and in accordance with school policies that require such actions, will quickly send signals to establish new norms within school cultures. Never allow students to go on believing that bullying will not be taken seriously. By not dismissing bullying allegations outright, the chances of an effective intervention are much better. So is the credibility of school districts, if matters culminate into legal controversies.

## SITUATION REVIEW PROCESS

What comes next in the response and investigation process obviously depends, but when a staff member brings a bullying possibility to a building administrator an incident assessment process is normally required. Here it is useful to consider Nancy Willard's *cyberbullying or cyberthreat situation review process from Chapter 2*. Available online in detail, this process calls for the creation of a situation review team that will be responsible for reviewing reports of cyber bullying and cyber threats. Willard also recommends that team members include an administrator, school counselor, technology coordinator, library media specialist, and school resource officer. We also recommend the person responsible for overseeing school safety and security to be on this team.

Depending on what sorts of emergency, safety or security teams that may be legally required per state laws, schools may wish to assign bullying cases to an existing team already formed. Based on the facts of the particular incident being investigated, not all team members are needed. However, a threat assessment and/or violence or suicide risk assessment should be conducted in standardized ways as spelled out in school policies or state education laws. Standardized investigation protocols will guide and ensure proper collection and preservation of physical, testimonial, and potentially even cyber evidence.

With an appropriate team formed and trained in advance, the first step in response to a bullying situation after it is reported should always be to deal with any immediate threats and to reasonably ensure that everyone allegedly involved is safe. Once the situation is *tactically stabilized* further evidence gathering can begin. This process should consist of attempting to identify the creator or sender of online bullying messages, and searching for additional material that may lead to evidence of an imminent threat. This will allow investigators to also preliminarily gain understanding of the nature and extent of offensive or abusive content involved, and whether state or local crime laws may have been violated. If evidence of a legitimate threat exists, the law enforcement authorities must be contacted immediately.

For off-campus incidents, an important burden for schools is to establish a clear nexus between the cyber bullying incident and a substantial disruption at school, which can be difficult to do. Questions should be asked to determine whether the cyber bullying is impacting on the school environment. Here administrators must use professional discretion in determining what constitutes an overall safe and secure environment conducive to learning and normal school activities as well as special events. Even if only one student is noticeably and significantly disturbed, it may be grounds for official action.

Begin investigations with interviews of the victim and any other witnesses such as peers or parents. The goal is to obtain as much information about the situation as possible in order to get a sense of the bigger picture. Did a male student send a nasty e-mail to another male student because that student stole his girlfriend, or did a student send repeated e-mails and post insulting comments on a Web site for no apparent reason? Did the victim know the cyber bully, or was the victim randomly targeted? If the victim knew the cyber bully, did they have a history of problems? How many students are involved? Has the situation been escalating in terms of its intensity, numbers of individuals involved, or Web-based social networking forums? Asking the right questions can lead to a greater understanding of how and why a cyber bullying situation happened.

## THREAT ASSESSMENT AND RESPONSE

In 2002, the United States Secret Service and the United States Department of Education issued a "Guide to Threat Assessment in Schools." The guide provides specific suggestions for schools to conduct a school threat assessment. The guide is also applicable for cases of cyber bullying that involve threats. Also called a threat assessment inquiry, the threat assessment process constitutes a thorough preliminary inquiry conducted by a school threat assessment team that can assist in making determinations as to whether a student of concern poses a threat. Asking whether a student of concern simply made a threat or actually poses a threat is a significant distinction. The process provides a basis for deciding whether to report or refer the incident to law enforcement. As stated in the guide, the inquiry process should take place immediately if a potentially threatening situation exists. If violence appears imminent, the police should be called immediately, and the school should follow procedures as outlined in their emergency or crisis response plans. According to the guide, the following information should be sought in an inquiry:[29]

- The facts that drew attention to the student, the situation, and possibly the targets.
- Information about the student including identifying information, background information, and current life information.
- Information about "attack-related" behaviors, which can include behavior concerns such as ideas or plans of attacking school/injuring self, attack-related communications or writings, recent weapon-seeking behavior, or rehearsals of attacks or ambushes.
- Motives such as revenge, attention, recognition, or wish to solve a problem otherwise seen as unbearable.
- Target selection (prior to attack).

Sources of information for the inquiry could include:

- School information
- Collateral school interviews with students and adults who know the student
- Parent/guardian interviews
- Interviews with student of concern
- Interview with potential target

Finally, information gathered from research and interviews should be guided by the following questions:

- What are the student's motives and goals?
- Have there been any communications suggesting intent to attack?
- Has the subject shown inappropriate interest in things such as school attacks/attackers, weapons, incidents of mass violence?
- Has the student engaged in attack-related behaviors?
- Does the student have the capacity to carry out an act of targeted violence (the intent and the means)?
- Is the student experiencing hopelessness, desperation, and despair?
- Does the student have a trusting relationship with at least one responsible adult?
- Does the student see violence as an acceptable or desirable (or the only) way to solve problems?
- Is the student's conversation and "story" consistent with his or her actions?
- Are other people concerned about the student's potential for violence?
- What circumstances might affect the likelihood of attack?

Threat assessment and response processes must take into consideration what is occurring in cyberspace as well as in physical places such as in the school building, athletic facilities, and on school buses. After all, the reality that social computing is mobile computing made possible by portable electronic devices means that cyber bullying can occur from anywhere and at anytime. A well-developed threat assessment guide provides an organized means to better determine cyber and physical possibilities of bullying, whether police need to be involved, and to determine who else should be contacted along with appropriate interventions for students involved as either perpetrators, bystanders, victims, or witness. Threat assessment instruments and process made known to staff, students, and parents demonstrates the commitment of schools to take action to protect and provide safety for everyone occupying school facilities or using its computer network(s), along with using the Internet while being physically on school property.

Determining whether someone actually poses a threat is not easy even though various levels of intimidation, coercion, and threats by and among students are very common. However, if efforts are not taken to investigate what could happen, tragedy may loom. Eric Harris reportedly made threatening comments online through Web postings, outlined harmful intentions online including his intention to kill a classmate prior to the Columbine Colorado High School shootings in 1999.[30]

Obviously the seriousness of facts, circumstances, and potential harm will guide the level of response, further investigation, and intervention measures taken. At a minimum, all incidents should be documented to create a record of caring and that can be referred to later if situations recur. Determining case level seriousness must be done carefully. We suggest that "less serious" mean an incident that does not involve threats or potential danger. Remember however, cyber bullying that involves public shaming or repeated insults can escalate to involve serious harm to the victim and lead to retaliation. Conversely, "more serious" include incidents that violate crime laws, require police involvement, include threats or actual injuries, involve several students, extensive Internet posts, and so forth. When in doubt, err on the side of caution. Take the extra time needed to investigate, document, and be thorough. In our experience, doing so in early cases following implementation of new policies and staff training pays off in the long-term as school communities come to realize that the bullying gig is up and will not longer be tolerated!

## INTERVENTION

School officials have many intervention strategies they can employ in bullying situations. These do not differ substantially from measures that can be taken in other instances of students violating school policies for one thing or another: verbal admonishments with stern warnings that repeat violations will result in harsher measures; staying after school or working on "thou shall but shall not" refection activities, being excused or suspended from extracurricular activities, special monitoring in between classes and during lunchtime, follow-up "how's it going, I just wanted to check-in with you" chats, and so forth. Suspending and expelling students in severe and repeat cases is also a legal option that school officials periodically face. Anything more serious will likely involve police and the juvenile justice system if that is not already the case.

Cases of cyber bullying that occur on school grounds should be handled in a manner consistent with other cases of bullying. Specifically, schools can discipline, reduce privileges, counsel, refer to treatment, or call police as warranted by the facts. Schools should always be looking at best practices in bullying prevention as certain practices such as "zero tolerance" and "three strikes and you're out" have been shown to have questionable effectiveness. However, it may be necessary in some cases involving particular hostility, involvement of weapons, and violations of crime laws to "work with" a student until the immediate situation is dealt with according to school policies, state and local crime laws, community standards of acceptable behaviors, and political realities involving parents and school boards that all public officials must contend with.

Unfortunately, it is the "less serious" types of off-campus cyber bullying cases that are difficult to formally discipline because they do not meet the legal standards of threats or substantial disruption of the school environment. Schools must consider the facts of the case to guide in the decision to intervene. For example, if a case of off-campus cyber bullying is found to be somehow connected to the school, such as starting in school and continuing online or vice versa, then schools can and should intervene. An appropriate intervention should be consistently applied and may include school discipline, warnings, referrals to additional counseling or treatment, further education about the impact of their actions, safe and appropriate computer applications, or communication with parents or police.

Even if formal discipline cannot be administered by the school, there are other options such as discussing the situation with the cyber bully and reminding them of the impact of their words and actions on others. Depending on the case, an informal referral to counseling may be the best option. The school should also provide support to the victim, and provide suggestions on how to protect themselves against cyber bullying. School officials must be educated themselves in order to provide guidance on how to deal with it, and prevent it from happening again. Schools should support the problem-solving effort. For example, they may offer recommendations such as not engaging the attacker online, changing screen names, or not using certain social networking sites that are more controversial. From a more global perspective, schools need to provide ethics instruction from a very young age and continue throughout. Although teaching ethics can be difficult, it remains a fundamental component of a cyber bullying response process.

## COLLABORATING WITH PARENTS

Depending on the facts of a cyber bullying incident, school officials may need to communicate with parents of the victim and the cyber bully. The victim may need further support from an administrator, teacher, or mental health counselor, but the parents should be informed and have input in the decision-making process. Parents or guardians of a cyber bully should also be notified, especially if an unfolding situation poses a threat. The same holds true for parents and guardians of bullying bystanders, who otherwise might be tempted to pile on or continue to quietly observe without standing up for justice and the rights of fellow students. Although notification to police is usually victim-driven, meaning that student victims or their parents normally decide whether to pursue law enforcement investigation and prosecution, school officials can help in an advisory role.

Schools officials broker all sorts of partnering with parents to effectively respond to or prevent cyber bullying. They should consider actively working with their Parent Teacher Association (PTA) or Parent Teacher Student Organization (PTSO) as much as possible, and to keep their school board informed of prevention and major response efforts. In addition, schools should provide opportunities to help educate and train parents about what bullying online now involves, and what must be done to address it. Given mounting empirical evidence from several very credible studies, it is unlikely that any school district is immune from cyber bullying. That is a fact that officials and parents need to come to terms with, along with the reality that everyone's child may be affected in some way.

## WORKING WITH STUDENTS

A key piece of any response option for schools is working with students involved in or experiencing cyber bullying whether directly as the principals in a case or indirectly as members of the student body. Again, the potential options vary depending on the particular unfolding incident(s) and larger community and school environments. What is possible and appropriate for an urban high school consisting of 3,000 students will not work or be appropriate in a rural school district that shares one building for all of its 500 middle and high school students. Yet the principles of and need for action to prevent and respond to cyber bullying apply to all school environments and students everywhere.

For the victim, support should be offered based on their individual needs. Some victims may need simple guidance on how to ignore or block harmful messages, or avoid harmful chat rooms or social networking sites. Other victims may need more extensive support that may include school-based counseling or external mental health treatment as determined in consultation with parents. Victims should be cautioned not to retaliate despite the instinct to due so, and to trust that the adults are there to help. Lessons in "think before you send or post" should be stressed, and it may be appropriate to help students learn to phrase messages in artful ways that deflate tensions online if messages or social networking forums cannot be ignored. Remember that for members of the digital youth culture, simply unplugging the computer may not be a viable option in their minds or for the reality of their lifestyle. Still, if victims can learn to avoid certain irritating locations in cyberspace as they do in their physical community, much can be avoided and gained to replace friends or activities that they once enjoyed.

Working with the cyber bully requires consideration of the nexus between school "grounds" of activity in conjunction with "grounds" for legal and official action as authorized by applicable statutory and case laws. The goals are to teach the cyber bully that their behavior is wrong, and to prevent and deter them from bullying again. In the survey of school building administrators conducted by Jim Colt, officials reported responding in many different ways to accomplish these goals, depending on the situation. For example, in response to students found to have cyber bullied in school 53 percent of administrators reported having suspended students out of school, 58 percent reported having suspended students in school, 72 percent reported using other disciplinary action, 80 percent reported using discussion/informal counseling, 80 percent reported discussing matters with the student and his/her parent(s), and 49 percent referred the bullying case to police.[31]

For cyber bullying that occurred off school property, 23 percent of officials surveyed reported suspending out of school, 36 percent reported suspending in school, 55 percent reported using other disciplinary action, 81 percent reported having a discussion or using informal counseling, 85 percent reported discussing with student and parent, and 47 percent referred to police. It is encouraging that schools appear to be taking action, and that that action seems to depend on the situation. Yet, that action must be consistent and in accordance with school policy to ensure that legal due processes are followed.[32] Overall, for those schools and officials who have yet to take action to prevent, educate and intervene, you are now aware of something—so do something!

# Advice for Students and Other Victims of All Ages

*Teachers see it and don't do shit. Kids with too much time on their hands make up crap and your reputation is ruined for life.*
*—20-year-old female victim*

Contrary to what most people may think, cyber bullying although primarily a youth problem, is not limited to teens and adolescents. Although we now have solid research evidence that the prevalence and incidences of online bullying peaks in middle school years, it continues for many youth through high school and college years and even older adults can also become involved. Stories about college student and adult cyber bullying are common. A female law student from New Orleans stated that a group of about 20 girls started to pick on her in her college for reasons she did not understand. When interviewed she reported they were repeatedly sending her text messages saying, "You're a bitch," "You're a loser," and "You're a fat pig," despite her weighing 120 pounds. If the cyber bullying keeps up, she says she will start going to a different college.

The 2004 Rochester Institute of Technology (RIT) "Survey of Computer Use and Ethics" found that among 873 college students randomly surveyed, 17 percent were harassed, 8 percent were threatened, and 6 percent were stalked online within the preceding year. Similar results were found in a comparative survey of over 500 college students attending the nearby

State University of New York (SUNY) at Brockport. Many students in these surveys reported they knew the perpetrator of the harassment or threats in person and prior to the cyber bullying. Another study also conducted in 2004 by the University of New Hampshire found that 10 to 15 percent of college students surveyed, reported experiencing some form of online harassment from either someone that they know, or from a stranger, and that it was occurring through e-mail and instant messaging. Among students surveyed, 13 to 14 percent reported receiving harassing e-mails or instant messages despite telling the sender to stop.[1] These survey findings do not reflect even more prolific cyber bullying via texting with cellular phones.

The authors believe that many adults simply age-out of bullying lifestyles just as most male criminals tend to grow up and stop committing crimes as a regular part of life. They get a job, marry, have children, accumulate things, rent or buy a home. As our responsibilities change our outlooks as human beings on what is important as well as how to go about becoming and remaining successful is of primary concern. Still, as many readers know, some adults bully other people when they are young and throughout their lives. For them, bullying is a lifestyle choice that, when effectively applied in particular situations, has enabled them (at least thus far) to remain successful in how they grapple with conflict and things that annoy them. Thus, youth bullies can grow up to become adult bullies when their aggressive behaviors are left unchecked, and it follows that adult bullies now exist online and off-line.

Obviously many adult bullies continue to embarrass, harass, intimidate, and/or threaten their victims even after being told to stop. Tragically bullying involving youth and adults affects workplaces just as it does school and home settings. It also may involve special and disadvantaged populations including the aged, developmentally challenged, and particular ethnic groups or those with sexual preferences who differ from those of the bully or a dominant group the bully affiliates closely with. In this chapter we conclude the book by briefly discussing all issues: bullying of particular concern to adults and special populations of bullying victims, including adults outside of and within workplace settings, elderly adults, and developmentally challenged and disabled persons. Then we take time to reflect on what we have covered and consider what the future holds.

## ADULT BULLYING

Adults bully adults and youths, and youths bully each other and sometimes adults. From featured cases discussed in the media, benchmark court cases reviewed in Chapter 5, and from our own interviews of dozens of bullying victims some of which have been shared here, we know bullying can extend throughout human lives and cultures anywhere in the world. Sadly, bullying is part of the human condition, but it does not have to be and it should not be. Regardless of the age of onset (in about 2nd grade for American students) we have learned how the evolution and egregiousness of online bullying now involves the creation of Web sites, doctored photos, fabricated stories, and insulting text messages. Cases include vulgar criticisms of school teachers and administrators, as well as college professors and other adults in positions of authority or responsibility. Parents and extended family members also fall prey to online bullies. Indeed being "friended" by someone online can ultimately ruin someone's cyber life. Recall that some Web sites specialize in listing people on the basis of how much they deserve to be put down, and that young adults as well as youth in the digital culture of today's interconnected world have come to expect, often dish out, and must tolerate online abuse, decadence, and crime as an online norm. That's just the plain and empirical truth.

Sometimes prevailing negative attitudes and online behaviors of youth culture extend from fixed locations (e.g., school, college, and home) into mobile computing environments and employment settings. This is where younger people invariably interact more with older people, including individuals who may themselves be victims or perpetrators of online bullying in the process of using computers and other types of information technology (IT) devices for personal as well as professional purposes. Like our 18-year-old hypothetical young adult from Chapter 1 who grew up using IT devices and the Net, millions of people now in their 30s, 40s or even older also grew up without the benefit of systematically delivered and reinforced Internet safety, information security, and cyber ethics education. In the process, men and women who did not age or mature out of bullying may have learned new ways to bully online. Consequently some older and young adults have slipped into cyber bullying behavioral patterns. Other adults are ripe for online assaults because they do not understand how to protect themselves, their systems, or data online. Elderly people, many of whom still remain uncomfortable with computers and the Internet, may be especially vulnerable to being taken advantage of when they are online.

In reality anyone can be bullied, threatened, or harassed online, and some people are also stalked online as well as in person. When adults are involved,

## THE DESTRUCTION OF JOY, TRUST, AND HOPE

**"Bullying and Cyber Bullying of an 80-Year-Old Grandmother Swindled Out of $60,000"**

In the words of the victim:

My grandson was the first born and I hate to say it now but he was my favorite. Guilty, guilty, guilty. I screamed. Not my grandson, he would never do this to me. There wasn't any reason. Anything he ever wanted ever since he was born, I gave to him. Anything! No way could this happen. I refused to believe it. Maybe that was a mistake, believing he was not guilty. But the words played over and over and over in my head, like a worn-out record—guilty, guilty, guilty, guilty . . . Shock, disbelief, and anger overwhelmed me. I froze with rage while flashbacks bashed my brains as if someone was beating me with a baseball bat. I was caught in a time warp of fear and helplessness. I remember this last year as suddenly and as real as yesterday. I still feel trapped and completely alone in this world. I am now a statistic because of my very own flesh and blood. The grandson that I would have given my life for in a heartbeat betrayed me. He thought he was above the law.

He was always a charmer, growing up. Later I saw a side to him that I never saw before nor could imagine. The sarcastic eyes and his arrogant smirk gave me chills. Even his body language was different. He even called me an idiot and an old fool. It was so surreal. I didn't want to live. I knew that these thoughts were crazy, but the mental wounds and emotional wounds just wouldn't go away and my health was jeopardized because of my nice life turned into a nightmare. I wanted to run and keep on running, but there was no place to run.

It only took a year for my grandson to swindle me out of over $60,000. My 18-year-old grandson just about lived at my house. We were always extremely close. One afternoon my grandson asked me if I heard about the lady who was my age and almost got killed by a home invasion. I told him no and then he told me that there was a rash of home invasions and the police weren't doing anything about the crimes. I told him that I wasn't scared. He worked on me for a couple of months using scare tactics about what was happening to all of the elderly people in the community and that I should get some type of security. He said that he would help me. I finally gave in.

A couple of days later, he said that he found a security company that worked undercover and were very successful at protecting the elderly in their homes and catching criminals. My grandson said that he would have them contact me. I got a call from the alleged company and they sounded professional, nice and knew what they were talking about. They told me that they were the best but expensive. After all, it was worth my life. Like my grandson kept on telling me: I couldn't take my money with me and he didn't want any of my money if I died. He wanted me safe and alive. So, I took the bait.

I arranged it with my bank to have my grandson handle the money transactions through my computer. My grandson was going to handle everything. It sounded wonderful. My grandson had come to my rescue and I was going to live a safe, long life.

Since I didn't know this company, I had my grandson handle all of the paperwork. I didn't discuss this matter with anyone because I was told not to tell a soul. People with good intentions sometimes slip out with confidential information, which made sense.

Tax time came and my son-in-law said that he would do my taxes since it was so simple. When he was going over my bills, he asked me what this security company was and I told him that it was for protection. He asked me why I needed protection and I told him about all of the home invasions on the elderly. My son-in-law wanted to know where I got my information from and I told him that it was my grandson. He confronted my grandson and he agreed to everything that he had told me. My son-in-law said that the story sounded fishy and hadn't heard about any home invasions. So, he contacted the local Better Business Bureau and found out the security company did not exist.

My son-in-law went to the cops and the cops went to my grandson. My grandson was arrested and charged with several offenses. I couldn't prosecute my grandson, I just couldn't. I love him and always will. He won't talk to me or give anyone the reason why he did it. I don't know what's going to happen from day to day. I don't worry about being safe because I really don't care what happens to me. The police said that I shouldn't feel alone. There's quite a bit of identity theft and fraud committed by children of elderly people . . . grandchildren even great-grandchildren, relatives, and best friends bully elderly family members into fraudulent situations all the time. If anything happened to me, God would be doing me a favor. I am completely devastated.

it may not be called cyber bullying, but the elements and results are similar if not the same. Remember that anything that makes someone stand out or appear different may trigger the savage insecurities of a bully. At times, celebrities become targets of adult stalkers who use technology as part of their repertoire. Actress Uma Thurman was recently in the news because a former mental patient was accused of stalking her in a number of ways such as repeatedly showing up at her front door and leaving her a frightening letter.[2] The stalker was also accused of sending harassing e-mails to Thurman's father and brother. He was eventually officially charged in New York State with stalking and aggravated harassment. Thurman resorted to hiring a private detective and installed surveillance equipment around her residence.

In another instance, *Star Magazine* editor-at-large Julia Allison recently told ABCNEWS.com that she has an online blogger stalking her.[3] She stated that the blogger follows everything she says and does on the Net: "She has references about me that I didn't know existed. She [the cyber bully] is a veritable storehouse of Julia Allison history and trivia." While Allison acknowledged that she receives much criticism online, she also stated that the blogger has crossed the line; that she is ". . . beyond the line of harmless activity and is obsessive." At the time of this writing, Allison had not involved the police and is still trying to figure out what to do.

These cases come to our attention because they do involve celebrities. However, common folks also experience bullying. Have you ever been bullied online as an adult? What would you do if you were in Julia Allison's situation with substantial financial resources to hire attorneys, private investigators, and security officers? What *would* you do? Would you fight back online? Would you file reports with police or other persons in positions of authority over the bully? Would you complain to the Web site administrators or your internet service provider (ISP) company? Or would you wait the bully out and hope they go away? Might you resort to vigilantism perhaps in cunning online ways that even exceed the methods used against you? Common people without much spare time, money, professional or political connections must typically rely on themselves to figure it out and/or "on the system" to do its job. That is why this book was written.

Cyber bullying is not controversial, except when it comes to responding to it as a victim, witness, or official with responsibility for doing the right thing and in ways that adhere to legal requirements of one's office. Response strategies are circumstantial and debatable. Some people take the position that when adults are public officials, celebrities, or post very detailed personal information about themselves online they are effectively inviting comments and criticisms from the general public. As with digital youth culture, other adults including people who administer their own blogs believe that sharing and receiving negative comments is to be expected, and "is all part of the game."[4]

Take a moment to reconsider Julia Allison's case and the questions we pose above. Now consider, *What would you do if you are put down online?* What have you done in the past if you have been bullied online? Does it depend on the circumstances including what as well as how something was expressed? Do you take into consideration that many adults are just clumsy in the way they express themselves orally or in writing? If you engaged the bully did you distinguish between constructive or at least considered criticism in your responses versus our cyber bullying elements (i.e., intentional online embarrassment, harassment, intimidation, or threats)? Clearly circumstances—the context in which posts are made, your available time, money, wherewithal and temperament among other factors—will vary and need to be considered. Our point however, is that bullying and cyber bullying does occur among adults, and even if not intended as such can be taken that way by sensitive and even thick-skinned people.

THE DESTRUCTION OF JOY, TRUST, AND HOPE

**"Maybe Words Cannot Kill, but a Mindset Can"**

As reported by author Nancy B. B. Meyer:

Dennis was a personal friend of mine and as close as a family member. He was a free-spirited guy who lived day to day. Dennis came from a large and financially poor family, but they were rich in love and devoted to each other. I knew him since he was a young boy. He was my son's first and best friend when we moved to where we now live. Dennis was a hard worker and nothing was ever above or below him. I never saw him in a bad mood. He was always jolly and carefree. Dennis's mom said that he was born happy and nothing much bothered him.

Dennis was also a good-looking guy with a great personality and girls loved him. The only problem that he had with the girls was jealousy on their part because of his free spirit. One Friday night he went out for a fish fry dinner. He sat next to a girl name Linda who started a conversation with him. Within the first 10 minutes, she played the sympathy, "poor me" story and told him that she had terminal cancer and had only a few months to live. Being the compassionate and sensitive human being that he was, Dennis's heartstrings were pulled—hook, line, and sinker. Shortly afterward they were an item.

Dennis told Linda from the start that he had many friends, including girls and he would not tolerate any jealousy. One morning, Dennis left his cell phone at home when he went to work. The phone rang, and although Linda didn't answer it, she did listen to the female voice message being left: "Dennis, don't forget dinner tonight at 7:00. I got some good wine to share and juicy pictures. It's going to be lots of fun. Can't wait to see you! Love, Carol." What Linda did not realize that the female caller was Dennis's sister who just got back after a month long trip with her husband, and that her call was a reminder about a family dinner at their parent's home, at which they would share some cool pictures. The word "juicy" was family code for anything that referred to something or someone they liked.

After Dennis got to work he called Linda to ask if he left his cell phone behind. "Yeah and some fucking bitch called and I found out about you sneaking behind my back and fucking around. If I catch you, I will stab you to death and I mean it!" Dennis said that he didn't know what Linda was talking about. Then, he realized that it was his sister and told Linda this. Linda apologized and things were smooth for a short while. After all, Dennis had to love her despite having terminal cancer.

Two weeks later, a friend of Dennis's came to the house to tell him that her mother died. Linda told her that Dennis didn't live there anymore and that she was the new owner. After the girl left, Linda started instant messaging Dennis telling him that he had better set his girlfriends straight or otherwise she would stab him to death along with his girlfriend bitches." Dennis laughed as he always did when Linda spouted off in this way. He told me once that words can't hurt a person, much less kill them. And then he would act his merry way, laugh, change the subject and ignore whatever unkind things happened or were said to him. In the process, Dennis "broke-up" with Linda many times, but she always played the cancer card. "Only a few months left to live . . ." she would say.

Linda's text messaging turned to instant messaging every hour accompanied with the usual threat, "I'm going to stab you if you don't call me with the hour." I told Dennis that it was not a laughing matter; there was nothing funny about it. As angry as I have gotten at people throughout my life, I have never thought about stabbing, killing, or harming a person. Linda would instant message him whenever she went on a rage, sometimes every 10 minutes throughout the day! Since all she had was time on her hands, the rages became more frequent along with the text messages—so did the stabbing threats. I constantly told Dennis to go to the police, but he would always laugh and take it with a grain of salt. "They're only words, Nancy, and words can't kill . . . ha ha." I told him it was her *mindset* that was so disturbing to me, who in their right mind would behave that way toward someone they loved?

One day Linda's words finally materialized. It was Labor Day weekend when I got a call that Linda had stabbed Dennis to death. Words have mindsets behind them, and mindsets can bring people to bully, threaten, and even kill. Dennis being dead is proof that threats, especially repeated threats that come in various ways from mindsets of anger, resentment, or jealously need to be taken deadly seriously, because they may ultimately be intended that way.

## ONLINE BULLYING IN THE WORKPLACE

Officially reported incidences of bullying and cyber bullying in workplace settings are comparatively rare to nonwork bullying situations, although some researchers believe rates of workplace bullying is "alarming."[5] If this is true, the reasons are probably due to a combination of youth having grown up among cyber incivility entering work forces that steadily rely on them and IT devices they along with older adults are more accustomed to using. So just as traditional bullying has found its way into cyber forms on the Internet, so too has schoolyard bullying transcended into employment settings where adults work.

As with their younger counterparts, adult bullies who lord power over others also engage in repeated, aggressive, and harmful behaviors against subordinates and fellow workers. Their actions cause stress, distress, disagreeable, and even hostile work environments that may constitute violations of organizational policies, labor contracts, or even employment laws. Bullying may involve a supervisor or manager abusing certain employees or can involve coworkers harassing each other in public or private places, online as well as offline. Some bullying involves sexual harassment or coercion of another variety (e.g., repeated unsubstantiated complaints about worker performance, etc.).

Executives including some famous businessmen such as John D. Rockefeller and Henry Ford have been described in the business journals as being bullies or "management tyrants."[6]

Bullying in the workplace is a significant societal problem especially when considering that so many people often leave their job because of a bullying supervisor. The economic implications of replacement employee recruiting, hiring, and training plus other costs associated with human resource complaints, distrust, and law suits are very great, perhaps even unknowable and immeasurable. Have you ever worked for a *jerk?* If you have, we empathize! Many principled, hardworking individuals are bullied at work, in school, and/or online. These are people who simply want to be left alone to do their jobs well and live in peace. However, even during tough financial times thousands of people throughout the world leave their positions because of a despicable manager who is given to bullying in one form or another: unreasonable demands, insults, degrading mannerisms, inappropriate touching, infuriating voice/e-mail messages, hang-up phone calls, and so on in ways that abuse power. Despite thousands of books written on managerial leadership, business etiquette, and professional ethics bullying and cyber bullying exist in the workplace. The worst bullies may even be sociopathic in their efforts to exert power and control over resources and people.[7]

## THE DESTRUCTION OF JOY, TRUST, AND HOPE

**The Ultimate "Bwitch!"**

Paralegal mother of three children:

My boss doesn't bully me in the typical physical, direct, bullying ways of men. She uses mind games. She's cunning, vicious, and obsessive. She's clever in her tactics and hard to detect. It will never end until she gets fired, because she is married to the brother of the owner of our company. She is arrogant and thinks her you know what doesn't stink. She has cost the company hundreds of thousands of dollars because of her arrogance to our customers and our boss knows it. He's just waiting for the right time to fire her. Meanwhile, everyone's life is a holy hell.

There are 50 employees and not one day goes by where she doesn't totally aggravate someone and they want to kill her. She pushes and pushes and pushes everyone into total mind frustration! Loss of work productivity is enormous. For instance, she'll tell someone that our boss needs a project done, which can take hours on the computer, if not days. After the project is done, she'll humiliate the person with a loud voice (always in front of other people) to say that she never said that the boss wanted that particular project. She is the biggest manipulator, intimidator, criticizing, name-calling, demanding, threatening, mocking, nasty looks, slamming, throwing things, and lying bitch I've ever known!

My boss goes through employees like a drugstore goes through pills. She really gets a kick out of making everyone's life miserable. She'll tell you to draw up a contract, or research some zoning laws, ownership, bankruptcies, wills, deeds, and anything to do with commercial land or buildings. After we do this, she'll write an intimidating letter on the computer saying that we researched the wrong information and imply that we are lying if we argue. Then, she spreads rumors to our boss that we're not cooperating, not doing our work, and that we are arrogant. She always gives us our duties verbally and then reprimands us on the computers. After so many times, if an employee doesn't suck it up and let her play her mind games, they get fired.

Whenever anyone gets fired, she's the one to tell them. She always has a big grin on her face when she gives them the fatal news. There is no exaggeration; she is really a sick person. I'm a single mother with three children and no support from my ex-husband. I am a paralegal and I need my job and she knows it. It's a hell. I go home shaking. I'm short with my kids and it seems like I am moody. I snap at the littlest of things! I'm stuck in my job. I have to put food in my kids' mouths. I'm not the only one in the workplace that gets bullied by a female boss. There seems to be a lot of it going on out there but again, the cliché is "girls are sugar and spice and everything nice." Totally false.

Whether workplace bullying is influenced by increasing pressures to succeed in a global marketplace, an environment that is conducive to bullying, individual narcissism and making one's career at the expense of organizations and personnel, or because of rogue employees who were probably bullied as children, results can destroy joy, trust, and hope for workers and managers alike. Results of workplace bullying also cause fear, decrease individual and team performance, and negatively impact the bottom line. Workplace bullying consequences are significant, and may probably cost organizations millions of dollars in annual losses! And just as traditional bullying among youth appears to be transcending more into online forms, cyber bullying by and among adults in workplace settings may also be increasing due to organizational reliance on interoperable computing and telecommunications technologies such as e-mail and texting that seemingly drive the very nature of work and associated stresses.

Although research is scant on cyber bullying in the workplace, a recent survey by the Dignity and Work Partnership in the United Kingdom revealed that 1 in 10 employees in that country believes cyber bullying is a problem in the workplace.[8] Specifically, 20 percent of workers surveyed reported that they had been harassed via e-mail in their current or past jobs, while 6 percent reported being victimized by text messages. As indicated above, e-mail is replacing office phones as a primary means of communication, and instant messaging and texting are also increasing as are industry specific and professional interest blogs. All provide technological means for a mean-spirited manager or co-worker to post unkind messages and other types of content. Further, once disinhibition takes hold—that feeling of online empowerment—online workplaces can become a living *hell*! Unfortunately, workplace bullying is currently only normally of legal and policy concern when it escalates into violent behaviors. At the national policy level D, the Center for Disease Control (CDC) and the National Institute for Occupational Safety and Health have for some time focused on incidents of workplace shootings and homicides, just as the U.S. Secret Service in partnership with the National Center for Missing and Exploited Children have paid attention to violence through their annual Safe School Initiative regional conferences.

## THE DESTRUCTION OF JOY, TRUST, AND HOPE

### "Cyber Bullying by a Manager Later Connected to Kidnapping and Sexual Slavery"

Adult female employee:

I was stalked, it was scary—I couldn't sleep at night—I developed anxiety and panic attacks—and I have always been an extremely independent woman. I have traveled the world starting at a young age. I threw away the e-mails that I was getting because I was extremely busy in my research plus all the other things going on in my life. It's so good to be back in the United States. As you know, I was there in Japan for four years—military (aero-engineering). I really loved the people, culture, and the food until the threats started coming via e-mail.

The Japanese are the most intelligent when it comes to computer savvy. I thought that my boss was the nicest guy in the world. I adopted him as a father figure and he adopted me as a surrogate daughter even though he had a family of his own. He was always very protective of me. The first week I started working at the company, my boss said that he would be there for me 24/7. He knew everything about me (even my social security number for military clearance purposes). My boss was a meek, gentle, protective Japanese gentleman. My intuition at times however, was that he could be overbearing.

One day he told me about "the epidemic" of women being kidnapped and used as sex slaves (not only young Japanese women but any young pretty woman). He constantly reassured me that the police were overwhelmed with the amount of crime in Japan, not only Tokyo, but all of Japan. It was about this time, when I had been in Japan for about a month, I started getting e-mails about how beautiful and angelic I was. I was flattered at first, in fact, very flattered because I had never gotten that much attention from men. I have always been the serious, focused, independent, nonflirty type.

The person e-mailing me did so for several months, and eventually become more lovey-dovey. Then the e-mails became really annoying. I finally went to my boss and told him about the e-mails. I showed him the e-mails, and pointed how the writer said I was beautiful and wanted to spend the rest of their life with me. They thought of me as a Japanese princess even though I wasn't Japanese. I told my boss that I ignored the e-mails but was having nightmares that caused me to wake up in the middle of the night with cold sweats. He would spend many nights with me, comforting, consoling, and protecting me.

The e-mails became threatening. The sender wanted to take me away to a private island where we could spend the rest of our lives together, alone! It made me wonder about the sex slavery issue that my boss had originally mentioned. My boss said that he would go to the police and handle it. I BELIEVED HIM! The threats were an extreme invasion of privacy that I never experienced before. They were CREEPY and SLIMEY. Sometimes I actually felt as though my skin was crawling, as if something or someone was controlling my feelings, but I couldn't put my finger on what was happening. The e-mails kept coming, sneaking into my work, mind, and life.

After three years of hell and totally trusting my boss with my LIFE, I went to the police. They had absolutely NO RECORD of the e-mail threats or of my boss working with them. The police told me not to tell my boss that I had consulted with them. They told me that there were other foreign women who had worked for this company and had similar experiences . . . the police set up surveillance and caught the perpetrator, my boss!

Now years later, I am still having nightmares and anxiety attacks. I have taken a different position because part of my former job requirement was to travel internationally. I can't do it anymore. I'm a changed person. I am no longer the fearless, trusting, independent person that I have always been. I refuse to leave the United States anymore. And I've given a great deal of thought to what happened to me, to my boss, and why. I believe there is a huge problem in Japan when it comes to scare tactics and men controlling women, some of whom are treated as second class citizens or merely objects. I think this begins among some Japanese boys who also learn to control computers at very young ages and that their attitudes about being in control extend to relationships with women. I think that may have been what happened to my boss, and ultimately to me.

## BULLYING OF CHILDREN WHO ARE DIFFERENT

Children identified as having special needs are especially vulnerable to being bullied. Youth ranging in age from 1-year-old to people in their late 20s and even older may be physically, emotionally, or otherwise developmentally challenged for their age. Their special challenges translate into special vulnerabilities, especially when it comes to the fast-paced interactions of digital youth culture with expectations for technology savvy and mental toughness. Issues of language processing, cognitive delays and dexterity limitations can also limit and disadvantage youth with special needs. The fact that they may look, sound, act, and be different than normal kids makes them all the more vulnerable to the extent that their interpersonal and online interactions are not carefully monitored, supervised, and nurtured.

Sadly, in the absence of research into this topic, we believe from conversations with professionals who specialize in providing education, occupation, and health services to disadvantaged youth that as a subpopulation they are susceptible to and even willingly participate in a limited range of cyber abuse and offending that includes cyber bullying.

As one professional acquainted with the issue reported, "this is an area that we are not expecting to see a problem, so the problem becomes more complex given the needs of the population we serve. In the case of one young adult who was victimized, she willingly participated in exchanging e-mail with a stranger who took advantage of her even after being warned about potential dangers involved. Currently very limited opportunities for professionals to even comprehend the threats that this client base may face when accessing the Internet . . . for me this is a world of technology that amazingly does not escape the interests of children and young adults with disabilities, who are just as curious and excited about things they experience online as other people . . . and what right do we have to limit their online opportunities despite their being so easily fooled by words?"

The Gay, Lesbian, and Straight Education Network conducted the National School Climate Survey in 2001, and found that 83.2 percent of lesbian, gay, bisexual, and transgender (LGBT) youth reported being verbally harassed due to their sexual orientation.[9] Yet, you don't even have to be LGBT to be bullied or cyber bullied because of it. For example, the bullying may occur either because of *actual or perceived* sexual orientation, which can begin with someone making up a rumor that someone is gay, or simply calling someone "gay," "fag," or "homo" online. This is made much worse given the youth culture, and digital youth culture that uses these words as part of their normal communication (that's gay), or meant as a joke (you're so gay or you're such a homo). Using the word "gay" is an extremely common expression among today's youth, and is often used as a random insult in everyday communications. It is interesting that the youth culture has become desensitized to the words, despite the negative connotations and meaning in today's society. However, as we learned through many stories in this book, when the words are used to attack someone's actual or perceived sexual orientation, the results can be destructive.

Finally, as we pointed out in the preface and elsewhere throughout the book, appearing different in some other way can also place someone at risk for all types of bullying. Whether someone is too tall or too small, too heavy or too ugly, individuals who choose to exploit a difference can do so through bullying behaviors. Recall that of the preteens who reported being cyber bullied in the Fight Crime research, the most common things that were said to them had to do with their appearance such as their clothes, hair, height, or weight (37% of victims reported this). Similarly, 38 percent of the teenagers in the Fight Crime research reported that the cyber bullying messages had to do with their appearance such as clothes, hair, height, or weight. It is important to recognize that bullies can find many ways to put down others and assert a position of power based on someone being targeted because they are different. As we have stated before, the bullies are often those who are in the popular or "in" group, and can use their status to oppress and marginalize those who are labeled "out." Further, as we will discuss later in the chapter, many of those who see this happening will either actively or passively take part in the bullying, because they do not want to be the next one who is "out."

## GENERAL STRATEGIES AND ADVICE

So what advice can be given to victims of all ages who are being bullied online? While there is no silver bullet that can be used for all cases, there are a number of things that can be done in terms of prevention and in response to cyber bullying. For prevention, the most important first step is to learn as much as possible about self-protection in the technological world and overall digital culture of cyberspace. Similar to personal protection in general, it is necessary to learn how to avoid becoming a victim in the first place, or at least reduce the opportunity for this to happen in all kinds of online situations. For example, advice for personal theft prevention typically includes locking valuables in a secure location, or not leaving valuables unattended. The equivalent in cyber safety and security tips also exist.[10]

Unfortunately, although such advice seems simple enough, it is often not internalized so that the behaviors change and lifestyles that involve routine actions become normal. In other words, people know how to prevent theft from occurring but often do not make needed changes until they are victimized. When applying this to cyber bullying, it is important to learn about Internet safety and cyber bullying prevention, and then practice safe habits daily and certainly each time you go online. For example, learning not to share passwords or private information is important to avoid being manipulated and bullied online, as is not engaging other people when they make irritating remarks.

Also, knowing "the rules" and "netiquette" in order to communicate on-line effectively and in ways that do not offend is important. Understanding legal rules is also critical. Know the laws that govern Internet usage in the United States and in your state and locality. Recognize that courts have ruled that once an e-mail is sent to another person, the sender loses control over its content that can be forwarded to others and even posted online although libel laws governing written communications always apply. Similarly, courts have held that there is no reasonable expectation of privacy when information is posted to social computing forums.

Appropriate communication online should also take into account the very public nature of online communications. Although there may seem to be a degree of privacy, once information is sent via-e-mail or posted online, that information is literally and figuratively out of their hands. Whenever a computer or other information technology is used, a detailed digital record of the data processed and/or transferred is stored on the hard drive of the device they used, on the server of the internet service provider if online usage was involved, and potentially on government or private sector databases. Therefore, digital footprints remain after one surfs the Internet, posts information to a Web site, or sends and receives e-mail or text messages. Using a cell phone also leaves a digital trail revealing information about who placed the call, who was communicated with, how long they communicated, and from where the call was placed and answered. Therefore, it should be remembered that placing increased personal information online means increased opportunities for someone to use that information in an inappropriate manner such as for cyber bullying.

Perhaps the best advice is to *think,* and *think again* before you send or post messages. Any and all content posted online is recorded on one or more (and probably several) computer systems. Once posted, consider something online "gone" and there forever. Although computer forensics experts may be able to recover and destroy online content, there are no guarantees about this. Just as someone in public may have happened to record something a person shouted without thinking, someone may have instantly downloaded, saved, forwarded, or reposted content posted online. As has often been said, "the Internet never forgets .com." Web.archive.org currently indexes Web pages and Web content on at least a weekly basis and has Internet data saved going back to the mid-1990s. For individuals who need to acquire content in cyber bullying investigations or litigations, this public nonprofit resource can be invaluable.

Also remember that things may not always be as they seem when communicating online. The Internet is full of false information, and it is very difficult to tell if information is truthful, completely made up, or a combination of both. Also, given connectivity to complete strangers, it is difficult to really know someone who may be considered a friend on a social networking site, or what their intentions may be. Learn to question online friends and the meaning of friendships. Discern whether for you these have the same value and qualities of relationships in "real life."

Further, online communication is very susceptible to misinterpretation. Written communication does not come with the audiovisual assistance that comes with face-to-face communication where tone and body language assist in understanding meaning. Therefore, it may be more difficult to tell if someone is intentionally cyber bullying or is just trying to be sarcastic and humorous. After all, few of us are really good writers, and even the best of authors write things they did not initially mean. Besides, people can change their minds about something they wrote. Again, one must be aware of the possibility that messages received and messages sent can be misconstrued. A simple rule of thumb when sending messages is to ask whether you would say that message in person. Treating others with respect and dignity while communicating online is not only a way to reduce confrontational situations, but is also the right thing to do.

Being a victim of cyber bullying can happen despite diligent efforts to prevent it. If one has been victimized, it is important to know that something can be done about it. First of all, if it is done by a stranger through a social networking site through messaging, via a chat room or bulletin board, or via online gaming, some options are to ignore it or stop visiting those sites or areas. If communication with the harassers is cut off, then the cyber bullying may very well end. Telling a harasser to stop may also work, but research has also shown that messages may continue. This could be because the bully is getting a sense of satisfaction knowing that they have succeeded in annoying or alarming their target. Other options are to use various blocking mechanisms that can be applied via Web site or instant messaging tools. Directly contacting Web site hosts, the ISP, or phone service provider is important because they have terms of use agreement policies that usually preclude harassing and bullying behaviors that allows them to ban bullies if warranted.

## APPRECIATING DIVERSITY AND STANDING UP AGAINST INJUSTICE

Individual cultural assumptions and values that create our attitudes of the world influence both the decisions we make and the priorities we set. This assertion can be applied to influence many injustices such as intolerance, discrimination, and bullying of people perceived as merely different rather than true threats. Unfortunately, individuals such as would-be bullies often make poor decisions about others based on their own untested and unexamined personal assumptions and beliefs. Their attitudes toward others different from themselves reflect a lack of knowledge, understanding, and acceptance of others and perhaps themselves. Bluntly put, many bullies are ignorant and arrogant people. Others are just mean or given to impulsively blowing up at other people for any number of reasons.

It is imperative that all stakeholders such as parents, educators, employers, and potential adult role models focus on promoting for our youth a sense of *understanding, respecting,* and *valuing* differences in others. Absent this positive influence, certain kids and young adults may form, buy into, and hang on to stereotypes about people different from themselves and then become lead or accomplice bullies when potential victims enter their lives. Developing appropriate attitudes toward others should be done not because it is politically correct or legally required as in affirmative action situations, but because it is the right thing to do and because the world we live in could use a good deal more peace and understanding among its peoples. To their credit, youth and young adults today appear to be far less hung up about differences in race and ethnicity perhaps in part because of digital youth culture and communicating so often with faceless people who they regard as a friend despite knowing them only on the basis of a nickname, an IM Buddy list name, or an e-mail address.

Just as traditional bullies like an audience, cyber bullies also like an audience and can use technology to reach an audience that is much larger. This implies the need to beware of inadvertently becoming a guilty bystander to online bullying when you encounter it. As we have seen, bullying can become very public as bullies seek to establish power and notoriety. When does a witness to online bullying become a guilty bystander for doing nothing *when they know they should?* There's your answer! We believe people know it when they read it or see it. From research we also believe that peers are present in most incidents of online bullying, but they seldom do anything to stop the bullying.[11]

Research has also shown that the majority of cyber bullying victims and bystanders failed to notify adults,[12] that some bystanders not only support bullying, but are predisposed to join in,[13] and that bystanders have many reasons for not standing up for justice, including that: The bully is or is not a friend, they believe it's not their problem or fight; the victim is a loser or deserves to be bullied, bullying will toughen the person up; deeply held views about the code of silence that exists among youth; it is better to be in the in-group than to defend the outcasts; and it takes too much mental effort to become involved.[14] We agree that doing the right thing takes effort and courage. Perhaps this explains why some school officials surveyed by Jim Colt believe the reporting of cyber bullying by bystanders and witnesses is declining despite research that verifies considerable amounts of bullying by and among online friends.[15] This can be problematic because if victims or their friends of youth cyber bullying do not tell adults, continued bullying and retaliation could result. Taking this one step further, if youth believe that their friends are trustworthy, caring, and helpful, then participating in behaviors such as cyber bullying is less likely.[16] The great irony is that cyber bullies often feel that it is fun and a source of entertainment. As expressed by a 9th grade boy, "I just pick kids that I don't like and then I bully them. My parents are getting me a computer and I can't wait till I start bullying on the computer. My brother said its fun. He's going to show me how to really mess up kids lives that you don't like or just kids you pick at random to mess their heads up. It's fun."

## CONCLUDING THOUGHTS AND LOOKING AHEAD

The digital divide that separates parental awareness about technology and the everyday use of IT devices by youth needs to change. Otherwise stated, there is a generational digital divergence that exists between youth and adults that needs to be addressed. This divergence exists on two levels and includes (1) the difference of perceptions that exists between adults and youth regarding cyber bullying, and (2) the discrepancy that exists between adults and youth regarding technology use and proficiency. Central to this concept is the need to address the increasing gap that exists between adults and youth in regards to communication, trust, and supervision issues surrounding the use of technology. Adults and kids are just not on the same page when it comes to technology. Therefore, prevention and intervention efforts should focus on establishing a model of generational digital convergence. More specifically, this would begin with efforts aimed at improved communication between adults and youth. Improved communication can result in both youth and adults developing a better understanding and appreciation of their differences of perspectives.

In order to achieve convergence, however, a key challenge is overcoming the issues of trust. In addition to open communication, perhaps one way to improve trust is for both adults and youth to teach and learn from each other. Adults should strive to be effective role models and should teach children how to behave ethically and respectfully. Adults should also be open to learning more about changing technology, and be willing to learn from their children about their online activities. Similarly, youth need to learn about safe and ethical communications while online, while at the same time teach adults about the online world and language. In short, both youth and adults play a shared role in the prevention and intervention of cyber bullying.

But this convergence cannot happen unless adults understand that digital youth culture is today a real social, economic, and political force with technological underpinnings. This reality is not merely by choice or convenience, however, as America and many other countries increasingly depend on information systems for everything from communications, management of financial systems, and commerce to education, transportation, and national security especially for protection of critical information infrastructure systems. Children from very early ages are being prepared to take their place in computerized societies. This is accomplished by their learning about and using IT in their schools, at home, and while on the move.

Standard Internet, Wifi, and cellular phone satellite communication systems now allow youth to connect from anywhere, including from the homes of friends, while riding school buses, playing outside, or hanging out in shopping malls. As we said, social computing is now mobile computing and vice versa. Consequently while using electronic media such as Internet-connected TVs, computers, and cell phones from places that are unsupervised, youth are now being exposed to a wide range of inappropriate content including that which is related to cyber bullying, other illicit online activities, and advertisements such as those that promote sex-related products and services.

Unfortunately unwary youth now growing up and routinely accessing the Net may not always understand "adult content" and the dangers that await them in cyberspace from many forms of cyber crime nor the meaning and importance of online civility. For example, most youth (and adult) users of the Internet do not recognize clever ways in which high-tech abuse and crimes are carried out as the result of what information security experts refer to as "social engineering"—online and/or in-person manipulation of people swaying them to give up confidential information about themselves, or about their personal or professionals associates or employing organizations. Acquiring someone's computer system or device password(s) enables cyber criminals or "friends" to pretend to be that person online for any number of purposes.

Teenagers today sometimes make up information about themselves or others while online in order to appear more appealing in various ways. Sometimes they create and maintain different profiles in various names with different online personalities and characteristics to fit into and/or attract different groups of friends. The Net effect (pun intended) is that deception is also ubiquitous among youth engaged in social networking. The RIT "Survey of Internet and At-Risk Behaviors" found that 23 percent of 8,665 4th through 6th grade students surveyed had lied about their age online within the previous year, while 7 percent had lied about their appearance online during the same time period. Comparable findings were found for thousands of 7th through 9th grade middle school students and 10th through 12th grade high school students. Indeed, lying about age online is now the most prominent form of cyber offending by and among youth.

Determining that which is real or true versus that which is not is often difficult in real-world settings. Contrary to the old saying, seeing no longer can no longer equate to believing (if indeed this was ever true)! This is because faked digital images and other content are so easy to create and post online, and many kids are doing just that, even as in their naivety many believe that what they read, see, or hear online must be true. All of this makes ripe conditions for cyber bullying to flourish. When considering additional RIT research findings that large percentages of middle school, high school, and college students now report sharing and/or having their password used without their permission, and infrequently if ever change their passwords even after sharing it, the implications for accessing computer account systems, for engaging online in deceitful ways, and for cyber bullying as oneself or while masquerading as someone else who may or may not even exist are ominous.

Responsible parents, teachers, and adults in positions of authority have known about and tried to deal with traditional forms of bullying for decades.

Aided by research in fields of study including education, psychology, health services, public policy, and criminal justice, professionals have explored the causes and effects of bullying to develop successful intervention strategies in some local community settings. In recent years some schools have created innovative and effective bullying prevention programs that engage students in discussions to promote ethical behaviors and intolerance of abuse in their learning environments. (Read more about this in Chapter 7.) Since the mid-1990s, numerous programs sponsored by government agencies, nonprofit organizations and businesses have also tried to intervene against traditional bullying that is steadily evolving into online methods to torment.

Unfortunately, as we have already emphasized, the Internet combined with new technologies (e.g., cell phones equipped with digital camera and Web content uploading features) are radically changing the ways in which bullying now occurs. This means that prevention and intervention efforts need to match and exceed cyber bullying tactics discussed in Chapter 3. How quickly the changes have taken place! Inherent aspects of cyber bullying include the widespread use of the Net and IT devices by youth, which although hugely popular, can be unsafe given that social computing forums remain largely unregulated. Further, practical and legal barriers to monitoring or banning hurtful communications in our society can limit the ability of parents, schools, or discrete prevention programs alone to effectively intervene.

In the new reality of bullying, low- to high-tech forms of abuse now combine to challenge society in ways not exceeded by traditional crime-related youth problems including truancy, drug and substance abuse, driving irresponsibly, property crimes such as vandalism and trespassing, and even violent crimes such as those carried out by criminal gangs. Research completed in 2001 reveals that approximately 30 percent of students in 6th through 10th grades have been bullied, or bully others "sometimes or more often" during a given school semester.[17] In addition, in the National Center For Education Statistics report, Indicators of School Crime and Safety: 2007, just over 1 out of every 4 12- to 18-year-olds reported having been bullied at school during the previous 6 months.[18] That equates to 6 students per class of 25! Rochester Institute of Technology's series of research studies completed in 2004–2008 echoes and builds upon these findings. They reveal that bullying continues throughout high school and college years, and that as young adults mature sexually online threats and harassment can escalate into cyberstalking. Of 873 randomly selected college students surveyed in 2004, 17 percent reported they were harassed online, 8 percent were threatened online, and 6 percent were stalked online all within 12 months prior to being surveyed.[19]

To counter bullying in the Digital Age, nothing short of a social, educational, and technology reform movement is needed, one that includes broad support from parents, government agencies and community-wide action inclusive of businesses in many employment sectors. This will not be easy. One significant issue is the difficulty in defining limits of normal abuse in relation to causing harm in society. Social scientists have long understood that what constitutes immoral or unethical behavior is not necessarily the same as socially deviant or illegal behaviors. What is perceived by one person as joking and horsing around may be viewed by another as offensive if not also harmful, violating of acceptable community standards and illegal.

Virtually nonexistent rules for civility in cyberspace further complicates any meaningful consideration of harmful online behaviors absent statutory crime laws that explicitly prohibit particular forms of behavior. Philosophical and legal distinctions between what is right or wrong are especially complicated in the subjective and inconsistent world of American juvenile justice systems (e.g., states have differing standards for prosecuting minors as adults and so forth). Some states and the federal government now have laws against online harassment or making threats online. At a practical level these laws seldom reach into online social computing forums in which youth and young adults voluntarily participate. Absent agreement about what constitutes illegal bullying, an incident may involve an insult and result in hurt feelings, yet considered to be merely unfortunate though normal or at least acceptable within the bounds of civil society.

One of the fundamental questions we have wrestled with in this book is: What online behaviors should be considered normal, acceptable, and legal on the basis of potential harm? This is very tricky because civil and criminal statutory and case law traditions recognize differing types and levels of mental reasoning among offenders. Committing a violation through negligence (i.e., what a person should have known might happen) is different from doing so with recklessness (i.e., knowing what might happen and choosing to do it anyway). These levels of what criminal justice professionals associate with a person's guilty mind are distinguished further from knowingly or deliberately committing a crime versus doing so with premeditation. As with all forms of crime and abuse in society, when it comes to bullying and cyber bullying, more than one level of culpability may be going on in the mind of any particular individual or persons involved in perpetrating an incident. Regardless of this truth, it is the substance of their actions and communications upon which decisions to intervene or prosecute must be made. Questions such as who was harmed, in what way, to what extent, through what means, and by which individuals under what circumstances matter tremendously when considering what can be done about bullying.

Therefore, as you review this book, please think about what is reasonable and justified under the circumstances of the cyber bullying cases we described, and what you would want, need, or hope for if your children or people you know were involved in similar situations. As you do, remember that bullying is universally accepted to mean interpersonal aggression that is deliberate, harmful, repeated over time, and involves people with more power attacking individuals they regard as being less powerful.[20] Also remember that cyber bullying is essentially an ethical issue, so another fundamental question involves how we should go about teaching what society generally considers to be ethical and responsible behavior.

The more we learn, the more we can become informed about and apply a critical component of prevention (i.e., promoting ethical behavior). Youth need our guidance to help navigate cyberspace responsibly. This means we need to figure out how to teach digital media literacy that includes Internet safety, information security and cyber ethics. We also need to consider frankly what it means in our busy lives and times to provide adequate levels of supervision and role modeling of positive online behaviors regardless of whether we are parents, school officials, business persons, community leaders, or members of the media. Adults and children must continue to openly communicate and establish the levels of trust needed to work on the problem, *together.* Society has many problems, it always has and it always will. Today cyber bullying is among the complex problems we face, demanding wise and sustained intervention in all ways possible.

# Notes

## CHAPTER 1

1. Barry, D., "A Boy the Bullies Love to Beat Up, Repeatedly," *The New York Times,* March 24, 2008. http://www.nytimes.com/ (accessed March 24, 2008).
2. Hewitt, B., Morrisey, S., and Grout, P., "Did Cruel Hoax Lead to Suicide?" *People,* December 3, 2007, 135–36.
3. *Primetime Live: Cyberbullying.* DVD. ABC News Productions. First aired on September 14, 2006.
4. Li, Q., "Cyber-Bullying in Schools: A Research of Gender Differences," *School Psychology International* 27, no. 2 (2006): 157–70.
5. World Internet Stats: Usage and Population Statistics. Retrieved July, 2008 from http://www.internetworldstats.com/stats.htm.
6. Lenhart, A. and others, "Teens and Social Media" (report from Pew/Internet & American Life Project, December 19, 2007). http://www.pewinternet.org/reports.asp.
7. Lenhart, A., Madden, M., and Hitlin, P., "Teens and Technology: Youth are Leading the Transition to a Fully Wired and Mobile Nation" (report from Pew/Internet and American Life Project, July 27, 2005). http://www.pewinternet.org/reports.asp.
8. Ibid.
9. Ibid.
10. Lenhart, A., "Cyber Bullying and Online Teens" (report from Pew/Internet & American Life Project, June 27, 2007), 1.
11. Lenhart, A., Madden, M., and Hitlin, P., "Teens and Technology."
12. McQuade, S., Castellano, Linden, E., Fisk, N. and Berg, S. (2004). RIT Computer Use and Ethics Survey. Unpublished manuscript: Rochester Institute of Technology.
13. McQuade, S., Gorthy, M. and Linden, E. (2005). SUNY Brockport Computer Use and Ethics Survey. Unpublished manuscript: State University of New York at Brockport.
14. McQuade, S. and Sampat, N. (2008, June 18). RIT Survey of Internet and At-risk Behaviors. Rochester, New York: Rochester Institute of Technology.

15. Prensky, M. Digital Natives: Digital Immigrants. NCB University Press, 9, 5 (2001).

16. Lenhart and others, "Teens and Social Media."

17. Wollack, J. & Mitchell, K. (2000). *Youth Internet Safety Survey.* University of New Hampshire, Crimes against Children Research Center.

## CHAPTER 2

1. Olweus, D., *Bullying at School* (United Kingdom: MPG Books Ltd., 1993).

2. Pellegrini, A. D., Bartini, M., and Brooks, F., "School Bullies, Victims, and Aggressive Victims: Factors Relating to Group Affiliation and Victimization in Early Adolescence," *Journal of Educational Psychology* 91 (1999): 216–24.

3. Sullivan, K., *The Anti-Bullying Handbook* (Melbourne, Auckland, Oxford, and New York: Oxford University Press, 2000).

4. Ibid.

5. Limber, S. P., "Bullying Among Children and Youth," *Proceedings of the Educational Forum on Adolescent Health: Youth Bullying.* Chicago: American Medical Association (2002), http://www.ama-assn.org/ama1/pub/upload/mm/39/youthbullying.pdf/ (accessed March 24, 2007).

6. Nansel T. and others, "Bullying Behaviors Among U.S. Youth: Prevalence and Association With Psychological Adjustment," *Journal of the American Medical Association* 285 (2001): 2094–2100.

7. McQuade, S. and Sampat, N. RIT Survey of Internet and At-Risk Behaviors: Cyber Victimization and Offending Experiences Reported by 40,079 K–12th Grade Students in 14 Upstate New York Counties. (Rochester, NY: Rochester Institute of Technology, 2008).

8. Lenhart, A., Madden, M., and Hitlin, P., "Teens and Technology: Youth are Leading the Transition to a Fully Wired and Mobile Nation" (report from Pew/Internet and American Life Project, July 27, 2005). http://www.pewinternet.org/reports.asp.

9. Lenhart, A. and others, "Teens and Social Media" (report from Pew/Internet & American Life Project, December 19, 2007). http://www.pewinternet.org/reports.asp.

10. Ibid.

11. McQuade, S., *Understanding and Managing Cybercrime* (Boston: Allyn & Bacon, 2006).

12. Ibid.; McQuade, S. and Sampat, N. RIT survey of Internet and at-risk behaviors, 2008.

13. Associated Press (2008). Girl, 12, Charged With Distributing Nude Pic of Classmate. Retrieved June 25, 2008 from http://www.foxnews.com/story/0,2933,370987,00.html.

14. Smoking Gun staff author. Teen Nabbed for Naked MySpace Photos—Cops: Boy Posted Explicit Shots of Ex-Girlfriend as way of "Venting" (May 21, 2007). Retrieved June 25, 2008 from http://www.thesmokinggun.com/archive/years/2008/0521081myspace1.html.

15. Denver News staff author. No Charges In Students' Nude Cell Phone Pics Prank: D.A. Says No Criminal Intent Found (March 26, 2007). Retrieved June 25, 2008 from http://www.thedenverchannel.com/news/11267621/detail.html.

16. Armour, Nancy. Blogs, Photo Sites Give Everyone a Peek at Athletes' Lives (May 27, 2006). Retrieved May 27, 2006 from http://sportsillustrated.cnn.com/2006/more/wires/05/26/2080.ap.bad.jocks.adv27.1331/index.html.

17. Olweus, *Bullying at School*.

18. Melton, G. and others, "Violence among Rural Youth," *Final report to the Office of Juvenile Justice and Delinquency Prevention* (1998), http://www.apa.org/pi/cyf/bully_resolution_704.pdf.

19. Nansel and others, "Bullying Behaviors Among U.S. Youth."

20. Dwyer, K., Osher, D., and Warger, C., *Early Warning, Timely Response: A Guide to Safe Schools* (Washington, DC: U.S. Department of Education, 1998).

21. Olweus, *Bullying at School*.

22. Nansel and others, "Bullying Behaviors Among U.S. Youth."

23. Cunningham, P. B. and others, "Patterns and Correlates of Gun Ownership Among Nonmetropolitan and Rural Middle School Students," *Journal of Clinical Child Psychology* 29 (2000): 432–42.

24. Olweus, *Bullying at School*.

25. Ibid.

26. Willard, N., *Cyberbullying and Cyberthreats: Responding to the Challenge of Online Social Cruelty, Threats, and Distress* (Eugene, OR: Center for Safe and Responsible Internet Use, 2006).

27. *A Dictionary of Psychology* (New York: Oxford University Press, 2001).

28. Suler, J., "The Online Disinhibition Effect," *Cyber Psychology and Behavior* 7 (2004): 321–26.

29. Ibid.

30. Lenhart, A. and Madden, M., "Teens, Privacy, and Online Social Networks" (report from Pew/Internet and American Life Project, 2007).

31 YouTube, http://www.YouTube.com/ (accessed November 23, 2007).

32. Ibid.

33. Espelage, D., "An Ecological Perspective to School-Based Bullying Prevention," *The Prevention Researcher* 11, no. 3 (2004): 3–6.

34. Espelage, D., Bosworth, K., and Simon, T., "Examining the Social Context of Bullying Behaviors in Early Adolescence," *Journal of Counseling and Development* 78, no. 3 (2000): 323–33.

35. Williams, K. P. and Guerra, N. G., "Prevalence and Predictors of Internet Bullying," *Journal of Adolescent Health* 41 (2007): 14–21.

36. Olweus, *Bullying at School*.

37. Williams and Guerra, "Prevalence and Predictors of Internet Bullying."

38. Ibid.

39. Sampat, N. and McQuade, S., "Digital Youth Culture and Social Networking," in *The Encyclopedia of Cybercrime*, ed. Samuel C. McQuade (Westport, CT: Greenwood Press, 2008).

40. Ibid.

## Chapter 3

1. Risling, G., "Woman Guilty in Cyberbullying Case" November 27, 2008 Associated Press.

2. Huffaker, D. and Calvert, S., "Gender, Identity, and Language Use in Teenage Blogs," *Journal of Computer-Mediated Communication* 10, no. 2 (2005), http://jcmc.indiana.edu/vol10/issue2/huffaker.html (accessed March 11, 2007).

3. Sampat, N. (2009). "Leetspeak," in *The Encyclopedia of Cybercrime,* ed. Samuel C. McQuade (Westport, CT: Greenwood Press).

4. Colt, J., "Building-Level School Administrators' Perceptions of Cyber Bullying Among Students Under Their Supervision: Implications for Prevention and Intervention" (doctoral dissertation, St. John Fisher College, Rochester, NY, 2008).

5. Lenhart, A., Madden, M., and Hitlin, P., "Teens and Technology: Youth are Leading the Transition to a Fully Wired and Mobile Nation" (report from Pew/Internet and American Life Project, July 27, 2005). http://www.pewinternet.org/reports.asp.

6. Lenhart, A., "Cyber Bullying and Online Teens" (report from Pew/Internet & American Life Project, June 27, 2007), 1.

7. Colt, J., "Building-Level School Administrators' Perceptions of Cyber Bullying Among Students Under Their Supervision: Implications for Prevention and Intervention."

8. Schoolscandals.com, http://wwwschoolscandals.com/final/postlist.php/cat//Board/CAWOODLANDHILLSTAFT (accessed April 30, 2008; site now discontinued).

9. As cited by Silva, Hector. "Modern-Day Bullying-Freeing Students From Fear," *SAANYS Journal,* 35 no. 3 (2006): 4.

10. cnnmoney.com, http://money.cnn.com/news/newsfeeds/gigaom/media/2008_11_20_19_year_old_commits_suicide_on_justintv.html (accessed December 3, 2008).

11. Lenhart, A., Madden, M., and Hitlin, P., "Teens and Technology," 2.

12. Perry, A., "Gaming Online," in *The Encyclopedia of Cybercrime,* ed. Samuel C. McQuade (Westport, CT: Greenwood Press, 2009).

13. Lenhart and others, "Teens and Social Media," 10.

14. Lenhart, A., "Cyber Bullying and Online Teens," 4.

15. Lenhart and others, "Teens and Social Media."

# CHAPTER 4

1. Wollack, J. and Mitchell, K., *Youth Internet Safety Survey* (report, University of New Hampshire, Crimes against Children Research Center, 2000).

2. Wollack, J. and Mitchell, K., "Youth Internet Safety Survey."

3. MNet Survey, "Young Canadians In a Wired World." Retrieved from http://www.media-awareness.ca/english/special_initiatives/surveys/index.cfm (2001).

4. Li, Q., "Cyber-Bullying in Schools: A Research of Gender Differences," *School Psychology International* 27, no. 2 (2006): 157–70.

5. National Children's Home, "1 in 4 Children are Victims of 'On-line Bullying,'" http://www/nch.org.uk/information/index.php?i=77&r=125 (accessed March 24, 2008).

6. Mobile Bullying Survey 2005, "Putting U in the Picture," http://www.filemaker.co.uk/educationcentre/downloads/articles/Mobile_bullying_report.pdf (accessed March 24, 2008).

7. Berson, I. R., Berson, M. J., and Ferron, J. M., "Emerging Risks of Violence in the Digital Age: Lessons for Educators From an Online Study of Adolescent Girls in the United States," *Journal of School Violence* 1, no. 2 (2002): 51–71.
8. National i-SAFE Survey, "National i-SAFE Survey Finds Over Half of Students Are Being Harassed Online," http://www.isafe.org/imgs/pdf/outreach_press/internet_bullying.pdf/ (accessed August 10, 2007).
9. Ybarra and Mitchell, "Youth engaging in online harassment," 319–36.
10. Ybarra, M. and others, "Examining Characteristics and Associated Distress Related to Internet Harassment: Findings from the Second Youth Internet Survey," *Pediatrics* 118, no. 4 (2006): 1169–77.
11. Li, Q., "New Bottle but Old Wine: A Research of Cyberbullying in Schools," *Computers in Human Behavior* (2005): 2–15.
12. Li, Q., "Cyber-Bullying in Schools," 157.
13. Kowalski, R. and others, "Electronic Bullying Among School-Aged Children and Youth" (paper presented at the annual meeting of the APA, Washington, DC, 2005).
14. Kowalski, R. and Limber, S., "Electronic Bullying Among Middle School Students," *Journal of Adolescent Health* 41 (2007): 22–30.
15. Patchin, J. and Hinduja, S., "Bullies Move Beyond the Schoolyard: A Preliminary Look at Cyberbullying," *Youth Violence and Juvenile Justice* 4, no. 2, 148–69.
16. Patchin, J. and Hinduja, S., "Offline Consequences of Online Victimization: School Violence and Delinquency," *Journal of School Violence* 6, no. 3 (2008): 89–112.
17. Burgess-Proctor, A., Patchin, J., and Hinduja, S., "Cyberbullying and Online Harassment: Reconceptualizing the Victimization of Adolescent Girls," in *Female Crime Victims: Reality Reconsidered,* ed. Venessa Garcia and Janice Clifford (Upper Saddle River, NJ: Prentice Hall, 2008).
18. Pre-Teen Caravan, "Cyber-Bully-Pre-Teen," *Fight Crime: Invest in Kids* (prepared by Opinion Research Corporation, Princeton, NJ, 2006).
19. Teen Caravan, "Cyber Bully-Teen," *Fight Crime: Invest in Kids* (prepared by Opinion Research Corporation, Princeton, NJ, 2006).
20. Research Topline, "Tech Abuse in Teen Relationship Study," Liz Claiborne Inc., 2007.
21. Williams, K. and Guerra, N., "Prevalence and Predictors of Internet Bullying," *Journal of Adolescent Health* 41 (2007): 14–21.
22. Ybarra, M., Diener-West, M., and Leaf, P., "Examining the Overlap in Internet Harassment and School Bullying: Implications for School Intervention," *Journal of Adolescent Health* 41 (2007): 42–50.
23. Raskauskas, J. and Stolz, A., "Involvement in Traditional and Electronic Bullying Among Adolescents," *Developmental Psychology* 43, no. 3 (2007): 564–75.
24. Lenhart, A., "Cyber Bullying and Online Teens" (report from Pew/Internet & American Life Project, June 27, 2007), 1–8.

# CHAPTER 5

1. Conn, K., *Bullying and Harassment: A Legal Guide for Educators* (Alexandria, VA: Association for Supervision and Curriculum Development, 2004).
2. Kowalski, R., Limber, S., and Agatston, P., *Cyber Bullying: Bullying in the Digital Age* (Malden, MA: Blackwell Publishing, 2008).

3. New York State Penal Law, http://public.leginfo.state.ny.us/menugetf.cgi/ (accessed June 4, 2007).
4. Smoking Gun Staff Author, "Teen Nabbed For Naked MySpace Photos—Cops: Boy posted explicit shots of ex-girlfriend as way of 'venting,'" 2007.
5. Essex, N., *School Law and the Public Schools: A Practical Guide for Educational Leaders* (Boston: Pearson Education, Inc., 2008).
6. Willard, N., *Cyberbullying and Cyberthreats: Responding to the Challenge of Online Social Cruelty, Threats, and Distress* (Eugene, OR: Center for Safe and Responsible Internet Use, 2006).
7. Ibid.
8. Essex, *School Law and the Public Schools*.
9. Ibid.
10. Ibid.
11. Shariff, S. and Hoff, D., "Cyber Bullying: Clarifying Legal Boundaries for School Supervision in Cyber Space," *International Journal of Cyber Criminology* 1, no. 1 (2007).

**List of Court Cases**

*ACLU v. Reno* (1997)

*Beidler v. North Thurston School District No. 3* (2000)

*Bethel School District No. 403 v. Frasern* (1986)

*Buessink v. Woodland R-IV School District* (1998)

*Coy v. B.O.E. of the North Canton City Schools* (2002)

*Dwyer v. Amato and Oceanport School District, et al.* (2005)

*Emmett v. Kent School District No. 425* (2000)

*Flaherty v. Keystone Oaks School District* (2003)

*Goldsmith v. Gwinnett County School District #1* (2003)

*Hazelwood School District v. Kuhlmeier* (1988)

*J.S. v. Bethlehem Area School District* (2002)

*Killion v. Franklin Regional School District* (2001)

*Kim v. Bellevue School District-Newport High School* (1995)

*Layshock v. Hermitage School District* (2006)

*Mahaffey v. Aldrich* (2002)

*Morse v. Frederick 555 U.S.* (2007)

*Muss-Jacobs v. Beaverton School District* (2003)

*Neal et al. v. Efurd and Greenwood School District* (2005)

*New Jersey v. T.L.O.* (1985)

*O'Brien v. Westlake City School Board of Education* (1998)

*Tinker v. Des Moines Independent Community School District, 393 U.S. 503* (1969)

*Wisniewski v. Board of Education of Weedsport CSD* (2007)

*Zeran v. America Online, Inc.* (1997)

## CHAPTER 6

1. Yurgelun-Todd, D., "Inside the Teenage Brain," *PBS.org,* http://www.pbs.org/ wgbh/pages/frontline/shows/teenbrain/interviews/todd.html/ (accessed May 1, 2008).
2. Ibid., 1.
3. CNN Video Report, www.cnn.com/video/#/video/us/2008/04/11candiotti. teen.beating.cnn/ (accessed April 11, 2008).
4. Colt, J., "Building-Level School Administrators' Perceptions of Cyber Bullying Among Students Under Their Supervision: Implications for Prevention and Intervention" (doctoral dissertation, St. John Fisher College, Rochester, NY, 2008).
5. Lenhart, A., "Protecting Teens Online" (report from Pew/Internet and American Life Project, March 17, 2005). http://www.pewinternet.org/reports. asp.
6. Macgill, A., "Parent and Teenager Internet Use" (report from Pew/Internet & American Life Project, October 24, 2007). http://www.pewinternet.org/ reports.asp.
7. Stansbury, M., "Study: Parents Clueless about Kids' Internet Use." *eSchool News.* Retrieved July 8, 2008 from http://www.eschoolnews.com/news/ top-news/?i=54295.
8. Ibid., 2008.
9. Woolfolk, A., *Educational Psychology,* 8th ed. (Boston, MA: Allyn & Bacon, 2001).
10. Berk, L. E., *Infants, Children, and Adolescents,* 3rd ed. (Boston, MA: Allyn & Bacon, 1999).
11. Huesmann, L., "The Impact of Electronic Media Violence: Scientific Theory and Research," *Journal of Adolescent Health* 41 (2007): 6–13.
12. Williams, K. P. and Guerra, N. G., "Prevalence and Predictors of Internet Bullying," *Journal of Adolescent Health* 41 (2007): 14–21.
13. Huesmann, L., "The Impact of Electronic Media Violence," 6–13.

## CHAPTER 7

1. Charach, A., Pepler, D., and Ziegler, S., "Bulling at School: A Canadian Perspective," *Education Canada* 35 (1995): 12–18.
2. Harris, S., Petrie, G., and Willoughby, W., "Bullying Among 9th Graders: An Exploratory Study," *NASSP Bulletin* 86 (2002): 630.
3. Teen Caravan, "Cyber Bully-Teen," *Fight Crime: Invest in Kids* (prepared by Opinion Research Corporation, Princeton, NJ, 2006).
4. Beran, T. and Li, Q., "Cyber-Harassment: A Study of a New Method for Old Behavior," *Journal of Educational Computing Research* 32 (2005): 2–20.
5. Holt, M. and Keyes, M., "Teachers' Attitudes Toward Bullying," in *Bullying in American Schools: A Social-Ecological Perspective on Prevention and Intervention,* ed. D. L. Espelage and S. M. Swearer (Mahwah, NJ: Lawrence Erlbaum Associates, 2004).
6. Olweus, D., *Bullying at School* (United Kingdom: MPG Books Ltd., 1993).

7. Ibid.

8. Will, J. D. and Neufeld, P., "Taking Appropriate Action," *Principal Leadership* 3, no. 2 (2002): 56–63.

9. Colt, J., "Building-Level School Administrators' Perceptions of Cyber Bullying Among Students Under Their Supervision: Implications for Prevention and Intervention" (doctoral dissertation, St. John Fisher College, Rochester, NY, 2008).

10. Teen Caravan, "Cyber Bully-Teen."

11. Greene, M., "Bullying in Schools: A Plea for a Measure of Human Rights," *Journal of Social Issues,* 62 no. 1, 63–79.

12. Olweus, *Bullying at School.*

13. Vreeman, R. and Carroll, A., "A Systematic Review of School-Based Interventions to Prevent Bullying," *Arch Pediatric Adolescent Medicine* 161 (2007): 78–88.

14. Greene, "Bullying," 63–79.

15. Ibid.

16. Colt, "Building-Level School Administrators' Perceptions of Cyber Bullying Among Students Under Their Supervision."

17. Patchin, J. and Hinduja, S., "Bullies Move Beyond the Schoolyard: A Preliminary Look at Cyberbullying," *Youth Violence and Juvenile Justice,* 4 no. 2, 148–69.

18. Colt, "Building-Level School Administrators' Perceptions of Cyber Bullying Among Students Under Their Supervision."

19. Ibid.

20. Toppo, G., Story from *USA Today* in the *Rochester Democrat & Chronicle,* May 5th, 2008.

21. Health Resources and Services Administration, "Best Practices in Bullying Prevention and Intervention," http://stopbullyingnow.hrsa.gov/HHS_PSA/pdfs/SBN_Tip_23.pdf.

22. Colt, "Building-Level School Administrators' Perceptions of Cyber Bullying Among Students Under Their Supervision."

23. Jernstedt, R., "The creation of trust," in *Inside the Minds: The Art of Public Relations* (Aspatore Books, 2001), 59–84.

24. Patchin, J. and Hinduja, S., "Bullies," 148.

25. Cohen, J., "Social, Emotional, Ethical, and Academic Education: Creating a Climate for Learning, Participation, in Democracy, and Well-Being," *Harvard Law Review* 76, no. 2 (2006): 201–22.

26. Ibid., 201–22.

27. Ibid., 201–22.

28. Ibid., 201–22.

29. "Threat Assessment in Schools: A Guide to Managing Threatening Situations and to Creating Safe School Climates." United States Secret Service and United States Department of Education, 2004.

30. rockymountainnews.com, www.rockymountainnews.om/news/2003/oct/30/missions-targeted-classmates (accessed February 14, 2008).

31. Colt, "Building-Level School Administrators' Perceptions of Cyber Bullying Among Students Under Their Supervision."

32. Ibid.

# CHAPTER 8

1. Finn, J., "A Survey of Online Harassment at a University Campus," *Journal of Interpersonal Violence* 19, no. 4 (2004): 468–83.

2. Maull, S., "Uma Thurman's Parents Testify at Stalking Trial," *ABC News,* April 30, 2008. http://www.abcnews.com/GMA/wireStory?id=4753494/ (accessed May 1, 2008).

3. Friedman, E., "The Price of 'Blogebrity': A Cyber Stalker," *ABC News,* April 25, 2008. http://www.abcnews.com/print?id=4719130/ (accessed May 1, 2008).

4. Ibid.

5. Harvey, M. and others, "Bullying: From the Playground to the Boardroom," *Journal of Leadership & Organizational Studies* (2006): 1–5.

6. Ibid.

7. Pech, R and Slade, B., "Organisational Sociopaths: Rarely Challenged, Often Promoted. Why?" *Society and Business Review*, 3 no. 2, 2007.

8. "One in 10 Workers Experiences Cyber-Bullying in the Workplace," *Person neltoday.com,* July 26, 2007. http://www.personneltoday.com/articles/2007/07/26/41707/one+in+10+workers+experience+cyber-bullying+in+the+workplace+.html (accessed January 1, 2008).

9. Kosciq, J. G. and Cullen, M. K. The GLSEN 2001 National School Climate Survey: The School-Related Experiences of Our Nation's Lesbian, Gan, Bisexual and Transgender Youth. (2001). Gay, Lesbian, and Straight Education Network, New York, NY.

10. See McQuade, S. *Understanding and Managing Cybercrime* (Boston: Allyn and Bacon, 2006), 245.

11. Nansel, T. and others, "Bullying Behaviors Among U.S. Youth: Prevalence and Association With Psychological Adjustment," *Journal of the American Medical Association* 285 (2001): 2094–2100.

12. Li, Q., "Cyber-Bullying in Schools: A Research of Gender Differences," *School Psychology International* 27, no. 2 (2006): 157.

13. Jeffrey, L., "Bullying Bystanders," *The Prevention Researcher* 11, no. 3 (2004): 7.

14. Ibid.

15. Colt, J., "Building-Level School Administrators' Perceptions of Cyber Bullying Among Students Under Their Supervision: Implications for Prevention and Intervention." (Unpublished doctoral dissertation, St. John Fisher College, Rochester, NY, 2008).

16. Williams, K. P. and Guerra, N. G., "Prevalence and Predictors of Internet Bullying," *Journal of Adolescent Health* 41 (2007): 14–21.

17. Nansel, T. and others, "Bullying Behaviors Among U.S. Youth," 2094–2100.

18. National Center For Education Statistics. "Indicators of School Crime and Safety: 2007." http://www.ojp.usdoj.gov/bjs/pubalp2.htm#indicators/ (accessed April 15, 2008).

19. McQuade, S. and others, RIT Computer Use and Ethics Survey. Rochester Institute of Technology, Rochester, New York, 2004.

20. Nansel, T. and others, "Bullying Behaviors Among U.S. Youth," 2094–2100.

# Bibliography

Armour, N. "Blogs, Photo Sites Give Everyone a Peek at Athletes' Lives," 2007, http://sportsillustrated.cnn.com/2006/more/wires/05/26/2080.ap.bad.jocks.adv27.1331/index.html (accessed May 27, 2007).

Associated Press "Girl, 12, Charged With Distributing Nude Pic of Classmate," 2008, http://www.foxnews.com/story/0,2933,370987,00.html (accessed June 25, 2008).

Atlas, P. and D. Pepler "Observations of Bullying in the Classroom." *Journal of Educational Research,* 92 (1998): 1–86.

Barry, Dan. "A Boy the Bullies Love to Beat Up, Repeatedly." *The New York Times,* March 24, 2008, http://www.nytimes.com/ (accessed March 24, 2008).

Beran, Tanya, and Qing Li. "Cyber-Harassment: A Study of a New Method for Old Behavior. *Journal of Educational Computing Research* (2005): 2–20.

Berk, L. E. *Infants, Children, and Adolescents.* 3rd ed. Boston: Allyn & Bacon, 1999.

Berson, I. R., M. J. Berson, and J. M. Ferron. "Emerging Risks of Violence in the Digital Age: Lessons for Educators From an Online Study of Adolescent Girls in the United States. *Journal of School Violence,* 1 no. 2 (2002): 51–71.

Burgess-Proctor, Amanda, J. Patchin, and S. Hinduja. "Cyberbullying and Online Harassment: Reconceptualizing the Victimization of Adolescent Girls." In *Female Crime Victims: Reality Reconsidered,* edited by Venessa Garcia and Janice Clifford. Upper Saddle River, NJ: Prentice Hall, 2008.

Caravan. "Cyber-Bully-Pre-Teen." *Fight Crime: Invest in Kids.* Prepared by Opinion Research Corporation, Princeton, NJ, 2006.

Caravan. "Cyber Bully-Teen." *Fight Crime: Invest in Kids.* Prepared by Opinion Research Corporation, Princeton, NJ, 2006.

Charach, A., D. Pepler, and S. Ziegler. "Bulling at School: A Canadian Perspective." *Education Canada,* 35 (1995): 12–18.

CNN Video Report www.cnn.com/video/#/video/us/2008/04/11candiotti.teen.beating.cnn/ (accessed April 11, 2008).

Cohen, Jonathen. "Social, Emotional, Ethical, and Academic Education: Creating a Climate for Learning, Participation, in Democracy, and Well-Being." *Harvard Law Review,* 76 no. 2 (2006): 201–222.

Coloroso, Barb. *The Bully, the Bullied, and the Bystander.* Harper Collins, 2003.

Colt, James. "Building-Level School Administrators' Perceptions of Cyber Bullying Among Students Under Their Supervision: Implications for Prevention and Intervention." Ed.D. dissertation, St. John Fisher College, Rochester, NY, 2008.

Conn, Kathleen. *Bullying and Harassment: A Legal Guide for Educators.* Virginia: ACSD, 2004.

Cunningham, P. B., S. P. Henggeler, S. P. Limber, G. B. Melton, and M. A. Nation. "Patterns and Correlates of Gun Ownership Among Nonmetropolitan and Rural Middle School Students." *Journal of Clinical Child Psychology,* 29 (2000): 432–442.

Dwyer, K., D. Osher, and C. Warger. *Early Warning, Timely Response: A Guide to Safe Schools.* Washington, DC: U.S. Department of Education, 1998.

Espelage, D. "An Ecological Perspective to School-Based Bullying Prevention." *The Prevention Researcher,* 11 no. 3 (2004): 3–6.

Espelage, D., K. Bosworth, and T. Simon. "Examining the Social Context of Bullying Behaviors in Early Adolescence." *Journal of Counseling and Development,* 78 no. 3 (2000): 323–333.

Espelage, D. and M. Holt "Bullying and Victimization During Early Adolescence: Peer Influences and Psychological Correlates." In *Bullying Behavior: Current Issues, Research, and Interventions,* edited by R. A. Geffner, M. Loring, and C. Young, 49–62. New York: Haworth Press, 2001.

Essex, Nathan. *School Law and the Public Schools: A Practical Guide for Educational Leaders.* Pearson Education, 2008.

"Exploring the Nature and Prevention of Bullying." *Ed.Gov.* http://www.ed.gov/print/admins/lead/safety/training/bullying/ (accessed June 21, 2008).

Fein, R. A., B. Vossekuil, W. S. Pollack, R. Borum, W. Modzeleski, M. Reddy. *Threat Assessment in Schools: A Guide to Managing Threatening Situations and to Creating Safe School Climates.* Washington, DC: U.S. Secret Service and U.S. Department of Education, 2002.

Finkelhor, D., J. Wolak, and K. Mitchell. *Online Victimization: A Report of the Nation's Youth.* Washington, DC: National Center for Missing & Exploited Children, 2000.

Finn, Jerry. "A Survey of Online Harassment at a University Campus." *Journal of Interpersonal Violence,* 19 no. 4 (2004): 468–483.

Friedman, Emily. "The Price of 'Blogebrity': A Cyber Stalker." *ABC News,* April 25, 2008. http://www.abcnews.com/print?id=4719130/ (accessed May 1, 2008).

Graham, S. and J. Juvonen. "Ethnicity, Peer Harassment, and Adjustment in Middle School: An Exploratory Study." *Journal of Early Adolescence,* 22 (2002): 173–199.

Greene, M. "Bullying in schools: A Plea for Measure of Human Rights." *Journal of Social Issues,* 62 no. 1 (2006): 63–79.

Harris, S., G. Petrie, and W. Willoughby. "Bullying Among 9th Graders: An Exploratory Study." *NASSP Bulletin,* 86 (2002): 630.

Harvey, Michael, Joyce Heames, Glenn Richey, and Nancy Leonard. "Bullying: From the Playground to the Boardroom." *Journal of Leadership & Organizational Studies,* (2006): 1–5.

Health Resources and Services Administration. "Best Practices in Bullying Prevention and Intervention." http://stopbullyingnow.hrsa.gov/HHS_PSA/pdfs/SBN_Tip_23.pdf.

Henggler, S., and M. Nation. "Violence Among Rural Youth." Final report to the Office of Juvenile Justice and Delinquency Prevention, 1998.

Hewitt, Bill, Siobhan Morrisey, and Pam Grout. "Did Cruel Hoax Lead to Suicide?" *People,* December 3, 2007, 135–136.

Holt, M., and M. Keyes. "Teachers' Attitudes Toward Bullying." In *Bullying in American Schools: A Social-Ecological Perspective on Prevention and Intervention,* edited by D. L. Espelage and S. M. Swearer. Mahwah, NJ: Lawrence Erlbaum Associates, 2004.

Huesmann, L. "The Impact of Electronic Media Violence: Scientific Theory and Research. *Journal of Adolescent Health,* 41 (2007): 6–13.

Huffaker, D., and S. Calvert. "Gender, Identity, and Language Use in Teenage Blogs." *Journal of Computer-Mediated Communication,* 10 no. 2 (2005), http://jcmc.indiana.edu/vol10/issue2/huffaker.html/ (accessed March 11, 2007).

Jeffrey, Linda. "Bullying Bystanders." *The Prevention Researcher,* 11 no. 3 (2004): 7.

Jernstedt, R. "The Creation of Trust." In *Inside the Minds: the Art of Public Relations.* Boston: Aspatore Books, 2001.

King, Jonathan, Carolyn Walpole, and Kristi Lamon. "Surf and Turf Wars Online: Growing Implications of Internet Gang Violence." *Journal of Adolescent Health,* 41 (2007): 66–68.

Kowalski, Robin, Susan Limber, and Patricia Agatston. *Cyber Bullying: Bullying in the Digital Age.* Boston: Blackwell Publishing, 2008.

Kowalski, R., S. Limber, A. Scheck, M. Redfearn, et al. "Electronic Bullying Among School-Aged Children and Youth. Paper presented at the annual meeting of the APA. Washington, DC, 2005.

Kowalski, Robin, and Susan Limber. "Electronic Bullying Among Middle School Students." *Journal of Adolescent Health,* 41 (2007): 22–30.

Lenhart, A. "Cyber Bullying and Online Teens." *Data Memo from Pew/Internet & American Life Project* (2007): 1.

Lenhart, A., M. Madden, A. Macgill, and A. Smith. "Teens and Social Media." *Pew/Internet & American Life Project* (2007): 1–44.

Lenhart, A., M. Madden, and P. Hitlin. "Teens and Technology: Youth are Leading the Transition to a Fully Wired and Mobile Nation." *Pew/Internet and American Life Project* (2005): 1–57.

Lenhart, Amanda and Mary Madden. "Teens, Privacy, and Online Social Networks." *Pew/Internet and American Life Project* (2007): 1–55.

Li, Qing. "Cyber-Bullying in Schools: A Research of Gender Differences." *School Psychology International,* 27 no. 2 (2006): 157–170.

Li, Qing. "New Bottle but Old Wine: A Research of Cyberbullying in Schools." *Computers in Human Behavior* (2005): 2–15.

Limber, S. P. "Bullying Among Children and Youth." *Proceedings of the Educational Forum on Adolescent Health: Youth Bullying.* Chicago: American Medical Association (2002), http://www.amaassn.org/ama1/pub/upload/mm/39/youthbullying.pdf/ (accessed March 24, 2007).

Macgill, Alexandra. "Parent and Teenager Internet Use." *Data Memo from Pew/Internet & American Life Project* (2007): 1–11.

Maull, Samuel. "Uma Thurman's Parents Testify at Stalking Trial." *ABC News,* April 30, 2008. http://www.abcnews.com/GMA/wireStory?id=4753494/ (accessed May 1, 2008).

McQuade, S. *Understanding and Managing Cybercrime.* Boston: Pearson Education, 2006.

McQuade, S. and N. Sampat. RIT Survey of Internet and At-Risk Behaviors: Cyber Victimization and Offending Experiences Reported by 40,079 K-12th Grade Students in 14 Upstate New York Counties. Rochester, NY: Rochester Institute of Technology, 2008.

Melton, G., S. Limber, V. Flerx, P. Cunningham, D. W. Osgood, J. Chambers Mnet. "Young Canadians in a Wired World-Mnet survey." (2001), http://www.media-awareness.ca/english/special_initiatives/surveys/index.cfm.

Moreno, I. Kids won't face charges for nude pix, 2007. http://www.rockymountain news.com/drmn/local/article/0,1299,DRMN_15_5421826,00.html    (accessed October 16, 2008).

Nansel, T., M. Overpeck, R. Pilla, J. Ruan, B. Simons-Morton, and P. Scheidt. "Bullying Behaviors Among U.S. Youth: Prevalence and Association With Psychological Adjustment." *Journal of the American Medical Association,* 285 (2001): 2094–2100.

National Center For Education Statistics. "Indicators of School Crime and Safety: 2007." http://www.ojp.usdoj.gov/bjs/pubalp2.htm#indicators/ (accessed April 15, 2008).

National Children's Home. "1 in 4 Children are Victims of 'On-line Bullying.'" http://www/nch.org.uk/information/index.php?i=77&r=125. (accessed March 24, 2008).

National i-SAFE Survey. "National i-SAFE Survey Finds Over Half of Students Are Being Harassed Online." http://www.isafe.org/imgs/pdf/outreach_press/in ternet_bullying.pdf/ (accessed August 10, 2007).

New York State Penal Law. http://public.leginfo.state.ny.us/menugetf.cgi/ (accessed June 4, 2007).

Olweus, Dan. *Bullying at School.* Cornwall, UK: MPG Books Ltd., 1993.

"One in 10 Workers Experiences Cyber-Bullying in the Workplace." *Personnelto day.com,* July 26, 2007. http://www.personneltoday.com/articles/article. aspx?liarticleis+41707.

Patchin, J. and S. Hinduja. "Offline Consequences of Online Victimization: School Violence and Delinquency." *Journal of School Violence,* 6 no. 3 (2008): 89–112.

Pech, R. J. and B. W. Slade. Organisational sociopaths: Rarely challenged, often promoted. Why. *Society and Business Review,* 2 no. 3 (2007).

Pellegrini, A. D., M. Bartini, and F. Brooks. "School Bullies, Victims, and Aggressive Victims: Factors Relating to Group Affiliation and Victimization in Early Adolescence." *Journal of Educational Psychology,* 91 (1999): 216–224.

Perry, A. "Gaming Online." In *The Encyclopedia of Cybercrime,* edited by Samuel C. McQuade, III. Westport, CT: Greenwood Press, 2008.

Prensky, M. *Digital Natives, Digital Immigrants.* Lincoln: NCB University Press, 2001.

*Primetime Live: Cyberbullying.* DVD. ABC News Productions. First aired on September 14, 2006.

"Putting U in the Picture." *Mobile Bullying Survey 2005.* http://www.nch.org.uk/uploads/documents/Mobile_bullying_%20report.pdf/ (accessed March 24, 2008).

Raskauskas, J., and A. Stolz. "Involvement in Traditional and Electronic Bullying Among Adolescents." *Developmental Psychology,* 43 no. 3 (2007): 564–575.

Reitz, Stephanie, and Jim Hawver. "Teens Put Twist on XXX Pictures." *Rochester Democrat and Chronicle,* June 5, 2008, sec. A.

Research Topline. *"Tech Abuse in Teen Relationship Study."* Liz Claiborne Inc., 2007.

Robertson, Ian. "Cyber Bullying Research Results Surprising." *CNews,* May 15, 2008. http://cnews.canoe.ca/CNEWS/Canada/2008/05/15/5572616-sun.html/ (accessed June 19, 2008).

Rockymountainews.com. http//www.rockymountainnews.om/news/2003/oct/30/missions-targeted-classmates/?prin/ (accessed February 14, 2008).

Sampat, N. "Leetspeak." In *The Encyclopedia of Cybercrime,* edited by Samuel C. McQuade, III. Westport, CT: Greenwood Press, 2008.

Sampat, N. and S. McQuade. "Digital Youth Culture and Social Networking." In *The Encyclopedia of Cybercrime,* edited by Samuel C. McQuade, III. Westport, CT: Greenwood Press, 2008.

Schoolscandals.com. http://wwwschoolscandals.com/final/postlist.php/cat//Board/CAWOODLANDHILLSTAFT (accessed April 30, 2008).

Shariff, Shaheen, and Dianne Hoff. "Cyber Bullying: Clarifying Legal Boundaries for School Supervision in Cyber Space." *International Journal of Cyber Criminology.* 1 no. 1 (2007).

Smoking Gun staff author. "Photos—Cops: Boy Posted Explicit Shots of Ex-Girlfriend as Way of 'Venting.'" http://www.thesmokinggun.com/archive/years/2008/0521081myspace1.html (accessed June 25, 2008).

Smoking Gun staff author. "Teen Nabbed For Naked MySpace," 2007, http://www.thesmokinggun.com/archive/years/2008/0521081myspace1.html (accessed December 10, 2008).

Stansbury, M. (2008). "Study: Parents Clueless about Kids' Internet Use." http://www.eschoolnews.com/news/top-news/?i = 54295 (accessed July 8, 2008).

"State of Wisconsin, Criminal Complaint Case No.: 08CF309." http://www.thesmokinggun.com/archive/years/2008/052106myspace3/ (accessed June 5, 2008).

Suler, John. "The Online Disinhibition Effect." *Cyber Psychology and Behavior,* 7 (2004): 321–326.

Toppo, Greg. Story from *USA Today* in the *Rochester Democrat & Chronicle,* May 5, 2008.

U.S. Secret Service and U.S. Department of Education *The Final Report and Findings of the Safe School Initiative: Implications for the Prevention of School Attacks in the United States.* Washington, DC: Government Printing Office, 2002.

Vreeman, R. and A. Carroll. "A Systematic Review of School-Based Interventions to Prevent Bullying. *Arch Pediatric Adolescent Medicine,* 161 (2007): 78–88.

Will, J. D., and P. Neufeld. "Taking Appropriate Action." *Principal Leadership,* 3 no. 2 (2002): 56–63.

Willard, Nancy. *Cyberbullying and Cyberthreats: Responding to the Challenge of Online Social Cruelty, Threats, and Distress.* Eugene, OR: Center for Safe and Responsible Internet Use, 2006.

Williams, K. P. & N. G. Guerra. "Prevalence and Predictors of Internet Bullying. *Journal of Adolescent Health,* 41 (2007): 14–21.

Wollack, J. and K. Mitchell. "Youth Internet Safety Survey." University of New Hampshire, Crimes against Children Research Center, 2000.

Woolfolk, Anita. *Educational Psychology.* 8th ed. Boston: Allyn & Bacon, 2001.

Ybarra, M., and K. Mitchell. "Youth Engaging in Online Harassment: Associations with Caregiver-Child Relationships, Internet use, and Personal Characteristics." *Journal of Adolescence,* 27 no. 3 (2004): 319–36.

Ybarra, M., K. Mitchell, J. Wolak, and D. Finkelhor "Examining Characteristics and Associated Distress Related to Internet Harassment: Findings from the Second Youth Internet Survey." *Pediatrics,* 118 no. 4 (2006): 1169–1177.

Ybarra, Michele, M. Diener-West, and Philip Leaf. "Examining the Overlap in Internet Harassment and School Bullying: Implications for School Intervention." *Journal of Adolescent Health,* 41 (2007): 42–50.

Yurgelun-Todd, Deborah. "Inside the Teenage Brain." *PBS.org,* http://www.pbs.org/wgbh/pages/frontline/shows/teenbrain/interviews/todd.html/ (accessed May 1, 2008).

**List of Court Cases:**

Beidler v. North Thurston School District No. 3 (2000)

Bethel School District No. 403 v. Frasern (1986)

Buessink v. Woodland R-IV School District (1998)

Coy v. B.O.E. of the North Canton City Schools (2002)

Dwyer v. Amato and Oceanport School District, et al. (2005)

Emmett v. Kent School District No. 425 (2000)

Flaherty v. Keystone Oaks School District (2003)

Goldsmith v. Gwinnett County School District #1 (2003)

Hazelwood School District v. Kuhlmeier (1988)

J.S. v. Bethlehem Area School District (2002)

Killion v. Franklin Regional School District (2001)

Kim v. Bellevue School District-Newport High School (1995)

Layshock v. Hermitage School District (2006)

Mahaffey v. Aldrich (2002)

Morse v. Frederick 555 U.S. (2007)

Muss-Jacobs v. Beaverton School District (2003)

Neal et al. v. Efurd and Greenwood School District (2005)

O'Brien v. Westlake City School Board of Education (1998)

Tinker v. Des Moines Independent Community School District, 393 U.S. 503 (1969)

Wisniewski v. Board of Education of Weedsport CSD (2007)

# Index

## About the Authors

SAMUEL C. MCQUADE, III, currently serves as the Professional Studies Graduate Program Coordinator at the Rochester Institute of Technology. He is a former Air National Guard security officer, deputy sheriff and police officer, police organizational change consultant, National Institute of Justice Program Manager for the U.S. Department of Justice, and Study Director for the Committee on Law and Justice at the National Research Council of the National Academies of Sciences. His textbook *Understanding and Managing Cybercrime* was published in 2006.

JAMES P. COLT is the Coordinator of School Safety and Security for the Monroe 1 BOCES school district. He is a former police officer employed by the State University of New York, and also served as a criminal justice instructor and school community safety specialist. He is the chair of the district-wide bullying prevention committee at Monroe 1 BOCES, and is an active member of the Monroe County Community Task Force on Bullying Prevention.

NANCY B.B. MEYER is an established community activist against bullying and cyber bullying. She routinely travels throughout the U.S. and other nations where she interviews young people about their bullying experiences. She has worked in schools and conducted community workshops about bullying, and has offered counseling services to students and parents struggling to manage familial, school-related, treatment and legal issues stemming from incidents of bullying.